Bull Canyon

By Lin Pardey:

Passages: Cape Horn and Beyond

Bull Canyon, a Boatbuilder, a Writer and Other Wildlife

Taleisin's Tales, Sailing towards the Southern Cross

The Care and Feeding of Sailing Crew

By Lin and Larry Pardey

Cruising in Seraffyn

Seraffyn's European Adventure

Seraffyn's Mediterranean Adventure

Seraffyn's Oriental Adventure

The Capable Cruiser

Storm Tactics Handbook

The Cost-Conscious Cruiser: Champagne Cruising on a Beer Budget Self-Sufficient Sailor

By Larry Pardey:

Details of Classic Boat Construction: The Hull

Videos, DVDs:

Storm Tactics

Get Ready to Cruise

Get Ready to Cross Oceans

Cruising Has No Limits

Cost Control While You Cruise

(All available online at https://thesailingchannel.tv/watch-outstanding-sailing-videos/pardey-sailing-videos/)

Biography of Lin and Larry Pardey:

As Long as It's Fun - written by Herb McCormick

Lin Pardey's Newsletter, Cruising Tips and Podcasts:

https://pardeytime.blogspot.com/

BULL CANYON

A Boatbuilder, a Writer and other Wildlife

Lin Pardey

PARADISE CAY
PUBLICATIONS
www.paracay.com

Arcata, California

Book and cover design: **Moira Durham**

Editing: **Ann Espuelas**

Copy editing: **JoAnn Neil**

Photograph page 273: **Eureka Photo**

Publisher's Cataloging-in-Publication

Pardey, Lin.
Bull Canyon : a boatbuilder, a writer and other wildlife / Lin Pardey.

p. cm.
Includes bibliographical references.
LCCN 2010940098
ISBN: 978-1-929214-67-9
ISBN: 978-1-929214-66-2
ISBN: 978-1-929214-32-7

1. Pardey, Larry. 2. Pardey, Lin. 3. Boatbuilders--California--Biography. 4. Journalists--California--Biography. I. Title.

CT275.P37P37 2011 623.8'092'2 QBI10-600237

LCCN – 2010940098

Paperback edi ion, 2024 - ISBN: 978-1-929214-32-7

Paradise Cay Publicatons

P.O. Box 29, Arcata, California 95518 USA

https://paracay.com

Phone: (707) 822-9063

E-mail: info@paracay.com

Trade distribution – Cardinal Publishers Group

https://Cardinalpub.com

For Bonnie Masculine and Allen Zatkin,
unwitting but well-loved victims of their sister's writing habits.

Contents

Note to my Sailing Readers

Many of you have asked, "When are you going to write about your sailing adventures on board *Taleisin?*" As we worked building this bigger sister to our first offshore cruising boat, we finished writing the four-part series that told of the wondrous times we had sailing on board *Seraffyn* to explore the far reaches of the world. At the same time, we wrote two practical books on voyaging under sail. These led to a demand from both readers and editors for ever more information on the how-to aspects of cruising. But even as Larry and I worked together on these practical volumes, I always wanted to return to the sailing narratives that spoke of the more personal aspects of our lives. Yet for some reason, every time I tried writing another book describing the adventuresome and romantic aspects of life afloat, I found myself stalled. Then I realized the genesis of the voyages we've had on board *Taleisin* lay in the story you now hold in your hand. This story had to be written before I could talk of going to sea. So, though the action in this book takes place on land, I hope you enjoy *Bull Canyon* and see it as the prequel to *Taleisin's Tales*.

Introduction

We were navigating by dimly remembered directions the first time we drove into the forgotten canyon. "Head out to Corona, then south for twenty miles and turn left onto the dirt track right across from the first eucalyptus trees you see," our friend had told us. "Then keep bearing right until you get to the Lone Palm Ranch. After that it's easy. Another mile and you reach the spot where the road has been washed out. Park there and walk along a couple hundred yards. The cottage sits on the bluff on the left side, overlooking the road."

It took us three hours of searching plus a flat tire to find the right dirt lane, to pick our way across ravines born of a hundred flash floods and to splash through the rocky stream meandering across our path. We failed to recognize the distinctly non-ranchy "Lone Palm Ranch." And the "washed out" road had been repaired since our friend's last visit so there was nothing to act as a landmark. It was only by luck that we finally found the cottage. By the time we had driven up the rutted driveway, we were covered in dust, tired, and hungry.

For the past three months Larry, and I had been looking for the "right" place to live. We needed a big yard for boat building and a quiet corner for writing. More important, we needed something affordable. This isolated spot, sixty miles southeast of Los Angeles, fifty miles inland, had sounded far from ideal when a friend mentioned it in passing. In fact, we'd ignored his suggestion to check it out for weeks, until we needed a reason to take a day off. It was the perfect excuse to get away from the tiny borrowed Newport Beach apartment where we were staying, tightly jammed between hundreds of water-front homes.

We climbed out of the car, more interested in food than exploring. We spread a picnic lunch on the weeds that carpeted the flat area in front of the battered, deserted homestead. Texas Umbrella and Chinaberry trees shaded us, and as we ate and began to relax, we could make out what sounded like a waterfall somewhere nearby, a chorus of bird calls, the gurgle of a stream. It was almost an hour before we ventured into the cottage itself. Constructed sixty years ago from stone, the three-room home had stood almost deserted for eight years, only inhabited now and then by illegal immigrants as they snuck through these canyons to evade border patrols and search for work in the valley below.

We walked slowly through each room, turning to take in the views from deep-set casement windows, touching the rough stones of the fireplace. Instead of seeing the rat droppings and dirty straw that covered the floors, we noticed only the beauty of the old red, slightly misaligned floor tiles someone had laid without the aid of a straight edge or a lining string. We looked at the ceilings, and instead of being put off by the old beehives, dripping honey and water stains that showed the roof leaked in what could be called prodigious amounts, we admired the warmth of the dark wood beams, how they contrasted with the pine paneling of the walls that had aged to a mellow gold. We didn't worry — then — about the lack of electricity or heat; instead, we were lulled into a romantic haze by dust-covered but gracefully rotund oil lamps and the greystone, ash-filled fireplaces in each room.

When we finally shut the sprung, peeling entry door, the sun was low in the sky. Its last beams highlighted the rose-colored, thick stone walls of the cottage, and there was a golden-pink glow through the jungle of weeds and ivy that covered most of the house. Even the scraps of rusting metal scattered like ravaged dog bones across the yard looked interesting in the late afternoon light.

As we left and inched down the rutted driveway that first day, Larry and I both felt a twinge of sadness to be leaving. It was sixty miles back to our garage-top rooms in Newport Beach, sixty miles that might have been a million. The peaceful setting, the old-fashioned house that begged to be lived in, the crystal-clear, smog-free air — it had already begun to work its magic, despite the obvious drawbacks. "Pretty hard to build a boat up here," I commented as we drove. "But I'd like to live in that place someday."

◇◇

And two months later, it was ours. After half a dozen weekend forays to Bull Canyon, we'd given up searching for a logical place to live and let our emotions and our parsimonious tendencies take control. We rented the stone cottage for the next three years for only the cost of our labor to fix it up. The friends who owned it had bought the 160 acres it stood on as an investment, planning to someday sub divide the land and bulldoze the house. But the old cottage had worked its spell on them, too. We were a solution to the problem of preserving the house from further decay until four or six years down the line when their other contracting projects were finished.

So decision made, we again drove up El Toro Road, a haze of dust billowing up around "Old Gold," our ten-year-old pickup, a rusty flatbed trailer bumping and groaning behind us. Now that the road was more familiar, I had time to soak in the sun-bleached colors of the desert growth, the startling reds and oranges of desert blooms as the truck juddered and clattered over the corrugated road. Even though I didn't see anyone about, I waved as we passed the rose-covered picket fence surrounding a pair of trailer homes that marked the last turn before *our* canyon.

Suddenly, something flashed through the tall yellow roadside grass. Then it came out of the grass and ran beside us, long legs striding out, head thrust forward, colors smeared by its amazing speed — that wondrous land-bound bird, the roadrunner. It paced alongside our truck until we had to slow down to cross the first washout before the foothills. The roadrunner kept going at top speed across the ravine, then into the thick green growth that marked the stream just ahead. "This is going to be a wonderful place to live," I whispered as I watched that long-beaked, brown-speckled bird lead us toward the hills that hid our new home.

"I think it's going to be quite interesting," Larry answered as he maneuvered the truck and low-slung trailer around some larger rocks that cluttered the ravine bed. "But we've got lots of work ahead of us."

The trail began to rise and grow narrower until there was room for only one vehicle. Larry slowed the truck to a crawl and pressed the horn at each blind corner. We would come to love this particular sycamore-shaded stretch of road; it would always seem to shield Bull Canyon from the real world, the hills closing behind us like a gate as we ascended out of the smog into clean, fresh air and made the turn toward the Lone Palm Ranch.

Pete Shomler, who owned the property uphill from the stone cottage, waved to us from a rusty red skip-loader he and his seven-year-old son Steve were using to smooth a patch of the Lone Palm's driveway. We'd met him during one of our previous forays to the canyon and now, as we slowed to a stop, Pete sauntered over and ran his eyes along the load of rough-sawn black locust timbers Larry and I had cut in Virginia, seasoned carefully for seven years, then carted across the country. "Funny-looking firewood you've got there," he said.

"That's not firewood," Larry replied proudly, "that's boatbuilding timber."

We chatted about the weather, the condition of the road, and then Pete stated, "You'll need a hand to get that rig up your driveway."

"No problem, we can handle it," Larry said, pulling away.

Since no one in the canyon had telephones, I often wondered how Pete had gotten the news of our arrival to the three other neighbors who were home that day. It might have been the dust plume that stayed suspended above the road long after we drove past; it might just have been the intuition even *we* began to develop after a few months of living in the canyon. But minutes after we reached our overgrown, tree-lined drive and attempted to back the unwieldy trailer up the slippery dirt incline, battered vehicles began arriving.

Massive, bushy-bearded Bob Steele, a 250-pound, 6'4" ex-boxer, stood in the bed of our truck to add traction, surrounded by two kids, two women, and two dogs. Pete directed the back of the trailer past trees and rocks. I watched the front wheels as Larry had to swing the truck close to the bank of the stream to make his turn. Twenty minutes of good-natured jibing and coaching finally got the load next to the old stone garage. Pete went back to his truck for a can of the Budweiser we later learned he carried with him like Greek men carry worry beads. When he came back, his son Steve waited politely for a quiet moment, and then asked, "Are you really going to build a boat out here on top of these hills? Are you Noah or something?"

I guess it did seem rather strange to our new neighbors that in the beginning of the eighth decade of the twentieth century, we'd decided to build a large wooden sailboat 2300 feet above the California desert, fifty five miles from the nearest ocean, nine miles up a dirt track in a canyon without electricity, telephones or piped-in water. But those who knew us well felt our choice made some kind of sense. In fact, Jimmie Moore, who leased the cottage to us, often shook his head and said, "If there is a harder way, Larry will find it."

We could see nothing but logic in our choice that day — beautiful surroundings, peace and quiet, helpful neighbors, no rent; so we just laughed at Steve's innocent comment, our minds filled with the camaraderie of the moment. But his words often came back like an echo during the next years.

We stored our wood in the cool depths of the stone garage that late spring day, and even though we wouldn't be back for several months, we didn't bother to lock the door. We figured no one would be interested in these water-stained, bark-fringed timbers but us. Then we said good-bye to our helpers, trying to remember each name against the time when we returned.

We left Bull Canyon and traveled back to Canada to get *Seraffyn*, the boat that had been our home for eleven years, and sail it as close as possible to our new-found canyon. We took our time finishing our voyage, reluctant to give up the life at sea that had become so familiar — we wanted to store up memories for those times when we knew we'd need the impetus to keep working hard on shore, but mostly to give us time to plan. Larry and I worked best when we had a joint goal, with some ground rules in place to ensure we stayed on track. Larry called it "having a plan A, plan B, and plan C just in case." So it was six months later when we secured *Seraffyn* to a mooring, then unloaded the amazingly small amount of personal belongings we owned to row ashore in Newport Beach, and began the drive toward our stone cottage, this time to finally settle in.

Chapter I

An Introduction to Reality

A brass bedstead, mattress and springs went into our homemade camper at the first stop on our way to Bull Canyon. Next came a dozen boxes of mismatched but potentially useful household gear — all, like the bed, treasures from friends' garages. Three boxes of boatbuilding tools we'd left in my parents' garage for more than a decade joined the load. On top, squashed between the uppermost boxes and the camper ceiling, sat a fine pair of plump new bed pillows, my mother's gift — blessed with the words, "I'm so glad you are finally settling into a home where I know you'll be safe and sound. Now I won't have to worry about you so much." The groceries we got at the final town we passed had to be crammed around me on the truck seat for the last of the drive "home."

It was late afternoon when we backed the truck as close to the door of the cottage as possible. The sun had already dropped behind the hills, and the November air quickly turned crisp and chilly. "You get a fire lit, I'll start unpacking," Larry said, as he felt along the top edge of the stone wall for the door key. "What do you want first?"

"The dishes, the pots, the food, then the bed, blankets, the...," I called over my shoulder as I loaded my arms with firewood from the shed that stood a few feet away from the kitchen door.

"Where should I put it all?" Larry called, as I backed carefully through the doorway, balancing my load. I turned and froze, transfixed by the chaos that confronted me.

Jimmie, who owned the cottage, had sent a few of his building crew to surprise us by installing a new set of kitchen cabinets. But the crew had obviously run short of time because all of the countertops lay helter-skelter on the floor. The sink sat in a box on the stove, and the bare innards of the cupboards held an assortment of plumbing parts, pulls and hinges. "Lin?" came Larry's voice from outside.

I took a deep breath, let it out. "No problem," I said. "Let's get the bed set up and we'll roast some sausages over the fire and call it dinner."

The fire I laid, guided by memories of my Girl Scout days, sprang into a warm flame almost instantly. I was delighted; if I could do this chore so easily, surely I could cope with anything this new life would offer. It was only as we came to know this house, this canyon, and other wood-fire-dependent homes, that we realized that this particular fireplace, set on its bench-height, red-brick hearth, was almost legendary, a classic engineering marvel. A retired Italian stonemason from a ranch in the next canyon had used almost forgotten logic as he laid its stonework sixty years before. It drafted so well that a small piece of paper set anywhere amidst the kindling got the fire going. The back of the firebox was carefully curved to insure heat reached out toward the farthest edges of the room within minutes. Banked toward the front, the fire roared and sparked, dispelling the first chill quickly if we came back to a cold house after a weekend away. Banked to the back, it burned slowly through the long winter nights and left hot embers to jump start the next morning's fire. No damper, no metalwork at all, except for a spark-arresting screen at the very top of the large square stone chimney, yet the fireplace never backdrafted or sent smoke into the room. And now I sat for a moment, as fascinated by the growing flames as the first cavewoman must have been as she dreamed of the comfort and protection fire would offer her family.

"Hey Lin, where do you want to set up this bed?" Larry called from the back of the house. "This bedroom is a mess and it's cold as H besides."

I didn't want to leave the glow of that fireplace so I called, "Let's set it up in here for tonight, we can move it later." Together we swept out the rat droppings and assembled that grandiose bed, fitted it with the crisp new pillows and blankets, set a rusty chrome and red plastic covered chair on each side to hold a burning oil lamp (the sole bits of furniture remaining from former occupants). After eleven years of sharing a three and a half foot wide bunk in the confines of a tiny cabin on a sailboat, the bed seemed enormous.

We dropped onto its soft sprung mattress and lay drowsily watching the fire fade to embers. As darkness filled the room, Larry wrapped me into his arms. My back nestled against his stomach. I was almost asleep as he whispered, "I'm proud of my little pioneer."

Some time later, I felt something race across the blankets covering my feet. I refused to scream. I wasn't going to let some silly mouse rattle me. I dozed off again.

That couldn't be thunder, I thought, as I poked my head out from under the covers to look at the moon-silvered trees at the front of the house. I remained absolutely still for two breathless moments and then the roar came again. I'll just pretend I didn't hear it, I thought, as I lay very still and tried not to wake Larry. I need not have bothered. The rolling stampede of a team of packrats shook the ceiling boards as those rodents played a game of soccer in the space between the ceiling panels and the outer roof. They had Larry wide awake, too.

"Stop that, goddammit!" Larry yelled.

Absolute silence.

I waited breathlessly for a minute, then broke out in relieved giggles. Then the next team of rats raced out onto their second-story playing field. "Stop that, goddammit!" I added my voice to the chorus. Silence again.

Both of us were reduced to giggles this time. But the rowdy, thundery stampede over our heads became oblivious to our shouts after a few minutes. We finally admitted defeat when we saw the size of the creature that scurried over us on a direct route from what we could make out as a ragged hole under the sunroom door to a hole in the paneling on the far side of the room. "You grab the pillows, I'll take the blankets," Larry said. "Let's sleep in the truck tonight. Tomorrow I'll buy rat traps." And with that, we left the warmth of the solid stone cottage for the cold of a slab of foam over a sheet of plywood surrounded by the thin aluminum shell of the camper.

The last embers of the fire greeted us next morning as we returned to the front-room battleground. I rekindled the fire while Larry cleared off the aged propane stove next to the wood-burning cook stove in the kitchen. With the bright November sun slowly warming the cottage, the smell of percolating coffee filling the kitchen, and the heat of the front-room fire dispelling memories of the rat-filled night, we began the first of what was to become an endless chain of shopping lists. Larry wrote as I washed a few dishes in the bucket of sweet, spring water he'd drawn from the main well a hundred yards from the house. "All we need besides some lengths of pipe, some connections and sealing putty," he said, as he turned another page of his notebook, "is a V-belt and we can connect the pump at the well and we'll have running water in the house, at least in the bathroom, by tonight."

I watched as he drove off toward the town of Lake Elsinore. A covey of quail sounded like a miniature tornado as they scurried across the driveway ahead of him. A light breeze rustled the eucalyptus leaves and the sun picked out the brilliant red against yellow of the last blooms on the acacia bushes that edged the weedy plateau in front of the cottage. It wasn't until I threaded my way back past the unfinished cabinetry cluttering the kitchen and into the box-littered front room that depression struck.

What have I gotten myself into? I sighed and sank down onto the warm hearth. My eyes followed a sunbeam up toward the two transom windows set high in the far wall and I saw the maze of cobwebs and old wasp nests that covered most of the glass. I looked into the fireplace and noticed for the first time the heap of ashes that would have to be shoveled out very soon. Every window in the sun porch was covered with cobwebs and torn screens. Holes chewed by rodents marred the bottom of every door in the house. I looked toward the kitchen and sunlight illuminated the tracks of drying mud we'd carried in from the dew-dampened dirt driveway. My mind imagined years ahead of fighting dust and mud combined with wood shavings from the boatshed we intended to build on the driveway beside the house. It would be right next to the stone garage, a perfect place to store our timber and supplies. It would also mean, though, that every time someone walked into the house they'd carry wood-shavings with them. But, there was no other flat ground anywhere on the 160 acres. My mind went round and round, "shavings, dirt, rats, dust, the winter rains will make it worse."

I'm not sure how long I sat staring at the disarray, my imagination creating ever more depressing images. But finally I snapped out of it. "Buck up old girl, make a cup of tea and get on with it," I said to the fireplace. Then I laughed, thinking how funny that phrase sounded here in America. And then I made my tea, warming my teapot as Larry's very British grandmother had taught me, while I waited for the kettle to reach a full rolling boil.

I'd just finished pouring myself a perfectly brewed "cuppa" when I heard a truck coming down the road. It sounded just like ours. "Wonder if Larry got lost," I muttered, as I ventured into the yard behind the cottage to look over the bluff and onto the road. I barely had time to note that the big pick-up truck was blue, not gold like ours, before I heard the sound of another vehicle coming up the road at what was a high speed for the blind corner beneath me. The combined speeds of the two vehicles must have been more than sixty miles per hour. The horrendous crash of two tons of full-sized truck head on against a ton of miniature pickup truck echoed across the hills. Then there was absolute silence. Beneath me the mini-truck lay at a crazy angle teetering over the edge of the stream, its engine smashed halfway into the cab while ten feet away the full-size truck lay skewed across the road, steam hissing from its shattered radiator, its fender crushed against the punctured front wheel.

I didn't stop to yell or even think. I bolted back through the kitchen door, looked quickly around for something, anything, that might be useful, grabbed the still steaming kettle and a roll of paper towels then skidded and slipped down the rough track to the road.

A tousled, dazed-looking teenager climbed out of the wreckage of the mini-truck. Blood streamed from a split across his forehead, and more poured from a gash that showed through the ripped trousers near his knee. "My wife's in there, help me, please, help Julie."

Inside the cab, a tiny, pale-haired girl lay absolutely still in the engine-filled cab. Blood ran from the corner of her mouth and from a split across her cheek. Her arm lay at an awkward angle to her body. The sun winked across the layer of shattered glass that covered her.

"I'm scared," she cried, when we wrenched open the bent truck door.

I'm scared too, I thought to myself as I squeezed her hand. But knowing she could speak made me braver. "Open your mouth," I said. I was relieved to see that the blood welling from a big cut in her tongue was already beginning to turn thick and dark as the bleeding slowed of its own accord. The first-aid lessons I had been forced to take as a first-year college student leapt vividly into my mind — breathing first, check that, then stop the bleeding.

She was breathing in a pretty normal sounding pattern, interrupted only by her crying. Her husband's bleeding should be stopped, I thought. I ripped handfuls of paper towel off the roll, then convinced him to sit on the tail gate of his truck and hold them against his wounds. Only when the bleeding slowed to a trickle around the bright red wads of paper did I turn toward the bigger truck.

A solid, six-foot-tall, probably 20-year-old was methodically tugging at the crumpled bumper of his faded blue truck mumbling in a monotone, "Knew I shouldn't have tried to take a short cut, got to get to work on time, got to..." His effort to pull the twisted metal away from his tires was obviously in vain. At least *he* wasn't badly injured, I thought with relief — he didn't present another problem out in the middle of the place that suddenly felt shockingly isolated. I doubted anyone would come this way until Larry returned from his shopping trip, one that could take him most of the day. My mind raced. I remembered seeing a phone booth about five miles down the road.

"Forget your truck," I said to the six-footer. "Walk down the road about a mile — there's a trailer and barn there, someone's got to be home. They'll go for help."

He looked at me, bewildered. "I'm not leaving my truck out here in the middle of nowhere. Someone'll steal my tools."

"No, they won't," I pleaded. "Get going. The girl in that truck is really hurt, she needs some help."

Slowly he shook his head, keeping his eyes carefully away from the other smashed truck. "No, ma'm, someone'll steal my tools."

I lost my temper, hauled back and did something I'd never done before. I slapped him across the face with all the force of my 115-pound, 4'10" body.

He staggered back.

I yelled, "Get walking. Get help and I'll take care of your goddamned tools."

He shook his head but did look where I pointed, and for the first time seemed to notice the blood running in slowly drying rivulets down the door of the other truck. "They need help," he mumbled. "Be sure you mind my tools, ma'm." Then he set off, ambling down the road as if he was out for an afternoon stroll.

Julie had moved out of the front seat and now lay in the bed of the truck. Her husband and I brushed glass carefully off her face and used some of the water from my kettle to clean blood from around her mouth and cheeks and away from the minor cuts on her arms and legs. Her arm still lay at an awkward angle, but slowly she stopped sobbing. Slowly the blood stopped oozing past the wads of paper the young man held against his head and knee. The realization dawned on me — no one was going to die. Even if we did have to wait for Larry's return, it wouldn't matter too much.

Suddenly the shock of the past ten minutes hit. I began to shake. "I'll be right back," I called, then rushed up the long driveway to reach the bucket we were using as a temporary toilet. Then I stood absolutely still for almost five minutes trying to get calm before I grabbed a bottle of Larry's whisky plus two glasses and returned to the accident-littered road.

I don't normally drink anything stronger than an occasional glass of wine, but I flung a mouthful of that whisky back, oblivious to the rush of the heat down my throat, then offered a small glass to the shaking young man. "You're awfully nice," he said to me as I reached over to hold his wife's hand again. I sure hope help comes soon, I thought.

Relief washed over me when less than twenty minutes later I heard the distant purr of a vehicle approaching. When I heard the downshift as it approached the steeper grade about a half mile downhill from us, I felt a twinge of guilt about the whisky, so I picked up the bottle and said, "It's probably not a good idea to let the ambulance crew see this." My patients (or was it victims?) agreed, and I hid the bottle behind the bushes by our gate.

A bright yellow, stripped-down Volkswagen, sans fenders or bumpers, exhaust pipe standing high over its rear like the tusk of a rhinoceros, roared into view. My sense of relief turned to something close to terror when two men jumped out, shotguns in hand the minute the "Baja Bug" scrunched to a halt.

"Get those fucking trucks outta the way," the burly, balding driver yelled. "I want to get up this fucking road before the damn sun drives all the quail into cover."

Only the tightening of Julie's hand in mine kept me outwardly calm. "There's been an accident," I said. "Someone has to go for help!"

The hunter climbed out of his car and marched up to within inches of me, glaring as he demanded, "Ya think I'm gonna waste my one good day off chasing after ambulances? Move those trucks."

The stench of liquor combined with sweat swept over me. I'd only once

before been in an encounter that included loaded weapons, and I didn't like it. Fear turned to anger as Julie began to cry again. "I'd love to move these trucks just to get rid of you," I stated in what I hoped was a commanding tone, "but I can't and someone else has already gone looking for help and you'd better get the hell out of here before the police come because this is private land and hunting is illegal and I'm going to report you even if they don't catch you for something else. So either help or get lost."

The hunter's mate began to climb back into the Baja Bug as he called, "C'mon, Ralph, she might be right. Let's go." But Ralph didn't budge. His attention was caught by the sound of a car approaching from uphill.

A battered white compact of unidentifiable make swung around the blind corner, brakes squealing as it skidded to a stop. I could almost hear the song its driver was singing before she saw the wrecks. The last words fell tunelessly from her lips. The car door slowly opened and a woman stepped carefully onto the road, bleached hair teased into a huge bouffant to complement pink-framed, heart-shaped sunglasses. Barbie-doll breasts were barely constrained by an embroidered brassiere that showed clearly through a lace-frilled, see-through top. White stretch pants clung to every curve of the legs they covered, and tooled leather boots kicked up spurts of dust as she strode purposefully around the wreckage.

"You must be Lin. Pete said you were really tiny and had long, dark hair. He loves long hair," she said in a sweet "welcome neighbor" voice as she ignored the drunken hunter and the weapon he clutched in his hand like a club. "What trouble you got yourself into? Another accident here already? Last month a guy killed a horse right here. What a mess, really ruined his car. Call me Sandy; I'm your nearest neighbor, at least just as near as Marlys. Sometimes, people think that — ," her words faded as Sandy seemed to register what was happening, finally seeing Julie in the back of the truck. "I'll be right back," she snapped as she ran to her car and took off before I'd had a chance to say one word.

The battered white car backed up the road at full speed. The two hunters were almost as stunned as I. Almost as soon as Sandy's car vanished from sight one of them spotted the glass of whisky I hadn't quite finished. "What's this?" he asked as he grabbed the glass off the tailgate. "Where's the rest of the bottle? Aren't you goin' ta show me some proper country hospitality? Hey, Don, show her those quail we got. I'll trade you a couple of birds for the bottle." Don hauled a long string of elegantly patterned birds from the Volkswagen. His partner grabbed them and shook the dead birds just a foot from my face, then held up his shotgun. "Don't like to threaten a lady, but you've got that bottle somewhere around here, haven't you?"

Before I had a chance to say one word the roar of another car caught his attention. He darted for his "Baja Bug" yelling, "C'mon Don, let's get outta here..." He was just opening the door when Sandy's car re-appeared on the downhill side of the wreckage, racing across a shallow spot in the stream at the end of a steep trail which lead up to Bob Steele's property. She skidded to a stop next to the hunter's Baja Bug. Sandy opened her door and climbed out just as the most aggressive hunter turned to face her.

"Okay, Blondie, get back in that car and show us how you got around to here," he said in menacing tones. Sandy calmly reached behind her back and pulled a .22 caliber pistol from her belt.

Whang! Whang! Two bullets kicked up dust right next to that hunter's foot. "Get moving, asshole!" Sandy growled.

"Calm down, little lady," the hunter whispered, backing slowly toward his car. He didn't take his eyes off Sandy for even a second as he climbed into his seat. I didn't either. In fact I was just as stunned as he was. He started the car and slowly headed down the road. Sandy called to me, "Keep them calm, I'll be back with help real soon." She climbed into her car and followed after the hunters.

A hundred yards down the road I saw the hunters slow until Sandy had to brake to keep from hitting them. "Get a move on it, buddy," she screamed from her car window. The hunter slammed on his brakes. Sandy calmly stopped, opened her car door slightly, leaned out of her window, rested her forearm against the window ledge, took aim and shot the back window out of their Baja Bug.

The hunters took off in a squeal of tires against gravel and dirt. Sandy followed at full speed and was soon lost to view as the road bent and disappeared behind a pile of boulders.

Julie and her husband, who told me his name was Tom, were actually laughing, albeit nervously, when I walked back to them. That's a good sign, I thought, as I tried to sort out the strange scene I had just been part of. It had all happened so quickly, I almost wondered if I'd somehow dreamed it all up. I spent the next ten or fifteen minutes wiping more of the dried blood from Julie and Tom's faces with the last of my water and paper towels, while I tried to reassure them (or was it me?) by asking them questions. They had plans, they told me, to fix up an old shack further up the canyon using money Tom had hoped to earn with his truck. He'd already arranged to deliver goods for the hardware shop in town.

Then we heard the sound of heavy vehicles approaching. A cloud of dust rose from down-canyon and soon three sheriffs' cars, an ambulance, a paramedics' truck, two tow trucks and five assorted pickup trucks came roaring up the road. Sandy's little white car was almost lost in the dust at their tail.

"Seems like you did a good job, lady," the ambulance man said as he lifted Julie onto a stretcher. "Report we got, expected two dead bodies. Looks like lots of stitches and a dislocated shoulder, maybe a concussion or two. You oughtta go have a strong drink — you're pretty pale looking yourself." Then I was completely forgotten as policemen wrote license numbers, tow trucks were hooked up, and ambulance crews slammed doors. Then each vehicle backed around to head toward town and radios prattled from the open windows of the emergency vehicles. I stood at our gate and watched as the caravan set off, augmented by the two wrecked trucks, Sandy in her tiny car again bringing up the rear. "Hey, lady, you living in the old stone house?" the sheriff, in one of the last cars asked. "Yes, I guess I am," I answered. "Okay, if we need a report we'll come back sometime." Then he drove off and all was absolutely quiet.

I heard the "tek, tek" of quail as I picked up my kettle, the empty paper-towel roll and the whiskey bottle. A red-tailed hawk soared lazily overhead as I headed up the driveway. I watched a flock of sparrows flitting past the window as I reheated the tea I'd never had a chance to drink. I sat down, cup in hand, wondering how such complete chaos had resolved itself into such apparent peace in the space of minutes.

Larry drove in minutes later and jumped happily out of the truck. "Hi, Pumpkin, hope you didn't feel too lonely out here by yourself," he said as he burst into the kitchen with arms full of plumbing bits.

Then he stopped. "What's wrong?" he asked, seeing the tears that had begun rolling down my face.

I don't think he believed a word I said until I led him down the driveway and pointed to the skid-marks, the sparkling litter of broken glass. Even then I think he had a hard time accepting the bizarre string of events that followed the accident, until Sandy Shomler roared into the driveway later in the day, yelling, "They caught those hunters. I gave the cops their license number as soon as I called the accident in. Intercepted them before they reached the freeway in Corona. Got 'em for drunk driving, killing too many birds, couldn't prove they did it on posted land, and something wrong with their car, too." She bit into one of the tuna fish sandwiches I offered. "Good to have company out here," she said, then launched into her version of the "Great shoot-out" as Larry listened in shocked silence.

A grumbling, clanking deluge of sound interrupted her dramatic presentation. The three of us rushed out onto the driveway to see a Caterpillar bulldozer lift its gleaming eight-foot-wide blade from behind a wall of damp earth. The driver, who I recognized as Bob Steele, our nearest neighbor, shouted something over the noise of his D6 Cat, but we couldn't really hear him. He backed down the driveway, lowered his blade and shoveled what was left of the water-worn ruts and center hump of the driveway in front of him.

We stood back as his machine worked its way over the pile of debris it had shoved to the top of our drive, then spread the excess dirt into a depression in the front yard, turning and worrying it like a giant dog trying to create a comfortable bed. When the dirt lay absolutely flat, the machine groaned one last time, then grew silent. Bob brushed off his hands, climbed down, lowering his huge bulk with care. Then he walked over to where we stood in slightly stunned silence. "Was on my way back from cleaning up a road at the Newhouse's, thought your driveway could use a clean up."

"It sure needed it," Larry agreed. "Beats doing it with a pick and shovel. I'd like to pay you for your work."

"Nope, consider it a housewarming gift," Bob said, following us into

the kitchen for coffee. "What's this I hear about Lin having to act like a nursemaid for some damn drunk hunters?"

It took us almost a year to realize that grizzly-bearded Bob, the ex-heavyweight boxing champion from the Marine Corps, was an inveterate gossip. The track leading up to his property was almost directly across the stream from our driveway. He'd come by every few days and offer his well-considered assistance, the loan of a tool or machine that was just perfect for the job at hand, a tree he'd dug up somewhere that would fit into my garden, or his own much-appreciated hard labor — just to have an excuse to stroll into the kitchen once the job was under control. He'd settle onto one of the high stools we soon got for the breakfast counter and begin to ask questions. He was so helpful, such an easy listener, it felt natural to share my thoughts with him. Only later did I realize his penchant for gossip, which we found to be completely free of any malicious intent, was also a sign of extreme inner loneliness. But on that accident-shattered morning, the wide, dirt-covered face, the block-like hands and green twinkling eyes seemed like those of a fairy godfather — he'd been the source of the one good thing to happen that day.

Bob listened to Sandy's version of "the story," then said, "You'd better get going. Pete's looking for you."

Sandy rose and left immediately, calling to me over her shoulder, "I'll sew you up some curtains, you just get the cloth."

"Where are you going to build this boatshed you talk about?" Bob asked. Larry led him outside and I watched their hands flying through the air as Larry described the shed he proposed building, half the size of a tennis court, two stories high. He pointed first at the house, then the garage just beyond it and at the old woodshed opposite the kitchen. Bob kept shaking his head and pointing toward his yellow and rust-colored bulldozer. I went out to join them.

"Bob says he'll move that hill and make us a flat area for 75 bucks," Larry said, pointing across the yard. "He'll do it tomorrow. I think it's a great idea, what about you?"

Great? I thought it was a fabulous idea. I couldn't believe one man on one machine could move half a hill for $75 but if this gentle giant said he would, he probably could.

Sandy's car pulled up the driveway and came to rest alongside Bob's machine. Pete Shomler climbed out. "Came to hear the real story of that accident and those damn hunters," he said. With his neatly-trimmed black hair, slight wiry build and almost military-like stance, Pete was a policeman who worked in a small city fifty miles to the north. He and Sandy lived with her two children in a house trailer set in the middle of 120 acres of land that Pete had bought for $200 down, $200 a month, three years before we heard about this canyon. Though their homestead was almost a mile and three hills away, on very still mornings we could hear the unmistakable bark of Mike, their bull mastiff, echoing through the canyon.

I left Larry and Bob to retell "the story" yet again and went back to get at least one or two boxes emptied and sorted before it became dark. The three men soon disappeared in the direction of the well.

An hour later I heard men's voices and opened the kitchen door to another pleasant surprise. "Hear that sound?" Larry almost shouted. "We got the pump working. We've got water to the house now. The big tank on the hill doesn't have any bullet holes in it for the lower two feet, so we can use it like it is for a while."

That evening, I climbed into the big brass bed in a wonderfully improved frame of mind. I'd had a hot shower in the ugly old concrete shower stall, courtesy of an ancient but amazingly efficient propane water heater. I wasn't going to have wood shavings dragged directly into the house every day. Our neighbors seemed friendly, helpful, and funny. Forgotten for the moment

was my sense of isolation, my shock at guns being flung around with the casualness of garden tools, the immense amount of work facing me.

I closed my eyes. Then I heard it: patter, patter, patter. I felt Larry tense against me. The rat feet paused. *Snap!* went the huge trap Larry had planted in the ceiling area over our heads. *Thump!* went the body of the rat against the ceiling boards.

We literally cheered. "Let's have a drink to our new home," Larry said as he re-lit the oil lamp on its chair-stand beside the bed. He brought me a glass of cream sherry and saluted with his whiskey and water. "Here's to the sweet smell of success."

Then the racket began. *Thump, thump, thump!* That rat wasn't dead. It was dragging the trap around with it.

"Do something!" I demanded.

"I can't climb into the attic to get it in the dark," Larry answered, distressed. "Let's go sleep in the truck."

Out in the truck again. Guns and bulldozers, rats, the screech of truck tires, my mother's voice whispering, "You'll be safe and sound, won't have to worry about you..." — all of these wove their way through my brain as I dozed restlessly through the night, startled awake a dozen times by the call of coyotes, the hoots of an owl.

Chapter 2

The First Thanksgiving

I was greeted by an ever-spreading puddle of water when I went into the bathroom at daybreak. Pinhole leaks studded the pipe leading down the wall from the copper toilet tank. "I'll find a bucket," Larry called.

Bucket in place, floor mopped up, I set to work brewing coffee as Larry climbed the rusty ladder that leaned permanently beside the kitchen door. I heard him clamber onto the roof, then open the ventilator cover that lead into the attic space over our front room/bedroom. "Take a look at this," he yelled. I ran outside just in time to see the black and grey body of a dead packrat come hurtling down to the driveway, still attached to the huge trap. A second trap and rat followed. "I think we're winning," Larry said as he climbed down and released the rats into the steel drum we were using as an incinerator. "Probably need to get a few more traps. Be a good idea if you do the shopping. I can stay here and get started on the plumbing."

"I've got to call my folks when I'm in town," I commented, as I grilled toast over the stove top flames. "I promised Mom I'd let her know if we were coming up for Thanksgiving. Today's Friday. Thanksgiving's only six days from now."

Larry looked up from where he was making a list of things he needed to fix the plumbing. I watched his brow wrinkle as he mentally switched gears. "Thanksgiving? You want to make a 230-mile round trip just for a dinner? Lin, if we start running up to your folks' place for every holiday, every birthday, every anniversary, we'll never get anything done. They lived without you for eleven years; they won't miss you now. We just can't get started on that routine."

"Thanksgiving dinner isn't *that routine*," I snapped back. "Thanksgiving is the one special holiday of the year, no gift giving pressures, no real expense to anyone, everyone pitches in so there's no arguing over who does what, just an excuse to forget problems and eat too much turkey. What's one day? It's my family and I've been away a long time and I want to get to know them again."

"It is not 'just one day', damn it," Larry said. He carried his coffee out to the rickety card table we'd set up that served as the only eating space we had. "We'd have to stay over night, then it's breakfast and talk and two days. Then it's Christmas and your father's birthday and your sister's anniversary and your niece's grammar school graduation..."

"It is just Thanksgiving and this whole project means as much to me as it does to you. I've got just as much work to do as you. It's not your family so you stay home. I'm going. I'll make you a tuna fish sandwich for *your* thanksgiving dinner." I stamped out of the front room to refill my teacup and hide the tears that rushed to my eyes. I was angry at myself for breaking the rules I'd made years before — don't lose your temper over little things, save the tantrums for real problems; and usually I could. But between the accident the day before, the sleepless nights, and the rats, I'd lost the will to control a temper I knew wasn't always in my best interests.

This unexpected outbreak shook Larry. He didn't say a word. I came back and sat on the hearth. We didn't speak for a few minutes.

"I've got a better idea," Larry said, a twinkle in his eyes. "Tell them to come here. We'll have a country Thanksgiving."

"Here?" I said incredulously. "There's no furniture, no kitchen counters, that damn antique toilet doesn't work."

"You tell me your family likes camping," he answered. "They'll have sleeping bags, air mattresses. I can make up seats from the old planks out in the shed. The propane stove works even if it is small and maybe we can light the wood stove by then. There's lots of water in the well. Go find someone who is a real kitchen carpenter and we'll hire him to fit the counters. He's got the right tools. I don't."

This sudden shift caught me off-guard. "No one's going to have time for our problems right now, it's only a week before Thanksgiving." But my mind was already screening the possibilities. I love parties, the bigger the better, crowds of people enjoying an outing I'd helped organize. If my folks came here they'd see how much work lay ahead of us. They'd understand why, unlike my brother and sister, who lived within ten miles of my folks in the house-filled valleys north of Los Angeles, I couldn't take part in all the family activities. Larry didn't have the same concerns since his relatives lived almost 2000 miles away. "Okay," I said slowly. "I'll call everyone and invite them here if, and it's a big if, I can find a cabinet maker and if we can get the toilet fixed," I said, as I gathered up my purse and Larry's list and headed towards town.

I had been a bit disparaging when, as a teenager, I read Dale Carnegie's books on the power of positive thinking. But that day did seem to prove his axiom — the right attitude could move mountains. I drove down the four-block-long main street of Lake Elsinore, population 5253, elevation 1258 feet above sea level, to the plumbing supply house. I described the pipe I needed for our antique pull-chain type toilet. I was sure the man behind the counter would say something like, "Haven't seen those in years." In fact he did seem a bit concerned as he headed into the cavernous warehouse behind the store. A few minutes later I heard a yell from the far corner of that echoing expanse, "Just as I thought, we're out of chrome ones. Can you use a plain brass pipe?" While I paid the amazingly small price for the perfect pipe, he directed me two miles down the road to a cabinetmaker he knew.

I turned onto a dirt road just off the two-lane highway that skirted the extensive mud flats around the drying remains of Lake Elsinore, then drove past a scattering of low cost WWII bungalows set on weed-covered, unused land. At the last one I stopped, checked the number, and then walked past well cared for flowering bushes into a garage workshop. "For Thanksgiving?" the lanky, sawdust-coated cabinet maker said, "Of course I'll help you out. Lady doesn't need these cabinets until after the first of the month. I'll be up tomorrow. No electricity? No problem, usually isn't any power where I get jobs. I'll bring my own generator."

I couldn't believe the way my luck was running, so I tried another test. "You wouldn't know of anyone who rents tables, would you?"

The man called to his wife. She yelled back over the sound of a churning washing machine. "The music store, of course." That led me to one of the luckiest finds of that lucky day.

The music store was the only pretty shop along the otherwise dreary main street. Scattered among the shiny new guitars and trumpets, drums and electric pianos, were antique dolls decked out in lace and ribbon, riding in immaculate perambulators and carriages. At the back of the shop stood a lattice work alcove filled with crystal punch bowls, huge artificial floral displays and ribbon covered draperies. "My son and I share this shop," a very well-groomed woman said as she rushed to lead me up steep steps into the unfinished attic. "My name's Jean. The music business is his. I rent bridal supplies and restore dolls. Only have six chairs I can rent you, the rest are at the old folks home for a month — will this table do?" When she showed me the twelve-foot-long folding table, I felt so relieved I began to tell her how I felt slightly overwhelmed at being a city girl and sailor dropped into the middle of "the country."

"A sailor," she said, "my son will love that. He's mad about sailing. He and his wife had a sailboat and went to the South Seas in it."

"What is he doing out here?" I asked.

"His wife took off with another sailor. Then my son had to sell the boat to settle things. Now he's working to buy another one. He feels this town is bound to grow. Decided to be in at the ground floor. He figures the way Orange County is getting over crowded, people are going to start moving out here soon."

Jean refused a deposit for the table and chairs, and when I asked if I could get some change to use the payphone at the corner she said, "Don't waste your money, costs double what you pay on a private line. Use the phone in there among the bridal displays. It's on a separate line and only rings in April and May. You can pay me when the bill comes in. It's all itemized." I sank gratefully onto the thick carpet in the corner of the gaily decorated alcove for the first of what was to become a weekly session the town folk and Larry would call, "Lin's phone day."

"Come out to the country for Thanksgiving?" my mother said when I finally got through to her at the high school office where she worked. "What a fun idea. I'll bring the salads." Her response was echoed by my younger sister and her husband, my older brother and his two girls. I was so delighted with the way this morning's argument was dissolving into a potentially fun-filled solution that I couldn't stop my telephone spree. I called Jimmie and Barbara, our nominal landlords. "Great idea! We'll bring a spare bed and leave it in the back room so we can have a place to sleep over when we come out there."

Mary Baldwin, a sailor friend of mine, who for once was in the same part of the world at the same time as I, said, "I'll bring Dean and dessert." The half dozen other friends I called said, "Can't come for Thanksgiving dinner, but we'll drive up on Friday or Saturday."

I drove up the ever-more-familiar dirt road singing, *We'll kill the old grey goose when they come!*

Forgotten was the mess of the cottage. I had a truck full of weapons:

heavy-duty leather gloves for cleaning the animal droppings out of the pantry, plastic gloves for scrubbing the mouse-nest-filled oven, more traps, rat poison, scrubbers, cleaning solutions, brooms. The truck skidded on the loose gravel as I came around one corner a bit too quickly. The squeal of my tires and the shower of pebbles startled a roadrunner from its weedy nest. I took off after it, laughing as the roadrunner stretched its long legs on the straight away that led toward the first ravine.

I had a hard time sticking to my tasks in the house when Bob and his bulldozer arrived later that afternoon. I kept running over to see his progress as boulders yielded to the stubborn push of his eighteen-ton machine and rock crumbled into sand before his blade. We did get one surprise: in one of the driest areas of Southern California, in a place where water is more precious than land, Bob dug up yet another spring. Soon, bubbling fresh water turned one corner of our future boatyard into a muddy quagmire. But the setback only made Bob and Larry laugh as they assured me a few pipes and a bit of digging would solve the problem.

Two tired but satisfied people fell into the brass bed opposite the blazing fire that evening. The toilet no longer leaked. Bob and his machine had moved "that hill." The propane lights in the bathroom and kitchen now

worked, hissing like two gossiping old ladies as they cast a white glow across the rooms. Larry had scoured every last bit of animal droppings from the front room's red brick floor. I'd scrubbed both stoves clean and rubbed the top of the wood-burning one with cooking oil until it glowed shiny black against its red brick casing. Tomorrow, I'd start on the pile of ashes that filled its fire box and clean out the two other fireplaces.

"Bob said we'll never get rid of the mice and rats until we get a cat," Larry mumbled as he pulled back momentarily from the edge of sleep. "But I told him 'no animals.' Don't want to fall in love with a pet, then have to go through the agony of leaving it behind when it's time to go."

We never heard the sounds made by two rats and four mice that our traps caught that night.

◇◇

"How will I recognize the cabinet guy?" Larry called as I started down the drive with yet another shopping list next morning.

"He's tall, fortyish, black, slim," I called back.

Fresh sawdust covered the concrete slab in front of the kitchen door when I drove up three hours later, and the high-pitched racket of a tiny gasoline powered generator sounded like a serenade to me. The first section of wide, wood-grained counter was in place along the far side of the room. Larry was upside down under it, plumbing the kitchen sink. After four days of washing dishes in a bucket, that was a delightful sight. Edward, the cabinet maker, said no thanks to the burritos I had bought at a take-out owned and run by a Mexican family across from the music store. (We later learned the fine burritos they served were only half the reason they were busy. Their shop also served as a clearing house for the ever-changing population of Mexicans who sneaked across the border to seek any possible job for three dollars per hour cash, at a time when unemployment in northern Mexico was running at thirty five to forty percent and good wages there were only two-fifty to three dollars a day. These hardworking illegal aliens were to become an important part of our lives in Bull Canyon.)

The three of us leaned carefully against the loosely installed central counter, and as the carpenter took sandwiches and coffee from his lunch pail Larry asked, "How long you been living in Elsinore?" He told us a story that convinced me that my new friends at the music store were right — people were beginning to move away from the city and they probably would settle in this sparsely populated area.

"I had a nice little cabinet shop about forty-five miles from here, in the middle of Watts," Edward said. "New wife, plus her two young boys. Then the summer heat, the frustration growing in the blacks who didn't have a close family like I did, it all burst out into the riots that killed three people. Burned my shop and half the city with it. From then on I didn't have a chance. I tried opening another shop with the money I got from the insurance company, but no one would insure me for a business anywhere near Watts. My car insurance rates tripled, I couldn't get a policy for my house. They later called it red-lining and made it illegal, but back then it meant I couldn't finance any new equipment because I couldn't cover it with insurance. So they drove me out of business. Then I saw my kids playing in the rubble of the riots, being influenced by other black kids who were picking up the hate that filled their folks. I didn't blame them for being angry, but I didn't see any future in it either, and I didn't want my kids growing up with a ghetto mentality. So I took my chance and got out. Sold everything I could for thirty cents on the dollar and looked for a small town where my kids could live with all sorts of folks — Chinese, Mexicans, blacks, whites. It was kind of hard leaving behind my friends, my wife's folks. They used to come and visit us out here but now it's only once or twice a year because they say there's nothing to do. And it is harder to make a living here. Back in Watts I had all the work I could handle, making cabinets and displays for the fancy offices only twenty minutes away around Wilshire and Downtown. I had low rent, could hire low cost labor. But I'd never go back. When I visit my friends in L.A. and see their kids, jealous of the rich guys who drive flash cars through the rubble of the riots for a laugh, when I watch my nieces and nephews playing along the railroad tracks while the folks just up the highway have paved tennis courts and big grassy parks, then I know I made the right choice. Not many rich folks in Elsinore yet, not a lot of spare cash and I have to hustle to make enough so my boys can go to college in a few years. But the kids have lots of open space, they ride horses and swim and fish down at the lake with all kinds of kids instead of hanging out at some all-black pool hall."

The city Edward talked about seemed further away than fifty miles. The real problems and tough decisions he'd had to make made our field mouse and house restoration trials fade to their proper proportions. That night we swept out each of the new cupboards and drawers, then polished the sweeping counters he'd so deftly installed for us.

Two days before Thanksgiving we woke in a house that was actually becoming home-like. The furniture was still minimal, but boxes no longer littered the rooms. Our favorite books lined the wide ledge between the sun porch and front room. We'd taped up unframed prints and paintings we'd gathered in our travels to decorate the paneled walls. Only occasional patters from above our heads or a few scattered droppings among my canned food in the pantry reminded us of the packrats and field mice who were, in fact, our nearest neighbors.

"I'll leave the house to you. It's time I got started outside," Larry said. "If I don't get that workshop built soon, we'll never get going."

I could appreciate his impatience. The cleaning tasks that faced me in the sun porch and back bedroom seemed surmountable now.

"When are you planning to get to work on your writing?" he asked, throwing a crook into my three-week schedule of painting the spare room, the window casings, planting gardens, trimming trees, exploring the hills around us.

"Hadn't thought about that," I answered truthfully.

"That's normal, you always think of excuses to put off writing," he said between mouthfuls of toast. "If you don't set aside time and just ignore everything else, you'll never get to it."

"I haven't got a desk," I said in self-defense. "Next week I'll go look for a desk."

"Use the card table," he answered with a knowing glance. "You wrote your last book on a pad perched on your knee. One reason I invited everyone here was, I knew we'd work hard and get the place livable if we had a deadline. It's nearly there. Promise me you'll start writing Monday morning after Thanksgiving. That's one of the reasons we decided to live out here, so you would have a quiet place to work."

I did try to think about his words as I began nesting further into my home. But the ocean and sailing, the subjects I was supposed to write about, seemed too far away, too foreign to fit into this life and were soon forgotten as I set about scrubbing the worst of the beeswax and old bits of hive from the inside of the kitchen windows.

"I'm going to have to move that wood shed," Larry announced at coffee-break time. "I need some place to keep my tools and I can't be walking back and forth across two hundred and fifty feet of yard all the time."

I looked out at the wood-framed concrete-covered shed that definitely was an eyesore, set as it was almost in the center of the clearing by the kitchen door. "How do you move a thing like that? It must weigh a couple of tons?" I asked.

"I've been thinking about it," he said. "See that boulder over by the euc trees? If I got a block and tackle secured around that and got the shed on pipes, they'd act like rollers. We could haul it with the truck. That boulder must weigh a hell of a lot more than the shed. Did you see how much trouble Bob had moving it? Almost brought his Cat to a standstill."

One thing I'd learned living with Larry for fifteen years was, if he said he could move it, he *would* move it. I'd seen him shift solid lead sailboat keels that weighed more than two cars using nothing but old bits of pipe. I'd helped him lift and move our five-ton boat with a second-hand car jack and a few wedges. So I knew he had studied the situation far more carefully than his casual remarks implied. He probably had surveyed the weapons at hand and already had a dozen items added to the ever present shopping list. But even more important, I knew that when he said, "I've got to move..." he really meant "we," and when "we" got going on a project, there'd be a lot of yelling and "Grab that timber! Quick! Haul up that pipe, yes, you *can* move it, hurry..." I'd end up exhausted, filthy and covered with Band-Aids. Larry would end up in the same shape. But "it" — whatever "it" was — would be moved, then we'd both end up laughing as we gloated over our latest triumph.

A light flashed in my mind: people, lots of people! Thanksgiving day! "Larry," I said quietly. "If we get that shed ready to move by Thursday, everyone can help us. Mary can drive the truck, Allen can —"

Larry cut me off, shaking his head. "You're always trying to get someone else involved in your projects — you and Tom Sawyer must have been first cousins! No one wants to work on their day off. They'll be dressed up, looking for some relaxation."

"But Larry, people love moving things, building things. It's like barn-raising, a reason for a party."

"Nope," he said firmly. "I won't take advantage of your family."

We finally reached a compromise when I offered to move five cords of firewood plus enough rodent nests and droppings to fill a fifty-five gallon drum from inside the shed. "You get it set up ready to move," I said. "Then on Thursday, I'll casually mention we plan to move it Monday. If the family volunteers, then so be it. If they don't, that's that."

When Bob Steele dropped by for his daily interrogation, I mentally scored a point as he said, "I'll drop off some long ropes I've got — good towing cables. Just wish I'd known you planned to move that shed. I'd never have agreed to drive out to Marly's folks."

Only one last problem remained by Wednesday evening. I came home with the twenty-eight pound turkey I'd ordered from a local farmer, plus four bags of groceries, the table and six chairs. I stored almost everything edible away in the rat-proof refrigerator or in the security of the truck cab. But that huge mound of beautiful bird wouldn't fit safely anywhere out of reach of the rodents who never seemed to diminish in number in spite of the four or six a day our peanut-butter-baited traps caught.

Larry, finally, came up with a solution. He wrapped the turkey in a piece of fish netting we'd brought from our boat, then hoisted it eight feet into the air above the foot of our brass bed using the hook that once held a large oil lamp. A bucket on the floor stood waiting for any drips as that turkey hung, slowly twisting through the night, the light from the fire dancing across its glistening skin to turn it into a pale duplicate of the full moon outside our windows.

I was up before dawn, remembering the yearly ritual of my childhood as I prepared the dressing, stuffed the turkey, then fashioned a roasting pan for it out of a dozen layers of aluminum foil stiffened by a hunk of old plywood. The pan just fit inside the propane oven. Then as the turkey began to roast, I stoked up the front room fire and sat down on the hearth with a cup of tea to watch the first soft rays of sunlight creep across Larry's still-sleeping face. We'd been through so many strange adventures together, and as I sat there that morning I had an almost intuitive flash of the stranger ones that lay ahead. But I instantly confined them to distant future, far away from this canyon that was just beginning to feel like a real home to me.

The aroma of garlic-and-sage-rubbed turkey slowly filled the pine-paneled room, and my thoughts were drawn back to the list of tasks I had to do before everyone arrived. As I basted the turkey, then formed loaves of bread and set them on the long, clean counter to rise, I surveyed my country cottage. Then I wondered, just as every daughter must, "What will Mom think?" Would she see only the peeling paint in the side rooms, the rotting ceiling panels in the kitchen, the old stains on borrowed tablecloths that couldn't disguise the rough legs of the rental table, the cracks in the few serving dishes we owned, the tree stumps and old packing chests that had to serve as seats for half of our guests? Or would she see the sweet-smelling boughs of pine, the cattails and brilliant autumn leaves I'd gathered to decorate the long table? Would she hear the crackle of the old wood stove as it warmed the kitchen and kept my fruit compote slowly simmering, and the sizzle of the turkey in the propane oven? Would she then envision, as I did, the romance of this hidden spot as it slowly yielded to my guiding efforts and became a real haven?

I need not have worried. Mom and I took a brief pause from the hustle and bustle in the kitchen where a laughing crew of women worked in warm harmony preparing candied sweet potatoes, pumpkin pies, minted peas and other traditional Thanksgiving treats, joking over the lack of electrical appliances, the need to stoke the wood burning stove every 20 minutes. Together we climbed up the hill to sit on the boulders next to the bullet-scarred water tank. We watched as seven quasi-engineers debated each move and Larry's booming laughter punctuated each success, as that ugly shed slid slowly along pipes and planks away from its home of sixty years.

"When your dad decided we should leave Detroit back in 1950 and move out here to California where there was more work, I dreamed it would be like this," Mom said wistfully. "Open, rugged, moldable, a place where I could be like the pioneers I saw in the movies." I nodded. Then we rose from our brief rest, and she pulled me back toward the house to dust off the battered but serviceable mahogany office desk, the four captain's chairs, and the double bed our landlords Jimmie and Barbara had brought to encourage our schemes.

"Remember, dinner is at four," my sister Bonnie and I reminded the crowd of shed movers as we distributed fresh baked chocolate chip cookies and tall glasses of lemonade. I found myself wishing I could get involved with the grunts and cheers of the moving team yet wanting to soak in every bit of the homeliness in the kitchen, where my sister's infant son Kurt lay cooing and smiling in his car seat crib right in the middle of the big central counter, surrounded by an ever growing array of food.

It was close to six o'clock when we finally got all seventeen men, women and children sufficiently clean and seated in front of the flickering fireplace at the overloaded table. I've never seen such a satisfied crew. Larry beamed as he said, "Sorry if we're late. I told them I'd settle the shed down by myself, but no one wanted to quit till it was right, sitting square and flat on the ground."

I looked around at the faces lit by candles spaced along the table, and in spite of my distinctly non-religious upbringing, in spite of the varied faiths of family and friends that surrounded me, I felt moved to ask, "Will everyone join hands for a prayer?" Then I dredged up the words I'd loved from my grammar school Thanksgiving pageant and began to sing:

We gather together to thank thee our maker,
For all of the blessing we count as our own,
For food and for friendship, for music, love and laughter,
For freedom in this world, for our country, our home.

My mother's clear soprano joined to fill the room and even my two normally restless young nieces sat quietly hand in hand between Larry and I for a minute after her sweet tones faded away.

More friends came by during the next three days to see our slowly maturing country boatyard. My family extended their stay and meals were a melange of leftovers and additions brought by each visitor. Nights saw the floors littered with sleeping bags and cushions. Afternoon walks turned into expeditions, as a dozen or more people helped us explore each path within a mile of our stone cottage. Family dogs chased rabbits, kids got skinned knees, and each evening found a half dozen of the younger ones asleep in the big brass bed while the fire roared and we adults sang to the accompaniment of two or three guitars — "Red River Valley," "Grandma's Feather Bed," "Bobby McGee."

Larry had his arm tightly around my waist as we walked to the head of the drive to wave good-bye to our last guest late Sunday afternoon. "Let's do it again next year," my brother Allen called. "You're on," Larry shouted back. Then we each picked up an arm full of firewood before heading back into the old stone cottage.

Chapter 3

The Long Road Home

I was a somewhat normal Southern Californian girl, raised amidst the growing web of freeways, shopping malls, and disappearing orange groves of the San Fernando Valley, just north of Los Angeles. With the glamour and apparent sophistication of 1950s Hollywood always on the periphery of my teenage vision, I'd tried, like most of my classmates, to mold myself into an imitation of Annette Funicello and her Mouseketeer companions. But a figure and face more suited to the tastes of Italian Renaissance painters than to *Modern Teen* or *Vogue* editors, an ear-to-ear grin that didn't quite fit my wide hazel eyes, plus an inability to stay neat for more than ten minutes at a time, kept me from joining the popular girls in my classes. So I gave up the idea of fitting in and instead chose idols like Joan Baez and Pete Seeger, and searched for stories about the few women I could find who chose or were thrust into lives of adventure.

By the time I was fourteen, I had grown to hate the restrictions of my family life, resenting the curfews my mother set as I headed out on each new date. I dreamed of the freedom I'd have as an adult.

As I bounded through high school in the early sixties, I experimented with being a civil rights activist just as seriously as I experimented with being a musician or a member of the debate team. I kept trying to find my niche, but each new experiment left me feeling confused. Yet one conviction held through all my teenage years. I knew I wanted to be "different." I couldn't define what different meant, but I sensed if I looked hard enough I'd recognize it when it happened.

Then, just before I turned eighteen, I walked out of my parents' home, my mother yelling, "Remember, the door is open. You can come back any time you want, but if you live here, you live by my rules."

I wanted to set my own rules. I got an apartment, sharing it with six other girls and one of their brothers, worked part-time driving a school bus and attended the local state college for as many hours each day as I could afford. When John F. Kennedy floated onto campus, I dreamed of joining his campaign for a Camelot world. Within a year, I became discouraged by the pre-equal rights prejudices of male instructors who found the idea of a girl who loved numbers to be laughable, by the "uselessness" of classes I was required to take, like Health Science, Social Anthropology or Composition 101, when my goal was a civil engineering degree. I blamed the instructors for my boredom but maybe I grew to be as tired of the discipline of school as I had the restrictions of my parents, so I joined the ranks of the quitters and reality struck. Now I was out on my own, working as a glorified accounting clerk, learning to wire programs into the first IBM commercial computers for Bob's Big Boy Hamburger Franchises HQ. I lived in my own apartment, which I tried to fix up with the guiding hints of Helen Gurley Brown in her book, *Sex and the Single Girl.* I may have been free. I was busy. But I was bored, and in spite of enough dates to fill most weekends, I was lonely.

Then Larry walked into my life.

Curly dark blond hair, laughing blue eyes, a full-cheeked, twenty-six-year-old face, a face that would have been more at home in a Scottish pub than in the Newport Beach waterfront bar where we actually met, and the lovely softness of a Canadian accent caught my eyes and ears. But what made me stick like a fly to honey was the adventure he offered when he said, "I'm skipper on a charter yacht. Spare time I'm building my own sailboat. I plan to set off cruising in a year or two."

I'd never heard of cruising. I'd only been sailing with my family in tiny, rented day-boats before I turned fourteen — and too "sophisticated" for silly days of sailing and chasing after my baby sister down by the beach.

It took three dates over the next few weeks before I'd been lured away from my "normal" life of assembling a better wardrobe, getting a better job, better education, better apartment, better man, better future. I wanted the excitement of not knowing where I would be next year or what I would be doing. Even more, I was lured by the promise of really being different. Larry offered me "different" on a platter as he described how he'd taken what sounded like only a few bold steps to go from being a sawmill worker in Vancouver, British Columbia, surrounded by the wrecks of cars that would some day be hot rods, to being a sailor bound for wonderful adventures. His life was filming movies in the warm turquoise waters of the Hawaiian islands as first mate on an eighty-five-foot schooner, or taking a gaggle of high-powered business men off to skin dive, surf and play on the wild sandy shores of Mexico as captain on a gleaming, fifty-four-foot ketch. I could picture his broad shoulders and slim hips swaying to the rhythm of the waves.

Less than three weeks after we met, I'd broken my apartment lease, quit my job and cut the final tenuous ties to my family by announcing, "I'm going to grab hold of my own life with this Canadian yacht skipper and see the whole world full-time, not just on two-week vacations."

"You are crazy," echoed in my ears as I ran from my family's entreaties that I choose security — boring, predictable security. On that bright spring day, my insatiable curiosity was stronger than any sense of logic.

"You *are* crazy," I said to myself as I tried to appear brave and nonchalant at the same time that I was seasick and scared, the day that Larry took me along on a short offshore voyage to introduce me to his world.

And the same thought occurred to me again as I worked with him in his boatshed trying to direct an unwilling piece of wood through a huge, whirring bandsaw, trying to keep my fingers clear of the threatening blade, yet not ruin the piece of mahogany that represented almost a day's wages. Larry had offered me adventures and I got adventures aplenty as we worked together for three years putting in sixty and seventy hours of work each week to build our first wooden cruising boat.

I learned a thousand ways to save money. I grew to judge every purchase by how many bronze screws I could buy for the boat if I didn't spend on this or made do without that. I got my shirts from the local thrift shop for fifty cents each, unconcerned if they looked slightly used. (They'd look far worse within a week when I wiped glue off my fingers onto my shirttails.) We cut living expenses to the bone by moving into the shop we had rented to build the boat. I turned the old office into a bedroom, the kitchen shared a corner of the bathroom, and our living room was the workshop where woodworking machinery sat next to overstuffed chairs we bought at the goodwill store. I loved every bit of it. It felt Bohemian. It definitely was different than the life my girlfriends back in the valley were living.

The most amazing thing to me — a girl whose most strenuous activity had been playing the piano or reluctantly washing my car on a Saturday morning — was that I loved the sheer physical work of the whole project.

I savored moments I spent helping to shape wood until it grew into the almost living thing called a boat, the excitement of learning to hold a tool correctly and then one day getting it to do my bidding without having to think each tiny step through. "Screws tighten clockwise, loosen counterclockwise, righty tighty, lefty loosey." Broken fingernails, glue-filled hair, bruised hands meant nothing when I applied another coat of varnish to something I'd actually helped build and watched the glow deepen the beauty of the grain-streaked wood. Then at night I'd lie in Larry's warm arms and listen as he spun a web of adventurous dreams. "She'll take care of us if we build her right," he'd say. Then he'd tell me stories of sailing friends who found lost treasures in faraway lands, who never had to work full-time for "the man" or punch a company time clock. "It's a bit riskier, but no risk, no glory," Larry would whisper in my ear instead of goodnight.

My family, on the other hand, was appalled by the specter of their "innocent daughter" throwing her life away on some itinerate Canadian sailing bum. "I didn't raise my children to live in a pigsty," my mother sighed as she walked through the sawdust-hazed combination bathroom-shower-kitchen-dining room of our rough boatshed/apartment. I laughed off her concerns, well aware she'd made yet another two-hundred-mile round trip intending to convince me I should recant and come home to normality and college. Two years into our joint boatbuilding project I came home from an evening of freelance bookkeeping work (days were saved for the much more important project, The Boat, and we earned our money in the evenings) to Larry's chuckled announcement, "Your father was just here. He came to have a man to man talk. Wants me to make an honest woman out of you. He's worried I'm using you to get my boat finished. Thinks I'll desert you as soon as it's launched then sail off on my own."

With the callousness of youth I barely considered my father's fears, just as Larry ignored his parents' anger against the "Californian hussy who's turning your head with talk of wandering irresponsibly around in a boat when you should be coming home to Canada to raise a family and settle down."

We worked together oblivious to their worries, growing ever closer, until after three-and-a-half years we couldn't think of any excuses not to get married. The rain poured down one late autumn day and flooded the boat yard, shorting the electricity to our tools. So we decided to take a break from our six-and-a half-day work week regime and lay luxuriously in bed and read. Then the tarpaper roof over our bed developed a leak. Larry got a pot from the kitchen and wired it to the exposed rafters above us. Twenty minutes

later another leak developed. "Looks like we can't stay in bed anymore," Larry sighed.

"What do we do now?" I asked, as I helped pull the bed onto its side away from the growing leaks.

"Can't play in bed, can't work on the boat, all our friends are working — be a good day to get married." So we got dressed, looked up the address of the county court offices and ran through the rain to our reliable, but slightly disreputable looking $200 truck.

"Guess we need a ring for this," Larry said, as he drove into the parking lot of the first shopping center we passed. "Show her every band you've got for under ten bucks," he announced to the bored looking salesman in the credit jewelry store.

"I'm only joking," he added as the man pointed to the two bands that cost less than ten dollars. The joke was on Larry as I tried on fifty bands to find the only one small enough to be worn by me that day cost $9.95.

We sat hand in hand waiting as the Santa Ana court judge supervised proceedings against a young Latino man accused of selling two ounces of marijuana to an undercover agent. When his lawyer called for a recess, the bailiff beckoned us into the somber, dark-paneled, desk-filled judge's chambers.

I'm not sure if it was the formality of the judge's chambers, his black robes and the grumbling rolling undertone of the thunder from the storm outside that made me do it. Maybe it was my delight with the nearness of our boat's completion, and my desire to please my sailing skipper/boat-building partner because his opportune entry into my life had changed its direction so completely. Maybe it was just good old Jewish guilt caused by my awareness of all the conventions I'd flaunted through the past few years. But when the judge finished his three-sentence sermon on the seriousness and responsibility of marriage and asked, "Do you Mary Lin... excuse me, but how do you pronounce your name? ...take this man to love, honor and cherish?" Like a fool, I piped in, "Love, honor, and *obey*." The judge looked startled, then smiled for the first time and repeated, "Do you, Mary Lin Zatkin, take this man to love, honor and obey?"

Larry could barely wait for the correct moment to kiss the bride. "Did you really mean that part about obey?" he whispered as he hugged me. Now, more than four decades later, whenever we sit amidst friends weaned and groomed on the feminist movement, I dread the moment when someone mentions weddings. I cringe as Larry starts out, "Want to hear the story of our wedding?" and I cringe again when he gets to the part about "obey."

The rain had stopped when we left the judge's chamber. The sun shone gently against the puddles and damp adobe-colored walls of downtown Santa Ana as we had a wedding lunch of chili and beans followed by lemon meringue pie at a café across from the old Spanish style courthouse. We saved our real celebrating until three weeks later when one hundred and fifty friends helped us launch five-ton, 24' *Seraffyn*, the boat we'd spent our hopes and dreams and hours building. She touched the water still speckled with a shower of inexpensive California champagne. Then Larry put up his hand for a moment's silence to announce, "Lin and I got married."

There was a resounding lack of interest, except from our parents. "Already thought you guys were married," several people said as they focused their attention on the far more important business of getting our boat ready for its first sail.

That small engineless sailboat, sans electricity, sans so-called modern necessities, did carry us toward the adventures Larry had offered me. We set off three months after she was launched, and for eleven years *Seraffyn* was our home as we crossed three oceans, seven seas and visited thirty-seven countries. We joined the rowdy festivals of Mexico and skin dived to our hearts content in the clear, lobster-filled waters of the Caribbean, climbed the volcanoes of the Azores, lived among the fishermen and working folks of Southern England and haunted the museums and bookshops of London. We sailed into the far northern reaches of the Baltic to celebrate the sleepless midsummer nights amid the energetic Finns, then stuck our noses behind the iron curtain of Polish politics and met the first organizers of Solidarity — before it became a force to shake the Kremlin. We got caught up in the wild gaiety of the Portuguese revolution and motorcycled through the mountains of France and Switzerland, then drank the wines of Spain and Italy. We experienced the tension of Israel as bombs went off a hundred feet from where I stood. Patrol boats pointed their menacing guns at us for half the night along the waters of the Gaza Strip. We knew the fear of being arrested in Tunisia for the twelve hours it took to convince authorities of our complete unawareness of a hidden military base that lay just beyond the point behind which we'd chosen to shelter. We lived through the terror of having the boat boarded by sub-machine-gun-toting Arab soldiers in the far reaches of southern Egypt while we lay at anchor riding out a raging gale without a translator in a thousand square miles. Adventure plagued us through the revolution-surrounded Red Sea and across the typhoon-streaked Bay of Bengal.

At first, we paid for these adventures by delivering yachts from one country to another for people who had more money than free time, or by working in boat building and repair yards along the way for three or four months at a time. Three years after we set sail, I wrote an angry letter to the editor of a sailing magazine that led to an invitation to write about our life afloat, especially since we were enjoying this amazing-seeming freedom for about $3,500 a year, an amount some people spent on a two or three week jaunt to Europe.

That first editor's eager acceptance of each story I wrote, and the checks he sent, began to give us even more freedom from the schedules imposed by the need to find work as we explored. Then Larry tried his hand at creating practical articles describing ways to improve boats and the gear on them, using the lessons we learned as we explored the shores of the Arabian seas and met Somerset Maugham-like characters along the Straits of Malacca. Rainy or stormy days no longer seemed an inconvenience as they became filled with writing projects, and we experienced the thrill of being invited to write for other, non-American sailing magazines. So, our yearly "freedom chip" fund grew until we could allow ourselves an extra $1,000 or $2,000 a year spending money as the lockers inside our small boat became ever more crowded with newly acquired (and in our minds, required) cameras, a typewriter, a filing cabinet.

Then about nine years after we set sail, there came the day when we both realized we were a bit weary of constantly moving onward, of never spending more then three or four months in one place, of always having to work to break down barriers in each new place we reached. We came to resent only seeing our families and old friends for a few days every three or four years. If you had pressed hard, you might even have gotten me to admit I was tired of adventures, tired of being different. Underlying this weariness was a desire to once again build something big, to watch a random pile of rough timber grow into the organized beauty of a finished sailing vessel under our own hands. And for me, there was the added attraction of being able to act like a "real" writer, with a stable desk and typewriter, access to phones and libraries for research, editors for reassurance. I was eager to explore the skills of my newfound profession.

We gradually finished our circumnavigation, crossing the pirate-plagued South China Sea and drifting north to Japan, then across the stormy, fog-shrouded lonely North Pacific to sail back toward the place we'd once called home, Newport Beach. Armed with our ability to earn most of the money we needed by writing for the nautical press, and the rest by doing occasional yacht deliveries, we were not restricted to a single locale as we began looking for a place to rejoin the so-called stable community of shore dwellers we'd left behind.

We searched from Nanaimo in Canada to San Diego in Southern California, leaving our boat in Vancouver for the winter. We stayed with friends, with family, hearing heartwarming reasons why we should choose a site near them for our project. We considered each potential building spot and found each had its drawbacks. We weren't comfortable with the hustle of cities. The traffic literally scared us after eleven years without a car. We couldn't afford the rents of quiet places on the edges of the city. The crude industrial complexes we'd have considered before when we were building our first boat at ages twenty and twenty-six didn't appeal to us as we came toward the edges of middle age. This time we were willing to keep our expenses down, but we didn't want to live in — as my mother had once put it — a pigsty, during the four years we knew we'd need to complete our new boat project.

Thus the little stone cottage grabbed our attention with its offer of the weekday solitude we needed to keep working, and its proximity to old friends who said they'd willingly drive an hour and a half to spend a weekend in the country. We shrugged off the extra work of rejuvenating the cottage by saying, "We'd want to fix up any place we rented to suit us." Though I'd had some serious doubts once we actually made the move out to the canyon, the warmth of our Thanksgiving festivities made me feel we'd finally come home.

Chapter 4

Settling In

On the Monday after Thanksgiving I did try to settle in at my newly acquired, slightly battered, executive-sized mahogany desk. Larry kindled a slow burning fire to warm my office-cum-living-room-cum-bedroom, then went out into the crisp morning to organize his newly situated tool shed. Positioning my miniature portable typewriter on the pull-out board that had obviously been designed for a much larger machine, aligning pencils, pens, paper, arranging my small array of reference files kept me busy for the first half of the morning. I'd positioned my desk in a corner with my back to two large windows to give me good working light. When the rays of the wintry sun began climbing down the canyon sides, I found this position had another advantage. If I needed an excuse to ignore the blank sheet of paper in front of me, I only had to glance sideways to find the welcome distraction of a squirrel cautiously searching for seeds, or a hawk soaring along the thermal updrafts of the canyon, or a lizard doing its early morning push-ups on the low stone wall behind the cottage. I did write a new shopping list that first morning, things I needed for writing. I did write "outline" on top of a page. I did do some serious thinking about what I wanted to write. I did take a half hour getting a perfectly arranged lunch ready before I called Larry. I did change the subject when he asked what I'd written so far.

He sensed my evasion and gently suggested, "I'm sure you need some things in town after all that company. I need some timber to start building my loft floor. Why don't you run in this afternoon? Tomorrow you can work until two thirty like we planned."

I leapt at this fully legitimate excuse to escape the self-imposed confines of my "office." I called encouragement to the roadrunner that raced alongside Old Gold as I bounced across the stream bed toward five days worth of mail that would be waiting at the local post office.

It took almost two more weeks to settle into a semblance of routine. The alarm would ring at six thirty. I'd stay hidden under the thick quilts as Larry, with indomitable patience, coaxed the ancient, poorly installed and idiosyncratic brick and cast-iron cook stove in the kitchen alight. First he'd lay a Boy Scout-style stack of paper and kindling in its fire box. Then he'd open the damper and both top plates, close the door leading into the front room, and, finally, open the outside kitchen door seven inches. Then he'd strike a match and light the paper below the kindling, count to fifty and open the window leading to the sun porch, close the kitchen door slowly, and cross his fingers. If all went well, the fire would leap to life and within five minutes the kitchen and adjacent bathroom would begin to warm and I'd leave my cocoon. If, on the other hand, something went wrong, billows of smoke would begin to pour out of every crevasse of that recalcitrant stove and Larry would rush around throwing every door and window in the house wide open while I hid under the covers until the clouds cleared. By now the billows of smoke were becoming a less frequent occurrence. (They only seemed to happen when we had guests from the city who then went away extolling the virtues of electricity and piped-in natural gas.)

I'd cook breakfast, staying as close to the stove as possible while Larry stoked up the big fire in the front room. By eight o'clock the house would be evenly warmed and we'd separate, Larry to his work in the slowly developing boatyard, me to work on the slowly developing manuscript in the far corner of the front room, opposite the bed. At two thirty, I'd either help Larry for a while, raking the eventual boatyard level, moving rocks and cutting brush, or I'd continue my assault on the cottage, painting floors, walls and window casements.

As I worked, I often wondered about the man who'd cut away the hillside to build this handsome stone building. My neighbors and people in the village fed me little tidbits about him from time to time. Everyone called him Old Man Payonessa. Antonio Payonessa, who had worked in the valley below us, had been a second generation Italian American. Like many children of immigrants, he dreamed of owning land like his forefathers had known in the rocky, dry hills of Calabria. Just after the turn of the 20th century, he bought two square miles from a county land auction. It was land that had been surveyed and divided up into townships in the aftermath of the great gold rush, sold to future prospectors then forgotten by their heirs so taxes remained unpaid until foreclosure put the land on the auctioneers block.

For the next ten years, Old Man Payonessa came out to spend each spare day tramping over the land he bought for ten cents an acre. He camped at each special spot until he knew its moods, then moved on to try another. From the stories our neighbors and folks in town related, we could imagine how he set up camp in the glaring sunlight of the desert summer and dreamed of a home surrounded by trees, how he camped on the ridge tops to survey the spectacular views but had to move when the cold, buffeting winds of winter threatened to tear his tent to shreds. He'd camped along the river bed when the first road was the narrow trail hacked out by mule riding miners in their search for gold, silver or any potentially useful mineral deposits and by herders looking for good grazing for the cattle and sheep that once fed in these hills. The flash floods of late autumn drove him away from the easiest access to water so he searched each ravine until he found an artesian spring that was dependable and far above the bottom of the canyon.

When he finally brought his new bride to see the place where some day

he promised a rose-covered cottage would stand, he had chosen a wondrous site, one that in our day and age would have been called ecologically and environmentally sound. Payonessa gradually cut and cleared a flat area thirty feet above the floor of the canyon, on a bluff at the side of a smoothly sloping hill that rose to form a perfect shade against the glaring heat of the long summer mornings. By the time the cold of the winter pressed upon these desert highlands, the sun had begun its southern migration to a dip between the hills so the stone cottage stood in sunshine until late in the day. Because it was well below the crests of the higher hills, the cold blasts of winter winds seemed to leap above it; we'd listen to radio reports of gales, yet walk out into a yard stirred only by mild breezes. I remember the shock of driving down the canyon one windy day to see dozens of trees felled by wind. The same winds, blocked by the hills near our cottage, had only blown away the last leaves of autumn.

Then came the breezes of summer. Payonessa had felt their desperately needed cooling power as the heat of the flat lands around the lake drew them down from the upper hills. He'd drawn his dream house so the big windows of each room would open to welcome the breeze inside but thick stone, windowless walls blocked the direct glare of the blazing summer sun.

Perhaps with a sense of supreme compromise he'd decided to build close enough to the one constant source of water, the abandoned well right next to the creek bed, so that when the artesian spring we now used couldn't provide enough for his needs, he could lift the extra with the help of a simple hand pump to keep his precious trees alive. Yet he was far enough from the bottom of the canyon to avoid the mosquitoes and flying insects that turned the course of the stream into a violin-like concerto each spring. The herd of insects rarely ventured far enough to drive anyone out from under the maturing chinaberry trees of the front garden.

From the day he decided on his site, Payonessa began planting trees, slow-growing ones interspersed with others that grew like the proverbial beanstalk. Even as he worked in town to earn the money for the concrete he'd need to lay his foundations, he made a pilgrimage twice each week during the long hot summer days to carry water to his trees, so that before the first of the thick stone walls rose to shoulder height, there was shade for the tent he camped in. The stones he used were right at hand and by the time they rose to the height he wanted, the land around the cottage was clear and ready for the gardens his wife planned in her mind. From stories other people told of the stone cottage, rose bushes did grow to cover the stonework, ivy sprouted and still covered the back of the house. I wish I'd seen the manicured gardens of Judith Payonessa where lawns were said to have felt like velvet, lilac and camellias were said to have perfumed the desert air. Now, only the shady grove of trees plus the remnants of iris, narcissus, naked lady lilies, ivy and two determined but ragged rose bushes survived the ten years of neglect the cottage suffered after Old Man Payonessa died and before we came to the canyon.

I tried to find a few minutes at the end of each day to clean up the flower beds Judith had tended so carefully, or to trim the branches of the chinaberry trees so the yard looked more like a park than a jungle. Then just as the sun dropped behind the hills across the canyon, an hour before the real sunset, the increasing cold would remind me to cart three armloads of firewood into the house — bits of sycamore to serve as kindling and kitchen stove fuel, split eucalyptus logs for the main fireplace. Then I'd light each of the half-dozen oil lamps we needed for the evening, and prepare our dinner.

The short winter days were both a trial and a delight. We had so much we wanted to get done that we resented having to stop at five thirty when the light faded. But the reward: some of the most relaxed, intimate evenings of our lives. We'd linger over a glass of wine discussing what we'd done that day, what we planned to do tomorrow. I'd read what I'd written about the sailing adventures that had led us to this cottage. Sometimes I'd get out our old log books and read the daily paragraphs that tersely described faraway-seeming events, like the wind that blew suddenly into our Red Sea anchorage, forcing Larry to climb out of a warm, dry bunk onto a rain-swept deck to struggle for two hours preparing and setting our storm anchor to back up the two anchors that we'd already set. Other daily entries mentioned simply "joined James and Anne for lunch and a visit to the Bonners." The brevity didn't stop us from spending the next firelit hour recalling that long walk through pressing tropical heat from our Malaysian river anchorage to the British colonial outpost where our friend James managed a five-thousand-acre rubber plantation. A visit to the Bonners meant climbing into a small, single-engine plane and taking off from a grassy airstrip cleared through crowding rainforest, then flying low over another forest clearing to scare any jungle creatures off the grass strip that served as a runway, before coming in to land.

Larry would urge me to include these incidents in my next day's writing, or to tell about the warm evening breezes as we sailed across bio-luminescence-lit seas on our way toward the unbelievable bustle of Singapore. "Tell your readers how clean it is living on a boat," he'd say as we contrasted this to the mud and dust that surrounded us now. My mind would begin to form Larry's ideas into logical additions to my own thoughts until it would be hard to remember whose words actually reached the final pages.

When dinner was ready the two of us would carry our plates to the card table next to the fireplace along with a notepad and pen, so we could add to the shopping lists I realized would be a constant part of our life in the canyon. Then, after dinner, I'd get out the guitar and we'd sing for a while as the fire slowly dwindled.

My daily dashes to the village gradually became twice-weekly as I filled the pantry and Larry accumulated enough building materials to keep him busy. Within a few months, I began to feel less like a roadrunner and more like a writer when I finally got down to a weekly visit to town for phone calls, mail, laundry and supplies. But it would be almost a year before either of us willingly missed a weekly visit to the local swap meet.

We had been to a few Sunday parking lot swap meets in places like Los Angeles and Orange County. We'd spent many years of our lives shopping in the marketplace stalls and kasbahs of less developed countries, but we'd never seen anything quite as exotic as "Pedlars Village — Lake Elsinore, California." Beneath that misspelled name, the huge yellow sign set high in the air at the junction of two-lane State Highway 71 and an equally unimposing Highway 74 proclaimed, "Y'all Come Heer!" Forty acres of scorched-looking dirt was divided almost in half by a line of towering eucalyptus trees. The half nearest Highway 74 stayed empty five and a half days a week except for a small fenced ring where on Saturday and Sunday, eight sleepy looking ponies plodded along at the edges of a metal wheel carrying shrieking children for 50 cents a ride.

Five hundred feet from the highway, a tiny, gaily-painted sign-bedecked booth divided the road into the village. And here reigned Jerry, the owner of the large square of flat land and mayhem. His ten-gallon Texas-style hat shaded a lined, sun-worn face seamed with the scars of a few too many wild bull rides. Its sweeping brim almost hid the blue eyes that seemed to mourn for a life that had been more real a hundred years before. His heavily tooled, perfectly-oiled, high-heeled leather boots increased his height so he reached a grand total of five feet, five inches. Behind Jerry was the dustiest, most haphazard collection of old trailers, sheds and stands we had ever seen. Row upon row of rickety stalls sold second-hand goods, old furniture, and bits of metal, battered books, records and "antique" jewelry. Some of the stalls were actually fenced areas as large as a normal home site. Their proprietors lived in trailers or motor homes, now firmly rooted by lean-tos, sun awnings, even complete free standing roofs built of rough timbers and plastic sheeting to protect metal tops that had long ago rusted through.

Rough-looking German shepherds and massive mongrels guarded collections of the most disreputable-looking junk I have ever seen. But as we worked restoring the stone cottage, I began to see bits of gold amidst that dust and rust. First it was 100 galvanized coat hangers — $1.50 for the lot; then the perfect piece of pipe to reconnect our main water tank — $2.80; the part to get our water pump going — 50 cents; the grating to fit our kitchen stove — $4; and the perfect hinge to match the others on our garage door — $1. As we began to know the lanes and alleys of Pedlars Village as intimately as our own land, we realized that our little patchwork cottage was probably built of bargains from this swap meet. The antique transom windows above my bed looked like souvenirs of some old schoolhouse in the valley, demolished years before and sold in bits and pieces. The rugged weed-fighting tools we found in our shed had definitely come from here.

So most Sundays would find us checking for the newest treasures the regulars had acquired during their weekly searches through garage sales, auctions, demolition sites and by offering "cash for junk." The front half of Jerry's land would be filled with pickup trucks and battered cars sitting side by side with shiny "city folk" cars. The air would be filled with the sound of competing country music radio stations, snarling dogs, and the yells of anxious mothers searching for their offspring who had wandered off to fondle "bunnies for sale." We'd buy beautiful fresh produce from the Mexican and Chinese families who kept gardens behind their small rented houses and carried it to the village to sell from the backs of battered trucks. Sometimes a treasure of an old Stanley plane or socket chisel made before hand tools were mass produced would turn up. Larry would justify adding it to his growing collection of boatbuilding tools by saying, "If I don't need it, one of my friends down at the beach will. Besides, how can I go wrong for two bucks?"

As we came to know Pedlars Village we learned that Jerry acted not only as cashier, banker and bouncer, but mayor, judge and jury for the 150 people who made their homes on his land. We also found the rough-looking accommodations in the village often belied the wealth of many of "Jerry's Folks."

Ruth, who sold the "antique" jewelry, could have afforded almost any home she wanted. Rumor had it that she owned apartment buildings in several cities to the north, but she preferred the free-wheeling society of this 40-acre corner. Ruth had made a lucrative business of offering cash for old jewelry. She'd wait all weekend in her rough wooden stand, dressed in run-down cowboy boots, a bandanna holding her windblown hair out of her age-hooded eyes, an old western style shirt tucked into a well-worn leather belt, arms covered with turquoise studded silver bracelets from Mexico. We rarely saw anyone spend more than a few dollars at her stand. But I often spotted harried looking women, babes in arms, one or two children tugging at dusty jeans, as they came to get some spending money by selling off Grandma's old-fashioned brooches, necklaces, and rings.

Then one day I spotted Ruth at the restaurant in downtown Elsinore. She looked closer to fifty years old than the sixty I'd have guessed at Pedlars Village. Wearing a rose-colored silk dress, leather high-heeled shoes crossed neatly beneath the table, hair coiffured in the latest style, heavy gold-drop earrings and old gold bangles quietly proclaiming her latest finds, she sat sipping a cup of coffee while across from her, one of the wealthy ladies from Newport Beach, part of her loyal following, eagerly viewed the latest treasures. The buyer paid with cash, discreetly folded into a bulging envelope.

"I'd never move from the Village," Ruth said to me some time later, "I'd miss my friends and I'd miss the excitement of spotting something real in a boxful of doodads someone found when they were cleaning out Aunty's cabinet."

The local sheriff kept an eye on the village and Jerry warned his villagers, "No fencing." But many of the less valuable items that went missing from homes in the valley or canyons above it eventually turned up here to be bought by one of a thousand shoppers who wandered around on sunny Sunday mornings. Shoppers ranged from locals on their way home from church, to city tourists searching for a bit of local color before driving toward the golf courses of Escondito, to sky divers headed toward Perris to would-be flyers bound toward the Ortega Highway Heights with hang gliders eager to catch high spiraling thermal lifts.

"Some day the police are going to close me down," Jerry said when I came to know him better. "If they don't it will be the health department or the zoning commission. Hate to see it, the place is a goldmine and these are my people, but if they let me stay open three or four years more, the town will have grown out to here. By then the new freeway from Corona to San Diego will come right through here and I can sell this land to a developer. So I can't lose either way. I only paid one day's rodeo winnings for all forty acres back when the lake was almost dried up and everyone said Elsinore was dead. Some day there'll be more water in the lake." Our conversations never lasted long; someone would always rush up breathlessly to announce, "Guys acting drunk over by the ice cream truck," or "John's putting too much junk on the path, no one can get to my stall." Then Jerry would touch the sweeping brim of his silver-trimmed hat with his broad-knuckled hand and say, "Excuse me, Miss Lin," and hustle off, his bowed legs marking double time as he went to settle yet another problem for "his people."

Just as we eventually got over the novelty of Pedlars Villages, our neighbors slowly got over the novelty of two city folk who were crazy enough to think they could build a boat in the mountains. Their visits dwindled to once or twice a week. Pete, who worked as a police guard at the Orange County jail for ten days straight, then had five days off, would stop by on his way home to see what we'd gotten done. After a quick survey, he'd lean back against his rusty compact pickup truck and begin a tale of life in the canyon "...before you guys moved in." Stories of drunk hunters who drove off the road, then came looking for help, the dead body someone found up the canyon five years previously, the "dirt bags on their damn dirt bikes" who tried every trail and sometimes ended up lost on his hilltop homestead. "I walk out with my shotgun, Sandy tells Mike to growl, and they take off," he said one day as he reached into the car for another can of Bud. A grey squirrel skittered along the roof of the stone garage fifty feet from where we stood. The squirrel paused as it reached the edge and looked our way. "Mind if I shoot it?" Pete asked quietly, reaching behind him toward a revolver that lay on the front seat of his car.

"You wouldn't shoot a lovely little thing like that?" I said, thinking he was just trying to tease the "city kid."

"Damn pests, covered with fleas, ticks, lice, filthy, eat through anything, worse thieves than packrats. You may think they're cute now, but as soon as the rains come you'll think differently. I shoot every damn one I see." He put his gun down and I gladly changed the subject, telling him we'd finally found the nest of the packrat that had stolen every single socket out of Larry's chrome-plated socket set. That two-pound rat had wiggled through a tiny knot hole in the floor of the tool shed and left a leaf, a nut or a piece of fungus in the socket set box in exchange for each glittery bit he took. When we located his hiding spot, under a pile of leaves beyond the eucalyptus trees, we found every socket plus more than fifty large bronze screws and an ancient pair of safety glasses. We hadn't missed the screws, but when we went to put them back in their barrel, we again found the edibles the rat felt were fair exchange.

Just as with the squirrels, we found the packrat's antics amusing those first few months. But by Spring, we'd grown tired of searching for missing bits and pieces at the packrat nest. When we found the third window screen gnawed through by a squirrel that had the audacity to sit on our hearth and chatter at us when we came in to eat lunch, we reluctantly began to set traps and poison bait to control the "lice-ridden, flea-covered nuisances." But with our aversion to scaring off the birds that made the trees around us come alive, we never let Pete shoot squirrels or rabbits on the land near the cottage.

Sandy Shomler, Pete's wife, brought the simple muslin curtains she'd stitched up for my kitchen windows late one afternoon. "Hell, Pete gave me a revolver for a wedding present," she commented. "Cop friend loaned us his mountain cottage for our honeymoon. Place was overrun with rats. There were already some bullet holes in the ceiling so Pete and I lay in bed shooting through the cracks, trying to get those rats — great fun!"

I'd come to take Sandy's stories with a grain of salt, but Pete later concurred on their honeymoon shoot-in. Rumor among the canyon dwellers was that Sandy and Pete met when he arrested her for a street offense late one evening. My curiosity got the better of me as we worked together threading wooden dowels into the curtains to hang them from the simple cup-hook hangers I'd threaded into the wooden sashes. I tried to lead the conversation to a convenient starting place, but finally blurted out, "Where did you meet Pete?" Sandy carefully patted a strand of lacquered blonde hair into place on her teased bouffant, pulled back her shoulders and announced, "Orange County Jail." Then, as if some worrisome thought flashed into her mind, her brow furrowed and she added, "You really should've let me embroider some flowers on these curtains. They look so sad with only that one brown stripe," she said. I never did get a more concise answer from Sandy, nor did I ask anyone else.

Bob Steele's visits still seemed to be perfectly timed to any new event in our lives; he usually had suggestions to help us solve each canyon-life problem we encountered. To lay the foundations for the shed, Larry had to dig almost 100 feet of trench, then settle and level the huge creosoted ex-wharf pilings we'd dragged home from a salvage yard at the edge of Riverside City. "Hey, Larry, why don't you borrow my Mexi-help, he's a mad digger, only three dollars an hour, and he's a lot faster than you. I'll send him down tomorrow with a real shovel," Bob said. Then he walked into the kitchen, plopped his bulk onto a stool, helped himself to one of the cookies I offered and said, "Saw Sandy's car here yesterday. What you two doing?"

Our first introduction to Bob's "Mexi-help" had us hooked. Mariano was one of six Mexican brothers who sneaked across the border to look for work in the U.S. They shared a tiny motel room at the edge of town with another group of brothers. Half of everything they earned, laboring at any job they were offered, got sent home to families in northern Mexico via postal money order on Friday afternoons. About once a month, one or the other of the brothers would be caught by immigration officials and shipped back to Mexico, only to sneak back across the border again within a week. But the brothers never failed to send someone to do the job if they got a message from us. We had spent almost three years living, working and exploring in Spanish speaking countries so we had a basic working knowledge of the language. We hired Mariano and his brothers whenever we could scrape up a few dollars extra or whenever Jimmie Moore, the real owner of the cottage, suggested he'd pay for help if we'd supervise. We gradually learned that over half of the workers at the farms and nurseries in the valley below us were illegal aliens. Even though unemployment among legal residents in Elsinore was said to be close to 14 percent that year, it was only these Mexicans who came up our long dusty road to ask, "Is there any kind of work for me? I work very hard!"

We never asked how or where the brothers slipped across the closely-guarded border seventy-five miles to the south. But, one day, Mariano, the oldest at twenty-seven, asked "Could you pay me for two extra days now and I will make sure your fire road is perfect and clear by the weekend? I have to bring my wife across. It is time to have our baby." Mariano was back at work two days later, but he carefully avoided talking of his wife. Six months later he proudly showed us his five-month-old daughter when he came to ask if we had any work for him that month. Whenever we did have work for him, Mariano would arrive at our cottage in the faded green 1963 Cadillac he shared with his brothers. He'd have dropped each of them at the jobs they found for the day, then he would maneuver the massive car into a well-shaded flat spot, arrange the back seat into a toy-filled playpen where he'd leave his bouncing daughter, then set to work clearing the fire road or cutting trees or trenching in plumbing.

"My wife has a full-time job at the big tree nursery," he told us. "If we can earn an extra $400, the lawyer in Murrieta said he could get us legal papers because my child was born in the United States. She is an American," he told us in his half-Spanish, half-English. "Some day I will be too."

Larry and I wondered if this lawyer's promises were fair or, if he, like others we had heard of, was taking advantage of these hardworking people. About two years after we first hired Mariano, he came dressed in his Sunday best, his wife and child gleaming like two angels in white. His attorney had told him he needed letters from as many people as possible saying he was a good worker and would make a good citizen. Our letter firmly in hand, he offered to work an extra day in exchange. Two weeks later, after what we later learned had been five years of paying off people to sneak him into the country, of paying others to carry money back to his family when the U.S. Post Office refused to send postal orders to Mexico because of the wildly fluctuating Mexican peso, of avoiding any chance encounter with the police or anyone who could turn him or his wife in to the immigration officials, Mariano arrived with a box of Mexican sweets to announce, "I have a legal working permit and now I can take a full-time job at the new factory in Rancho, California, because I can get a social security card. So I can't work for you, but when you need, I'll send my brother Manuelo. He needs to earn $400 for the lawyer now."

"You know, it's ironic, isn't it?" Larry mused that evening just as I began to nod off to sleep.

"What?" I asked groggily.

"Mariano's ancestors explored and settled this land. They were here two or three hundred years before any Americans even saw it. They built the first roads, drew the first maps, and named every city from San Diego to San Francisco. I'll bet it pisses him off to have to sneak across an imaginary line into what was a territory of Mexico for almost three centuries. Seems sad he had to break the law just so he and his wife could work for the minimum wage."

If Larry hadn't started his late night philosophical meanderings we might never have heard it: Rrowwerr, rrowwerr. The other night sounds echoed familiarly around this new one. The screech owl called from his favorite tree behind the house, mice scurried overhead, the yip, yip, yip of a coyote echoed from down canyon. Then we heard it again: rrowwerr. "Something's wrong," Larry said. "I'll take a look."

"It's probably some mountain lion or a lynx and you'll get more than a look if you aren't careful," I said as I burrowed deeper into the quilts.

"Come on, Lin, there usually aren't any big animals around here. Bob's been putting you on," he said as he pulled on jeans and a jacket then found the flashlight we kept on top of the refrigerator. I saw the beam of light flash around the front yard. I heard scrambling sounds and Larry yelled, "Come see this!"

"What is it?" I called back.

"C'mon, you little bedbug, get your clothes on and come see."

I had no desire to climb out of that warm bed and said so.

"Come on, Lin, I really need your help, hurry!"

So I pulled on some clothes and went out to the far corner of the front yard where a magnificent Himalayan pine spread its drooping branches.

There, ten feet up, huddled in the glare of Larry's light, was a small grey and white cat. "Hold the light while I climb up and get it," Larry said. "It's a wonder some coyote didn't eat it."

He carried the amazingly placid three- or four-month old kitten into the house and searched out a can of evaporated milk. "We'll have to find a home for it. Maybe you can ask around when you go into town on Friday."

"Maybe we should keep it," I said, as the kitten rubbed his back against my leg and his purr reverberated like a smooth running engine. "Bob says the only way we'll ever keep the mice down is to get a cat."

"Nope," Larry answered. "We both decided, no animals. We'll be moving on in two or three years and we can't take animals with us. So we don't need any emotional attachments. Hell, I still miss the dog I had when I was fourteen."

By Friday the matter was settled. "Better put cat food on your list and a flea collar too," Larry said at coffee-break time as Shadow Cat stretched his head toward the ear scratching he knew always waited for him if he got close to Larry. "He's not a pet, he's a working part of the place. How many rats has he caught so far this week?"

That long-haired mouser more than earned his keep as he quickly controlled the rodent population around the cottage. He knew we needed him. His pride was tangible the day he dragged a ten-inch-long packrat out for our inspection. But most enjoyable was his penchant for following us everywhere we went.

Our neighbors watched him scouting the edges of the road just ahead as Larry and I took Sunday morning walks to the far edges of the land we were beginning to think of as ours and along the streambed where I searched for flowers and leaves to decorate our dining table. Shadow soon lost his real name, to be called "Dog" by all who knew him.

A month or so later when Bob Steele stopped by for one of his weekly inspections, I came out with a tray of coffee and fresh bread to see the two men perched on a workbench, Dog between them purring contentedly.

"How's the rat problem?" Bob asked. "Haven't heard many complaints lately."

"Thank God that little cat got lost and wandered in," I replied. "He's solving my biggest problem. Haven't seen a mouse turd in the house for a week. Haven't had to set a trap. It's great."

Bob began to laugh. Every bit of his huge frame began to shake. Tears formed as he tried to stop. They rolled down his wind-wrinkled face. We looked on in puzzlement until his mitt-like hands brushed away the tears. "Wandered in? That goddamned kitten was no more lost than I am. I got tired of your stubborn attitude and picked it up at the city pound. Kept it at my place for a few days to make sure it was healthy. Then I waited until I saw your lights on late. Had to climb up the bank and into that tree half a dozen times before that silly cat stayed put. I made such a racket I was sure you'd hear me. Wouldn't have done it if you'd had a gun around. Marlys and I have been laughing ourselves silly about it ever since."

Now it was our turn to laugh as we imagined 250-pound Bob sneaking around, climbing trees at night with a tiny cat tucked inside his jacket front. We chuckled for weeks, each time we watched Dog's antics, each time we contemplated our pest-free sheds and whenever the three of us walked home to the tree-shaded stone cottage on its bluff above the quiet creek.

Chapter 5

Translation Station

Tom T. Hall's gravelly country tones greeted me when I brought Larry a hot mug of coffee. I caught the last words of this latest hit about loving little baby ducks and old pickup trucks. "Good timing," Larry stated, turning up the volume on his battery powered radio. "They're going to play George Jones' new one next, a real tear jerker. You'll probably love it."

To me that cereal-box sized radio, which now hung from a nail driven into a eucalyptus tree at the edge of the boatyard, had been just one more item successfully crossed off the endless shopping list. To Larry, it became a constant source of amusement. Because of the hills surrounding us, and the radio's limited power, it would only receive one station loud and clear, "WHWB, your country music station from Riverside — home of Don Williams." Larry would turn that radio on as soon as he went outside. At noon he'd come back humming, *"He stopped loving her today..."*

A few days later Pete Shomler heard Larry's companion blaring away and said, "See you like country music, too."

"It's all new to me. I call it my Translation Station," Larry answered. "Helps me communicate with the locals."

I, too, came to feel the pull of these songs as I spent more time working with Larry in the boatyard, songs designed to involve the listener, ballads describing a simpler life than that found in the rush of the huge cities to the north. We hummed along as a lonely country singer, lured to Hollywood by the promise of fame and fortune, dreamt of the cowboy she'd left behind in Montana. We laughed at the antics of the cowhand trying to act like a gent, and agreed with the wisdom of the old gambler on the midnight train as he advised the young gambler that any hand could be a winner, or a loser, too.

Soon a Willy Nelson tape made its home next to my favorite Segovia Classic Guitar favorites, and Tom T. Hall nestled up to the Mamas and the Papas. In the evenings, we'd turn on our battery-powered cassette player to learn the words of a new country song, then try to sing it ourselves while the fire burned down and evening grew quiet.

Help me make it through the night...

◇◇

The first real rain of the California winter fell soon after the New Year. It fell right through a dozen cracks in the roof, and an array of pots and pans littered the floor after five hours of downpour. But as the rain eased and the spring-fed waterfall across the road from the cottage began to gurgle so loud we could hear it even with the windows closed, we laughed at this minor problem. We could call it minor because Jimmie Moore had already promised he'd be down that weekend with a crew to put a new roof on the cottage. He was as good as his word, and in two days, five of us had re-roofed the whole place and added overhanging eaves that gave the old stone cottage a lilting, friendly look.

Our next problem was far more difficult to solve. The rains that came again later that week pounded down for two days. The heavy drops found no chinks in our new roof, but they did turn Larry into a restless, house-bound, prowling nuisance. He soon grew bored with editing my work, with outlining an article he wanted to write, reading, scheming and planning. By the end of the second day, I knew getting a boatshed built was the only way to guarantee both of us continued sanity. Our canyon neighbors had made dozens of suggestions. "Got a friend over in Riverside who's tearing down some storage sheds," one told us. We went and looked. The sheds weren't tall enough. Bob Steele said, "Call my friend who makes prefabricated workshops." We did — too expensive. Jimmie Moore came by, restless and looking to fill his day since work on his three construction sites was shut down by the rain. "Tell you what. You build a good solid framework that can become a horse barn when you finish your boat. I'll give you the plywood to make the walls. It'll only cost me 30 sheets of plywood. I've got half of that left from a house I just finished. You'll get a good shed for half cost and I end up with a barn that improves my property value." As soon as Jimmie left, Larry set two oil lamps on my desk and began to sketch. By the time I had dinner ready he had covered four sheets with building ideas. "Look here. We'll build eight main frames, put a truss across from here to here. It'll be a piece of cake."

Just as I'd learned that when Larry says, "We'll move *it*," things get moved, I also knew that when he says, "*It* will be a piece of cake," *it* rarely is.

"Sounds like a great plan," I said as he propped his favorite sketch against the pitcher full of cattails that decorated our rickety dinner table. "Only problem is, how are we going to get a building permit for something that large? Don't you need an architectural drawing, approvals, soil tests, inspectors?"

"You'll take care of that," he replied as he tilted his hand back and forth next to the sketch, trying to be sure he liked the cant of his imaginary roofline.

"Thanks a lot," I groaned. "What do I do? Go visit the building inspector and say, 'Don't worry, we'll build it right'?"

"Bob Steele says the inspector for this area doesn't ever really come

out and look," Larry said. "When Bob went in for a permit for his barn the inspector told him to ask for a storage shed permit and not give any details. Said if there weren't any toilets, no one would care because it wasn't going to affect the neighbors. Don't see why the inspector will feel any different about us building a boat barn. Our neighbors are all so far away we really can't affect them!"

I didn't share Larry's optimism as I drove nineteen miles to the county sub-offices in Perris. Bob Steele was building his barn far from the road where no one would ever see it, whereas ours would be visible for a half mile before you got to our driveway. But when I asked the inspector, I began, "We live up on El Toro road, the property across from Bob Steele and Pete Shomler. We're in the old stone house. We need to build a storage shed about seventeen feet high..."

The inspector gave me a wink, looked over his shoulder to be sure the only other person in the office wasn't listening, "Now this chicken coop you want to build, that will be eleven dollars for a permit. It's got to be fifty feet away from any dwellings."

In my eagerness to follow Bob Steele's instructions, I almost corrected him, then I caught on, gave a quiet chuckle and said, "Don't worry, we'll build it right. Have to be strong for the long-legged chickens we'll be raising."

He laughed and filled out a form, then said, "That will save us both a lot of trouble, because I sure don't want to be driving out to El Toro when the rains come."

A week after the building was sketched, I came out to see the huge, rough-looking timbers Larry was laying on the ground to form a life-sized outline of the shed he had sketched. The roof rafters swept across an area almost as wide as the stone cottage. The frames to support them stood two stories high. They seemed huge and unbelievably heavy as they lay on the ground ready to grow into a full-sized, three-dimensional version of Larry's sketch. "Looks great," I said. "Only problem is, how are you are going to get that frame and rafter into the air? It must weigh a couple hundred pounds."

"It's closer to four hundred pounds, but I've got it all figured out. You run down to the hardware store and get me..." The list had sketches of metal bits, plus a large assortment of nails and bolts. I came back just before dusk to see him lean a ladder against the towering eucalyptus tree that would give the eventual shed its welcome shade. He scaled its thick trunk until he was three stories above the ground. "Quick, Lin, clear this line. It's fouled on that timber," he called. I jumped out of the truck and ran to clear the rope that dangled from his waist, then watched in complete awe as he casually rigged a bridle around the tree, then hauled up the heavy lines he needed for the next step of his project.

"There must be an easier way to do this," I called as he scrambled from limb to limb, adjusting his lines and bridles.

"If it was easy," he called down, "everyone would be doing it."

How often I'd heard that motto as we rushed through life together. Somehow it summed up the most difficult-to-explain aspect of our relationship — the one that made it most rewarding. When we first met, Larry and I talked long into the night about the frustrations of working long hours for someone else, someone you probably didn't respect or like much, just to earn money to go out and buy something that didn't work quite right, that seemed to break as soon as the guarantee ran out, or, to hire some specialist who didn't do the job well or who left a mess behind that was more work to clean up than seemed justified. "If I just get on with it, I seem to get what I want almost as quickly," Larry told me. "And if I don't like it, there's only myself to blame."

At first I'd agreed with him in theory. Then, as he urged me to learn some new mechanical skill, to do something myself instead of calling for outside help, I, too, caught his fervor. For all his impatience with anything resembling paperwork or routine, Larry could be infinitely patient whenever I asked him to show me how to use a new tool or to explain the way some mechanical thing worked. His was an amazingly mechanical mind. He seemed able to repair anything that worked with gears and pulleys. His hands could control any mechanical or woodworking tool after only a few minutes of practice. Our most intimate moments often occurred as he patiently explained the workings of a pump or small tool, or in this case the block and tackle lifting gear he was setting up. Most of these moments would start out as a simple question. Larry would then pull out a pencil from his ever present work apron and grab a scrap of wood, a sheet of paper and begin drawing rough sketches. My simple question would lead to an evening-long discussion of the power of blocks and tackles. We'd sometimes lie in bed late at night, marveling at how simple some project would be if we just did it step by step.

Larry's extreme confidence, which at times seemed to border on arrogance, had become one of the most important aspects of our relationship. He was, unlike many of the less confident men I'd dated, eager to acknowledge and therefore encourage other peoples' accomplishments even to the extent of giving me credit for an idea that had really been sparked by him in the first place.

Years before, when we'd first been together, I had listened and tried to follow his explanation of some boat project he had in the shop. I asked him, "Why couldn't you do it this way?" Two days later I accidentally overheard one of his friends ask, "Why you doing it like this?"

"Lin's idea. She's got a great engineering mind," Larry replied, pride in his voice. "Saved lots of time, saved money!" I was so pleased by that indirect praise that I began wanting to be part of each project, and soon Larry began using me as a sounding board, saying, "If I can't explain it so you can understand what I'm trying to do, I probably haven't worked it out well enough in my own mind."

As I gained some mechanical skills and began to join in most of the planning, I came to agree with his general "do it ourselves" philosophy in practice, too. There was an indescribable joy in doing yet one more thing without calling in the "experts," a sense of beating the system even if doing it was physically hard — or maybe especially when doing it was physically hard.

The next morning at coffee break, he said, "Mind coming out to help for an hour? I'll be ready to set the first frame in place soon." I enjoyed the break from my desk routine. The winter sun filtered through the trees and warmed my back as I hauled on the rope Larry handed me. But best of all was the feeling of power I had as I pulled that heavy framework slowly skyward. The system of blocks and ropes Larry had rigged controlled the upper end of a long timber that worked like a crane arm. At its end was a heavy-duty block and tackle that hooked under the middle of our first workshop frame. I hauled on the rope with all of my 115-pound might. The frame moved upward six inches. Larry put props under each side and the center to hold it while I took another grip and hauled again. Inch by inch the rafters moved skyward as he ran from side to side checking alignment, propping, watching. With a final heave, I had that first 400-pound outline of our shed upright. My hands burned and ached as I hung on the end of the rope while Larry nailed temporary struts to hold it upright. "Okay, Lin, you can go back to your office. I'll get another frame ready for us to put up after you finish typing this afternoon," he said.

I was exhilarated by the sheer size of the building we were creating. The blister that formed on my palm as I hoisted the second frame went unnoticed. I'd caught the fever that Larry seems to get whenever he stops planning and finally grabs ahold of a piece of wood to start building. "Let's get another frame up today," I called as I ran to the house to make sure the pot roast in the oven wasn't burning.

We weren't surprised when Bob Steele drove in a half hour before dusk. Those two huge frames could be seen a half mile down-canyon. He inspected the block and tackle as Larry rigged it, stood back for a minute while Larry helped me haul in the first few feet of rope until the frame was just off the ground. Then Bob said, "What a waste of time." He grabbed a long board from our scrap wood pile, put it under the frame, told Larry to get some shores ready, then shoved the framework upright and held it while Larry nailed temporary stringers from it to the two frames we'd already set in place. "Now that's the way to raise a barn," Bob said. "Where's the next frame?" He'd cut our frame-raising time to minutes so we couldn't say no when he offered, "Not working tomorrow. Get the rest of the frames ready and I'll come by at noon and help you shove them in place."

I left my desk about ten times the next afternoon to watch through the kitchen window as those huge frames arced skyward to turn Larry's sketch into reality. It was good to have Bob's help, to see it happening so quickly, yet deep down inside I felt almost cheated, like Bob had stolen something from me.

Now, years later, I can see how this whole manly-strength syndrome undermines and steals the confidence of women who are trying to grow into the sport that defines my life. In sailing, as in many areas of life, sheer brute strength can make things happen quickly, and often more easily. That is why many women find themselves unwittingly stepping back whenever a man, any man, offers to use his strength to hoist a sail, lift an anchor or take over any of the myriad tasks that could be accomplished, albeit slightly less quickly, by using skills (and the confidence) that can only be earned by direct physical participation. I contrast this with some of the newer breed of women who have been encouraged to challenge the male dominance of sports. They often have learned to sail competitively, eliminating the chance of letting a man give them a hand by having other women as crew, competing against other all-women teams before moving on to mixed racing, mixed crews. Some are making it onto top levels, from round-the-world racing, to world class dinghy championships. But as Monica Collins, one of these women, told me, "To get there you have to shove some guy out of the way and grab hold of that winch yourself. Learn to work it even if it makes your muscles ache! The guys hurt, too, when they spend a day working the winches!" But on that sunny day in the canyon, my disappointment had nothing to do with a quest for an equal footing with these powerfully-built men. It wasn't that I felt any pangs of jealousy as I listened to Larry and Bob exchange ribald comments and shout together,

"Shove, shove, shove," in a camaraderie of sheer strength that women rarely share. It was more that I missed the feeling of power, the sense that I, too, could control and contribute to the creation of something more solid and lasting than the words on a shopping list, a meal that was soon devoured, a cleaned room that would soon be dirty again, or a manuscript that could be hacked up by an editor just to make my story fit in between some late arriving, cash-paying advertisement.

◇◇

We were enjoying a brunch out in the bright winter sun about three weeks later. The boatshed was completed, Larry had laid the keel for the boat, I'd sent off an outline for the book we'd promised to write, there had been no more rain, and life seemed not only under control, but wonderfully balanced. Shadow Cat, alias Dog, prowled the edges of the raked front yard and flushed a pair of quail from the bushes near the bank. We heard the sound of a light truck climbing uphill and, through the bare branches of the winter-shorn trees, we spotted Lee and Betty Newhouse heading our way.

"Brought these beehives to set near your spring. Wanted to put them in place before the really heavy rains came," he said as he stopped at the top of our driveway. Lee and his wife Betty lived three quarters of a mile downhill in a green barn-style house with goats, geese, chickens and turkeys penned in a yard right beside the road. When the breeze blew from the south, we could hear the geese greeting the sun. Fifty-five-year-old Lee, dressed in his perpetual bib-type overalls, baseball cap creased beyond recognition by metal-stained hands, had drawled a warm welcome the very first time we met. "Y'all come meet Ma," he had insisted, urging us to walk past a mélange of rusting trailers, old tractors and two broken-down mobile homes plus a converted bus/workshop toward a straw hat that topped a large figure covered by a Hawaiian print muumuu. "Ma, come greet your new neighbors," he said. Betty rose awkwardly from the patch of roses and geraniums she was tending, "You all must think this looks like some Okie farm," she said as she grabbed my hand and gave it a firm shake. She looked around her and laughed, "Come to think of it, that's probably because we're Okies. Come from Oklahoma and proud of it." There wasn't any good answer we could give to counter her statement. Rusting hulks of used-to-run vehicles, bales of wire, and old bedsteads littered every flat spot. The place was an eyesore in that wilderness-like canyon. But it was the realization of a dream to these people who had spent twenty-five years trapped in a rented house in Fontana, California, while Lee worked as a welder for the power company.

They'd bought the land for $100 down and $50 per month several years before then spent every weekend and every extra dollar clearing and building on it while they worked to raise three children back in Fontana. Two years before we arrived, when their last daughter left home, they stopped paying rent and moved to their half-finished house in the canyon. Lee was stoical about the fifty-five mile drive to and from work each day because now he could put the rent money into improvements and work all weekend and every evening on his "Rancho Casa Nuevo." He'd done a few welding jobs for us as we settled in. Then one day he'd offered Larry a deal he couldn't pass up. "Y'all got good wild flowers growing at the spring aback your shed. Let me set a few beehives; give you a jar of honey for each hive, each six months. You'll get more flowers with the bees there. I know my little lady likes that. Yours probably will, too."

So this Sunday we stayed back as Lee yelled we should. We watched him cover every inch of his body in thick clothes, gloves, and neck wrapping. His head disappeared into a net-covered contraption. Then he lit a fire inside a container that he had obviously welded up for this job and started pumping smoke over and into the six beehives in his truck bed. "Puts the little devils to sleep," he yelled toward us.

"Don't think you'll see more than one or two of them bees around the house after the next rains," he said when he'd set the hives. He took the cup of coffee Larry offered and sat to talk, "Just for a minute or two." Though Lee usually seemed relaxed, he acted nervous and uncomfortable once he finished the coffee. The conversation wandered aimlessly until he finally blurted out, "Ma's been wondering… you folks legit?" We both must have looked puzzled, because he blushed, rubbed his rough hands across his chin and carried on. "Well, Ma says she never sees you drive off to work, doesn't see anyone coming to bring work to you…"

We laughed as we remembered Pete Shomler's stories of "dirtbags" who grew marijuana in the hidden folds of this canyon country, or the smuggling ring that had been found hiding cases of Mexican rum in a cave a few miles uphill from the canyon.

"We are legit," Larry answered almost brusquely, and gave a wink in my direction. So I said nothing for a moment until Lee began to blush again.

"You rich, then?" he mumbled. I found that very funny as I remembered the hours of scrubbing, painting and rat-eradicating behind us, the hard time we were having finding a generator to provide Larry's shop with the electricity he desperately needed, yet stay within our quite restrictive budget.

"Don't let Larry give you a hard time, Lee. We're using our savings, got enough for the next six months. We don't pay any rent, our landlord pays for all the materials to fix this place up, and all the furniture is borrowed. Meanwhile, we're getting a bit of money as freelance writers, and if that goes well, we'll be able to keep this project going with just me working for money. If it doesn't, Larry will have to take on contract boatbuilding work. He can drive down to the coast to do the measuring and then bring the work back here to our shop."

As I explained to Lee, I began to realize that in a way, we were rich. We didn't have to drive down out of the peaceful canyon every day onto the two-lane highway to join a never-ending parade of rushing cars and lumbering trucks that started twenty miles away in Corona where eight-lane freeways fed millions of workers into the factories and offices of Orange and Los Angeles counties. We didn't have the fixed overheads of mortgage payments, car payments, credit card loans, telephone and utility bills.

As we walked the Newhouses back to their truck, Lee said, "In a year or two I'll have the place paid off. I'll save a bit, then stay at home full-time and make our spending money with my bees and welding gear. Then I'll be a free man, too."

Later that day, as Larry and I raked up shavings in the boatyard, the translation station played a new Johnny Paycheck hit. Its words brought Lee Newhouse's dream to mind. I could imagine he, like the singer, was waiting impatiently for the day when he could say to his city boss: *Take this job and shove it.*

Chapter 6

And Then the Rains Came

I'd been pleased with the heavy rain that began to fall early that February morning. The hills around us needed the moisture. Besides, it gave me an excuse to spend the afternoon inside, cooking a prime rib roast, basting slowly, browning vegetables and baking fresh Maltese-style bread, hard crusted and hearty, dusted with a light film of flour just before it came from the oven. I bustled around, stoking the fires in the kitchen and front room, stacking extra wood on the hearth. At coffee time, Larry came in from his shed singing, "I'm not Lisa, my name is Julie..." as I was blaring out the same words in accompaniment to the big multi-band, battery-powered radio that now lived on the kitchen counter.

Bob Steele drove in just after dark, mud splatting across the yard as he skidded around the top corner of our driveway. "Have to get some gravel up here or you'll be fighting mud all your life," he said as he unlaced his heavy work boots. "Where the hell's Marlys? I told her to leave work on time. She loves that damn job more than me."

I knew Marlys planned to arrive as early as possible. Donna Fargo, whose plaintive voice had kept her songs in the country music top 40s, was performing live at a country music club forty miles from the cottage. We all had tickets. The show didn't begin until nine, but the drive could take longer than usual in the rain.

I wasn't surprised Marlys preferred her office to her home in Bull Canyon.

She had been working as a semi-professional pool player and go-go dancer fifty miles north of the canyon to pay her way through business school when she met Bob. With his outgoing personality and bigger than life appearance, plus her love of organization, they'd quickly built up a chain of employment agencies affording them a luxurious ranch style house in the Riverside suburbs, complete with the requisite fancy cars, barbeque, extensive swimming pool and constant round of family visitors. Marlys had loved it. Bob loved it until the challenge was over. One day, without consulting Marlys, he sold the company, the house and his big car, then arrived home in a pickup truck to announce, "I've bought a ranch. Now I'll build you a real ranch house." He didn't tell Marlys it would take eight years to build what eventually turned out to be a 4000-square-foot monolith. He didn't tell her the 14-foot camping trailer he bought from a junk sale for $18 would be their only living quarters for all those years. She wasn't quite prepared for the quiet of the canyon after her fun-filled, dancing, pool-playing nights and chic businesswoman days. Her friends and family soon tired of the long drive plus the lack of comfort when they arrived. Marlys hated the scorching heat of summer at their hilltop home, hated the rain and mud of winter when the bare dirt around their trailer turned to a soupy quagmire. So she got a job twenty miles to the south as the office manager of a growing electronics firm, more for the companionship and sense of physical order than for the money. She did seem to spend an inordinate amount of time at her job, but the electronic firm was new, growing fast, and her work was exciting.

We saw a flash of car lights coming through the rain from uphill about forty-five minutes after Bob arrived. "Can't be Marlys, going the wrong way," Bob grumbled. But it was. Her big red Pontiac skidded just as Bob's truck had, and pulled to a stop next to our door.

Marlys rushed in, her dark red hair in all its five-inch Afro-style permed glory sparkled with raindrops. Her clear, rosy complexion glowed as the heat of the fire warmed her. She stood an elegant 5'9" in her tweed pants suit and silk and lace blouse. "Bob, don't be angry," she began, as he rose. "I left work early. But when I got to the wash below the narrows I found a car stuck, water up to its doors and no one in it. So, I didn't dare come across. I went back and drove around to Santa Rosa Mine Road. Came in through the orange groves. That road is slippery but passable."

Bob seemed almost pleased with Marlys's tale of adventure. "If it doesn't stop raining we'll all pile into my truck. It's got mud tires. The back road is the quickest way to Riverside. We'll go that way," he said. "Wonder if my lakes are filling now?"

"You and your lakes. Wish I'd never bought you that Cat," Marlys said as she settled down at the table.

I caught the end of her comment as I came in from the kitchen with the roast. "What does a cat have to do with lakes?" I asked.

"Bob was complaining about my job so much. Kept saying I hated Bull Canyon. So last year I saved up and bought him a real country birthday present. A D-6 Caterpillar bulldozer, secondhand, but in real good shape. Well, Bob didn't get off that dozer for most of the year. He built roads everywhere on our land. Then he began digging lakes. Said the springs would gradually fill them up, but all that happened is now we've got seven big depressions with muddy green spots at the bottom."

"Come on, Marlys, lay off," Bob said. "We've been having a drought the last few years. Give us one good rainy season and we can start raising catfish. Heard there'll be a big market for catfish soon. Lots of southerners are moving out this way."

Tears were rolling down my cheeks as I laughed at Marlys's tales of Bob's exploits on his Cat. How he had to have a bigger one and traded her gift in on a D-8 model only to find it was too wide to go up the winding road that ran across a corner of the land we lived on, across the stream and along the edge of a steep, 500-foot high hill to reach the plateau where their unfinished house and unfilled lakes lay. "Took Bob a week to bring his newest Cat home, building the road as he went," Marlys said.

I got up to add more wood to the fire.

"You using the old pallets I dropped off?" Bob asked.

"I sure am. Thanks, they burn well," I answered.

"How you cutting them up?" Bob asked.

"I'm learning to use a handsaw by cutting them up."

"Next time I've got the Cat down here, I'll run over those pallets and break them up for you. Save you lots of work," Bob told me earnestly.

"Don't let him do it," Marlys shouted. "He did it for me and all I ended up with was a bunch of kindling and a mess of wood ground into the dirt in front of the trailer."

◇◇

Eight hundred enthusiastic fans jammed the tables around the big, country-style dance floor and cheered as Donna Fargo sang "*Funny face, I love you...*" I looked at the tooled leather boots of the dancing crowd, the pearl-buttoned cowboy shirts and tight Levis. I watched the women in their designer Western clothes as they added stylized dips and twirls to the formalized two-step that held echoes of old-time square dances. Then, as the evening mellowed, I began to notice a new group of dancers, their two-step less flamboyant, their leather boots more worn, their faces and hands tooled by the harsh desert sun. The women they danced with didn't have the perfect shapes, the skin-tight Levis or the fashionable hairdos of the Coca-Cola cowgirls who had dominated the floor earlier in the evening. Instead these women matched their men, strong-armed, probably strong-willed and probably in from the hills or desert for a once-a-month treat. I chuckled inwardly as Donna sang, "*I was country when country wasn't cool.*" Here we sat, Marlys in her business suit, Bob in clean but nondescript working clothes, Larry in his boating shoes and favorite sailing sweater, me in clothes that a British shop assistant had assured me would be fashionable for many years. Though we lived in the wide open spaces, though our roads were dirt, though our water came from wells instead of city mains, though coyote, lynx and occasional deer roamed past our windows, we weren't country at all, but transplants and probably misfits. These leather-skinned men and probably many of the dolled-up Riversiders were the people who made the oranges and lemons grow, who tended the oil-drilling rigs, the farms and ranches and lumber mills that fed the appetites of the city dwellers to the west. And now their way of life was being threatened by ever encroaching freeways, housing tracts and the lure of higher-paying, high pressure jobs in factories and offices, by mortgages and divorces while Donna Fargo crooned, "*Stand by your man...*"

The rains continued to fall as Bob drove us home. By morning, when a huge, low-bed truck and trailer arrived at the bottom of Bob Steele's winding, mile-long driveway, the normally two-inch deep stream alongside the road was running two feet deep. We went out to watch Bob load his bulldozer for its journey fifty miles east where he had a contract to clear storm drain channels. "Won't be needing it here in the canyon," he had told us the night before. "No one needs any work done and it might as well be earning its keep." I interpreted that to mean that Bob was tired of Marlys teasing him about the uselessness of that huge tractor.

The rain kept falling. I found the wet weather perfect for writing, painting inside the cottage, lining shelves, but Larry hated it. He had drawn full-sized plans for the boat on a huge plywood floor in front of the boatshed. The persistent rain, already double the normal yearly totals, was causing the paint on the floor to flake. The lines he'd so painstakingly drawn were becoming obscured before he could use them to make patterns to help him shape a backbone from the solid balks of timber that lay scattered outside the shed.

The radio reported flooding in the valleys to the north. They broadcast warnings for people to stay clear of creek and wash beds. Flash floods were now a danger if the heavy band of rain approaching from the northwest arrived before the runoff from the previous day's rain found its way down to the sea.

It was about three in the morning when I felt Larry climb out of bed. "It's raining pretty hard," he said, "I'm going out to check the boatshed. Make sure my tools are all under cover in case the roof leaks." He took the big flashlight from the top of the fridge and went out clad in yellow sailing boots and orange foul-weather gear. I put another log in the fire, then lit an oil lamp in the kitchen and made up some hot chocolate. When he didn't come right back, I didn't worry. I knew he'd call if he needed me. I climbed back into the cozy brass bed and was startled awake what seemed only minutes later. "Damned little stream behind our boatshed has become a regular river," Larry told me. "Burst its banks and flooded right through the back door of the shed. Place is a foot deep in mud. Had to dig a trench to lead the water from the shed." It was almost five thirty. Larry was covered in mud and brush. I re-warmed the chocolate as he took a hot shower. Then we went back to bed.

We were dragged awake at seven thirty by shouts and pounding. A bedraggled Sandy Shomler stood in the pouring rain outside the back door. "Car's stuck in the creek. Got to get the kids to school." Larry towed her clear and came back for breakfast. "Sandy's getting some extra food in just in case there are washouts on the road. We might not be able to get to town for a few days if there are. Why don't you do the same?"

That afternoon, as I drove carefully down canyon past the Newhouses' barn house, I stopped to yell "hello." Lee and Betty were clearing brush from the uphill side of the culvert that funneled our stream under the road. "Can't let it plug up," Lee called through the driving rain. "Would take the road with it, leave you guys stranded." The normally complacent creek surged against the road in the narrows. It had already nibbled sizeable chunks out of the edges of the bank on the sharper turns. The big washout below the canyon was a hundred-foot-wide river of brown surging water. As I hit the river, I put the gas pedal to the floor ploughing boldly through just like Larry had coached me, a five-foot-high curtain of spray flying from the wheels of the truck.

In town I noticed a sense of jubilation among the business people that was at odds with the grey lowering clouds outside their shops. "The lake's filling," every retailer told me. "Hope it rains for days," the owner of the service station said as I filled up a spare can of kerosene, another of gasoline.

There is a local saying, "The fortunes of Elsinore rise and fall with the level of the lake." Back at the turn of the century, Elsinore had been a sleepy town that served as a stopping place on the dusty road leading inland from San Diego to Riverside. Then in the early twenties, the Hollywood crowd discovered the two-mile-wide, five-mile-long lake with its hot springs and fine climate. The guardian Ortega mountain range served as a barrier between the ocean and the valley to keep Elsinore dry and warm in winter. The low rim of the Gavilan hills on its desert side calmed the worst of the scorching summer winds. Its spas became a major attraction for tinseltown personalities, and soon a railroad line led straight from downtown Los Angeles to end beside the lake. Amy Semple McPherson, a wild-eyed and some say less than scrupulous evangelist, built a huge castle in the hills overlooking the lake and subdivided the land around her headquarters into lots that she sold or gave as gifts to those who donated to her cause. Soon a dozen more castles sprouted, along with casinos, spas and a fishing-pier amusement park. Old photographs on the walls of the town pharmacy showed famous people dressed in the skullcaps and flapper skirts, the boater hats and white shoes of the roaring twenties, as they stepped onto the Lake Elsinore pier from flying boats while big bands played in the central plaza.

But then came the destitute thirties and a five-year drought. The lake shrank until it was little more than a large puddle surrounded by miles of dried, cracked mud flats. The town almost died, the castles were deserted. But through the years, just enough people were attracted by the climate, the cheap land prices and quiet atmosphere to keep the post office and market open. Elsinore thrived for brief periods whenever the lake rose. Occasionally, someone bought one of the old castles and tried to restore it. A state park at one end helped make the lake a nice place to camp for a few days of fishing if the water level was high enough. By the time we moved here, a hang-gliding craze had brought a bit of extra cash to the village; the Ortega mountains rose as an almost vertical 1,500-foot cliff on the western side of the lake and the low population meant few power lines for gliders to hit and plenty of open spaces for them to land.

The lake had receded to less than one square mile in size. Its surface lay 1,245 feet above sea level, or twenty feet below the level that made it a scenic and usable lake. Now, with over nineteen inches of rain during the past six weeks, the lake was filling and the manager to the supermarket told me,

"It's up to 1,252 now. If it reaches 1,260, the town council is going to apply for a government grant to drill some wells to keep it that way. Then this town can grow." He seemed almost ready to jump into the air and click his heels together as rain pelted down while he helped me load ten bags of groceries into our truck.

Bob Steele was just as jubilant as he came trudging up our drive before I'd stored all the groceries in the pantry and jammed vegetables into the old propane fridge. "Truck's stuck. Can you give me a quick tow, Larry?"

"Sure, why are you smiling? That's the third stick this week," Larry answered.

"My lakes are filling!" Bob shouted.

The two men were back ten minutes later for hot chocolate spiked with brandy. I took their wet jackets into the shower to drain as they unlaced their workboots and left them on the old towel I'd spread just inside the door. I leaned on the inner side of the counter while they perched on stools, their stocking feet planted firmly on the rungs.

"Bob, you've gotten that truck stuck three times since the rain started," Larry teased.

"Not really. I only needed help to get clear once," he retorted.

"Ya, but you had to dig and pile rocks under your tires once," I added.

"You guys just haven't been driving out as often, but I saw you ask Lin to check under your wheels the other day when you started to slip."

"If you only have to get out and appraise the situation, it's not a stick, agreed?" Larry suggested.

"Okay," Bob said, "but if you have to even bend over to put a rock under your wheel, it's a one-point stick, and if you have to use shovels or a pick, or any sort of tools, it's a two-pointer."

"On that basis, if you ask someone to help, it has to be a three-pointer," I added.

"And if you need a tow or shove, it's four points," Bob said, finalizing the system.

Pete Shomler gave a knock and opened the door just then. "Saw Bob's truck, wanted to know how the road up to his place is. Safer to go across the stream here than at my place. You mind if I cut through your land?"

"Take off your shoes and come and have a cup of chocolate — add some brandy if you like it," I offered.

"Not going to unlace my boots," Pete said. "Too much work."

Bob looked at Pete's mud covered workboots. "Guess you'll just have to stand there then."

Pete gave an angry glance at Bob, then at me. "What's a little mud on a stone floor. Sandy cleans it up at our place. That's her work."

"My wife has better things to do with her time," Larry retorted.

I left the kitchen as a palpable silence began to form. "Thanks for the offer, Lin, but should be getting on, see how things are at my place," Pete called after me.

Before he could turn to go, Bob said, "Don't get stuck, we're counting points now." He and Larry began describing their system. Pete added some refinements. A few minutes later I came back from adding another log to the fire, to find Pete sitting at the counter, his stocking feet wrapped around the rungs of the stool, while Larry poured him chocolate laced with brandy, and the laughing went on as the rain continued to fall.

We noticed all sorts of small creatures sheltering in our buildings as the rain relentlessly pounded down and low-laying areas and gullies flooded. Shadow Cat, alias Dog, was kept busy full time as field mice tried to make nests in the ceiling. Ground squirrels scattered whenever I went into the stone garage on my twice-a-week forays for the wine and supplies I stored there. Packrats hid in the corners of Larry's storage shed and even rabbits began to sneak under the cover of the eaves. By the time twenty-two inches of rain had fallen, I was sure I'd spotted a cougar flashing into our stone garage early one morning. But Larry teased me, saying, "No wild cat would live anywhere near the smell of humans." Then he, too, saw the long, low-running flash leave the garage one evening as the rains continued to fall and the streams continued to grow and the neighbors continued to come by to ask for a tow. "That animal could be a really big dog, but let it be," he said, late one night as the moon shone through the clouds that had broken apart for the first time in a week. "I wouldn't deny any creature a dry place to sleep. Can you believe we've had almost forty days of solid rain?"

We woke to a cloud-free sky the next morning. We spent (or was it wasted?) most of the day cleaning the debris left behind by the rain, clearing the stream bed behind the boatshed and scrubbing mud from the front porch. We took a walk along the narrow road that climbed up the hill to Bob and Marlys' plateau. We commiserated with Bob about the damage the rain was doing to the inside of the partially-built house that stood two hundred feet away from their disreputable-looking trailer. We admired Bob's lakes, which had reached within a few feet of the top of the twenty-foot deep depressions he'd dug. The waterfall just below the lowest lake, normally fed only by a spring, was leaping ten feet beyond its natural rim in its rush to join the stream below. The stream now swirled alongside our road like a fair-sized river. As we descended from Bob's plateau, enjoying the rare warmth of the sun, we could clearly see how our road now had its edges made ragged by rushing water. Ruts crisscrossed the road and threatened to widen into washouts if the runoff from the saturated hills grew any stronger. The weather forecasts for the next week promised no rain *if* the bands of heavy clouds a hundred miles out in the Pacific kept to their normal path and dumped their rain far out in the ocean as they should.

Late that same night something dragged us from our sleep. Larry's arms were around me and I could feel him tense as a high-pitched yowl came again from behind the house. The yowl was joined by a wild, chilling growl. Larry leapt from the bed. "The cougar's got my cat," he yelled, as he fumbled for his shoes, then dashed through the kitchen and out the door. I found my shirt and got the flashlight I kept in the pantry.

I shone it across the driveway and up the hillside toward our huge iron water tank. Larry, armed with a shovel and flashlight, nude except for shoes, was chasing our garage animal around the tank. "Cougar's got my cat," he yelled again, as the howling animal dashed a second time around the tank, Larry in hot pursuit. When my light flashed into its eyes, the animal screeched off through the heavy desert brush and up the hill. There was a moment of quiet as Larry leaned up against the tank to catch his breath. Then I heard a small meow. I turned my flashlight toward the roof behind me. Dog stretched and yawned three feet above my head, obviously bored by all of the unnecessary efforts being made to rescue him.

"He's not a pet, just a working part of the place," I teased as I lay beside Larry in the warmth of the quilt-covered bed. I'd been assured by the radio weatherman that tomorrow would be clear. So I ignored the clouds that drifted across the silvered moonlight flooding through our windows as I drifted off to sleep.

But instead of dumping their moisture over the wintry sea, the rain-filled clouds swept onshore. The coastal mountains started to shed their topsoil. Debris rushed downhill to block the drainage canals crisscrossing the cities below. Larry and I lingered over morning coffee in the fire-warmed kitchen as rain pelted down. Commentators on the radio had a dozen theories for the deluge — misplaced upper atmosphere jet streams, dust from a Mexican volcano intensifying the cloud cover, sun spots. It was late February, we were only halfway through the rainy season, and already the rainfall was triple that for a normal year. The hillsides were eroding away wherever the vegetation was thin. Trees, accustomed to firm ground around their roots, were toppling as the soil became saturated. Our driveway ran with mud and threatened to turn back into the rutted mess we'd encountered when we first came to see the cottage.

"Think I'll go down the road and see if any culverts are blocked," Larry finally said. "Couple of days ago a bush blocked the one above the Newhouses. Started a real dam-up of brush and weeds. If the water backs up much, it will wash out a hunk of road."

I was glad to hear him drive off as the rain lightened to showers. He'd become like a prowling animal every time it rained. Though we now had the shed complete, most of the timbers he had to cut for this stage of the project were stored outside and were soaking wet. Inside the shed, the constant dampness had turned the floor into clinging mud. I had seen Larry live patiently through days of calm at sea, or sit comfortably reading thousand-page-long history books while week-long storms trapped us on board in some foreign port. But now he had no patience at all.

He'd come into the cottage for a cup of coffee four times each morning and call to me, "Don't let me disturb your work," then proceed to ask me to look at his sketch for some new ideas. Each rainy afternoon he'd say, "Want to drive into Riverside for a movie? We could pick up the parts for our saw on the way." I understood his frustration. He is one of the most goal-oriented people I've ever met. Life was right if he could see a definite step made toward a pre-defined goal each day or week. Through the years his determination had infected me. The very rains that held him back were setting me ahead. I had a growing stack of pages in the cardboard box behind my desk. There was little I could do out in the boatyard. So I felt no guilt as my afternoon hours were spent painting and scrubbing cupboards and closets. I went eagerly to my desk that morning, ready to be lost in the far reaches of the sunny Mediterranean as I wrote of Spanish fishermen and bank robbers and Gibraltarian smugglers.

It must have been two hours later that the room began to lighten and a watery sun broke through the scudding clouds. My head and wrist ached from the hurried scribbling I'd been doing in the almost trance-like state I sometimes fall into when writing is going well. I stood up to watch through the window as cloud shadows scurried along the hillside across the road where rushing water leapt off the top of the normally placid falls. As I watched, I wondered if other people who composed music, painted or wrote fell into that same sort of state, a state where everything seemed to flow from some source other than their conscious mind. Did their minutes disappear? Did they feel completely at peace and only vaguely tired when hunger or thirst called them back to reality? I know the words I re-read when I'd had a morning like this were always satisfying and rarely needed much re-working, though at times I could barely decipher the scrawled pen marks I'd left behind in my rush to record thoughts on paper.

I heard a muffled roar as I stood deep in thought. A tidal wave of rusty colored water seemed to fill the V in the hills just upstream of the waterfall. Mud and water flew out into empty space and hung for the blink of an eye, then plunged earthward in a roar that sent me two steps back against my desk in surprise. Spray flew thirty feet in the air and the strong wind blew a spattering of mud stained water across the window. "The dam, Bob's dam," the thought flashed through my mind, "It's gone!"

I ran for my jacket and boots, and then headed down the road. The stream now roared like a river as water from Bob's seven lakes rushed unhampered over the waterfall, augmented by the heavy runoff from the two inches of rain we'd had that morning. The impatient river tugged at bushes that usually were five feet above its level. Rotting vegetation around the bases of the sycamore trees broke free and joined tumble weeds and sagebrush to litter the roaring water. I watched as a bush snagged on a rock, then seconds later, the pressure of the water behind it tore out a chunk of the hard-packed dirt we'd driven over each time we came home. The chunk diverted the stream for only a few seconds. Then before my eyes the road seemed to dissolve and fall away.

The river's rampage lasted less than ten minutes before Bob's lakes were emptied, but only a few feet from where I was standing there was a yawning, five-foot-deep abyss across two-thirds of the road. I walked slowly downhill, marveling at the damage the flood water had wreaked in its rush to freedom. I was halfway to the Newhouses' place when Larry came driving up the road. He burst out laughing when he saw me. "Ya should have seen him!" Larry called as he rolled down the truck window. "Never seen him run before."

"Who was running. How's the road?" I wanted to know.

"Road's gone. Good thing we got in extra food. But Bob, you should have seen him. I was working uphill from where the Newhouses were up to their waists in water, pulling brush out of the big culvert. The road was already eaten halfway through on each side of it when they got there this morning. Bob Steele was about halfway between us, pulling the bigger branches out of the stream...then all of a sudden a wall of water came raging down. I got in the truck and headed down to help the Newhouses. If that culvert plugged, it was all over. Then I saw old Steele, running toward me, water sloshing out of his boots, beard flying, puffing like an old locomotive — yelling 'Don't tell 'em my dam burst, don't tell the County!'"

I got in and rode back to the big culvert with Larry, remembering how Bob had talked about building a proper concrete spillway on his earth-dam during one of our evening get togethers. "Yaa, sure!" Marlys had retorted that night, "You don't do nothing that means getting off that bulldozer." Now each of us stood on either side of a fifty-foot chasm, staring at the huge galvanized culvert that sat like a beached whale, five feet from the new course of the rushing stream.

No one said a word about Bob's dam as we picked our way across the washout, jumping from rock to rock in the rare sunlight. A half-mile downhill we came to another huge chasm just above Lone Palm Ranch. Ellie Moyer, the ranch's owner, stood on the far side, her mink jacket thrown open, her rubber boots covered in mud. When she saw our squadron, she called excitedly, "It was like a dam burst! I could see the narrows fill up with water, then a minute later, the road was completely gone — must be a half-mile of it missing below my ranch."

The spectacle of a huge, bearded mountain-man managing to somehow look like a kid with his hand caught in a cookie jar was too much. Everyone broke out laughing as a crimson blush grew slowly out of Bob's grizzly beard to spread upwards across his wind-chapped cheeks.

The sound of approaching horses seemed utterly appropriate at that moment. Two handsomely groomed quarter horses trotted along the good section of road. Bob introduced Mrs. and Mr. Heck, who lived almost three miles beyond us, well past the end of the county road. "We couldn't get our car out to work towards Riverside, figured this way wouldn't be much better. Seems we were right," Mrs Heck said with a laugh. "So, we're out for a ride while there's some sunshine. Might as well enjoy having a few days off. We'll call the county for you when we're near a phone." We watched them ride off down stream, their horses carefully picking a way between tumbled boulders and waterlogged brush. No one commented when Bob mumbled, "Sure hope they don't tell 'em about my dam."

We were climbing over the crumbling sides of the last chasm below our truck two hours later when we heard horses splashing uphill along the rushing stream. "We got a phone call through to the county," Mrs. Heck called, "asked them if they owned El Toro Road. They said they did and I told them, "If you can find it, you can have it!"

We laughed as we continued homeward. Life wasn't too bad. The sun was definitely helping our moods as the worst puddles around the house began to dry. Larry said he and Bob planned to go uphill later in the day to see if they could do a bit of digging to clear a way out to the north, above the flood caused by the broken dam. I was feeling quite sure the road crews would be out in a few days to open at least a one-lane track. They couldn't leave five families stranded. So the thought of being locked in the lovely canyon for a week or so didn't faze me as I ticked off a list of the food I had in the pantry, the projects I had planned. Then we turned on the radio. Our dam-burst began to pale in significance as news reports filled every minute.

"Ortega Highway closed, California Highway patrol reports seventeen miles of pavement have slid off the mountainside."

"Highway 71 closed between Corona and Elsinore, two bridges washed out."

"Six hundred families forced to flee as the rising waters of Lake Elsinore threaten to cover their homes. Evacuation efforts continue."

This was the biggest news in the whole United States, first on every broadcast. Even the president, Jimmy Carter, was offering his condolences. Reports of closed highways, houses sliding off hills, schools and factories inundated by flooding from San Diego north to San Francisco filled our kitchen. The Army Corps of Engineers had been called. All of their efforts were barely making a dent and more rain was forecast within a week. "Our road is probably going to be low priority this week," I commented.

"Sure wish Bob's bulldozer was here," Larry said. "Could just about build our own road with that."

The skies did stay clear for the next week, the days were warm. But even as the runoff from the hills slowed to a trickle, each possible track out of the canyon was impassable and would stay that way until the storm-saturated earth had a chance to dry. So we stayed at home, Larry happily chopping away at huge hardwood timbers, whistling like the birds that flitted through the blooms of the desert brush, me contentedly adding to my pile of typed papers, and clearing ivy away from the cottage windows as an excuse to be out in the warm afternoon sun.

I really liked the special closeness that grew in the canyon during those flood afflicted days. Only Marlys managed to go to her job that first week. She'd been outside the canyon when the flood struck, so she stayed with friends in Elsinore and hiked in on the weekend to get fresh clothes. The rest of us seemed to meet almost by instinct at Ellie's house late in the afternoon to talk about the attempts everyone was making to keep the constant runoff from mountain springs in proper channels so it wouldn't wash out the remains of our driveways. "Bob got four more points for a stick," Pete Shomler said with a laugh as we sat having a drink at the Lone Palm. "He not only had to get out and use his shovel, he had to go get his old tractor. I used it to tow him out."

Ellie reminded us that floods had happened here long before the county had maintained the road past our homes, when four-wheel drive vehicles or horses were the only useful transportation choices. "There were only three couples living up here — must have been twenty-four years ago, old Payonessa and his wife at your place, Lin, the Abernathys over on Lindell road. We all got together to play bridge one long weekend. Ran out of vodka before dinner. Tom drove into town to get more. Rain came down. We didn't see him until he came riding back on a mule he'd borrowed the next day. We were all still playing bridge, no sense anyone leaving, couldn't have gotten anywhere. Sure were glad he brought some mixer back, too!"

Fifty-five-year-old Ellie was an amazingly open person. She'd joke about the facelift she was saving for as easily as she'd tell of being a frightened, unmarried, pregnant twenty-year-old when she went to work for Tom's family run cabinet-making business. "His family was appalled when he decided to marry me. He was twenty years older than me, never planned to marry. But he said he wanted to be sure my child had a name. He turned out to be a good father, too, even if it wasn't his. He'd already found this land, and with a youngster on the way he decided to make it our country weekend hideaway. We came out here to live most of the summer — it's a lot cooler than Riverside — wasn't too far for Tom to drive back in to work. Good place to raise my Shepherds," she told us as she petted one who snuck in to lie at her feet. As Ellie's son gradually took over the business, she and Tom began to cut their ties to Riverside. Though they'd cleared and planted lovely trees and created a flower-edged pond next to the single, towering palm tree, they'd never built much of a house. Four years after Tom's death, it was still just a jumble of lean-tos attached by a roof. Inside the rough walls, marble-topped counters leaned against hardboard partitions, unedged plywood doors opened into a sun porch with a leaded glass, carved mahogany liquor cabinet and matching bar. In many ways, the cottage was a direct reflection of Ellie. With her high cheek bones and rail-slender body, she looked like an aging high fashion model, hair died a bright autumn red. It seemed to accent the lines of her long, chain-encrusted neck. She was always elegantly groomed, but smoked an endless chain of cigarettes as she drove around the dusty roads in her twenty-five-year-old, mint-green Cadillac, two or three uncombed, floppy German shepherds in the back seat, patched, knee-high rubber boots on her feet, high heeled sandals next to her on the seat.

A week after the dam burst, the heavy whoosh of a helicopter broke into our lives. I ran out to see it swinging low overhead. Its pilot leaned out of his bubble and pointed uphill, urging us with hand signals to head that way. Then he swung toward the Steele and Shomler homesteads and zoomed away. Within ten minutes, the handful of people living in the upper reaches of Bull Canyon had gathered at the crossroads uphill. All ten of us were in a festive mood as the helicopter settled to the ground and two army officers stepped out. "If you designate one person to go out with us, we'll take them into town to shop. We can only come in once a week." That drummed home, as nothing else had, just how bad the situation outside our canyon really was. The army was already thinking in terms of weeks! "There are over two thousand miles of roads washed out or in bad condition. The Ortega Highway won't be open for two or three months," he told us as we scribbled shopping lists. I desperately wanted to be the one to fly in that magnificent machine, not to be away from the canyon, but just to have a joy ride. But Jo Caphart, a widow who lived by herself in a trailer at the top of the hill, explained, "I need some prescription medicine, and I have to sign for it." So I watched with envy as she climbed in to fly straight up, then off over the hills.

Two hours later the same helicopter flew low over our cottage, this time with a cargo net full of hay swinging below its skids. I grabbed my purse and drove uphill, and within minutes I was glad it was Jo who'd gone to town. "These tomatoes are too soft," groaned one neighbor. "That's not Budweiser, I like Bud...", groaned another. The helicopter pilot's last words should have been a warning, but instead we took them as assurance in the calm, late afternoon, "Don't worry. All of southern California has been declared a national disaster area. So the National Guard is coordinating the clean-up efforts. They'll take care of you and your road."

Chapter 7

The Great Stick

After ten days with no rain, Bob Steele and Larry spent an afternoon laying rocks alongside the road above the stone cottage. Then with infinite patience, we nursed our truck out to the highway and headed toward town. More rain was predicted, and from the mess we'd seen in the village, we didn't expect the county crew to be working on our road within the next few days. So instead of retracing our route after doing some much needed shopping, we decided to leave our truck below the washouts. With the truck there, we could hike three miles downhill and not risk breaking an axle or adding more dents to the body if another part of the upper road unexpectedly collapsed.

Sun streamed through the bare branches of the sycamore trees as we hiked in to the canyon. The rope-handled wooden wine box that I used as an attaché case swung by my side, tapping out a rhythm as we went along. Inside it, a dozen eggs and seven beautiful tomatoes crowded the mail we'd picked up from town. Larry, loaded down with a duffle bag full of fresh food, often turned to help me over downed trees and slippery spots as we negotiated the narrows, sometimes having to climb forty or fifty feet above the stream to find a clear path.

At the Lone Palm Ranch, Ellie came out to hear our tales of the ever-rising lake below us. Town papers told of seven hundred homes and trailers being inundated as the water reached 1265 feet above sea level — and still kept rising. We'd seen the roof peaks of dozens of homes a mile from the slowly creeping shoreline. The Army Corps of Engineers had cut the town in half in its attempts to dig a drainage ditch and prevent more homes and businesses from being lost. To get from the post office to the grocery store, which normally lay a half-mile apart, we'd had to drive twelve miles. We'd stopped to watch a bulldozer clearing the lake outflow ditch, we told Ellie, and saw it scoop up a glistening silver three-foot-long carp along with weed and flood debris. The canyon, in spite of its access problems, seemed to present a more ordered world — the electrical outages of town didn't worry us, since we didn't have any electricity in the first place. The closed roads didn't delay us since we didn't have to commute to work each day.

But after two more weeks of flood-enforced seclusion, the charm began to wear off. When Sandy Shomler stomped up our driveway with both arms in casts, I could sympathize with the madness that had led to her accident. She'd been going stir crazy. "Had to get away from the hills, had to get into town and see people, just for a day. Pete suggested going out on his dirt bike." So they'd both climbed onto the tiny machine and headed down their long driveway toward town, half-carrying, half-nursing that one man machine through the washouts and ruts. Halfway into the narrows a bank collapsed under them. Now Sandy grumbled, "What a bore, can't even sew. Pete bought lots of ammo just before the rain and I can't use it, squirrels are going to overrun the place. Besides, my roots are showing. I hate it when I can't do my hair."

Our days were still punctuated with "stick stories" as we waited for the roar of the county road crew machines. A half-dozen times a week, someone would try to get in or out the back way and sink into a mud hole or end up dangling over the edge of a crevasse when yet another section of road gave out unexpectedly. "Mind giving a hand, I'm in a real four-pointer," Bob called as he strode up our driveway. "I've already got my tractor down here. Pete's on his way, too." Bob had decided to go out visiting and charged across the stream dividing his property from the road. Now his truck was stuck right in the center, water washing against its doors. I stood well back as the three men moved rocks, shoveled, swore and tugged. The unmuffled roar of the old tractor echoed off the hill to combine with the trucks growling low-gear tones. Bob's truck shuddered and slid clear. Pete stopped the tractor fifty feet up the road. "Leave the tractor there," Bob shouted, as he and Larry unhooked the tow cable. Bob climbed into his truck while Larry and Pete walked back to get their well-worn tools. I thought Bob was reversing in his truck to say thanks, but as he came closer, I could see a wicked grin spreading across his face. He continued backing up until his heavy-duty mud tires were only an arm span away from the two men. Then just as they looked up, he shifted into low gear, hit the throttle, spun the wheels and covered them both in mud and gravel. His booming laughter spread across the canyon and hung there like an invisible cloud and I almost joined in as I felt the pure evilness of his act. "Only a 250-pound ex-boxing champ from the Marine Corps could have gotten away with that," I thought. Larry evidently had the same thought because he looked at Pete's mud-spattered face, then down at his own filthy work clothes and broke out laughing. Pete did too, then said, "I think we're all going a bit stir crazy."

Larry and I were both glad to pack our gear and climb into Bob's mud-tire equipped truck five weeks after the dam burst. We had been invited to present sailing seminars at four cities a day's drive to the north. Bob was driving us twenty-three miles around the back way to where our truck still waited below El Toro Road's washouts. Then we'd be on our way to the luxury of hard surfaced roads, telephones and electricity.

The heavy rains had affected almost every town we drove through. At Moss Landing, one hundred miles south of San Francisco, a 120-year-old cedar tree had toppled when strong winds loosened its waterlogged roots. It just missed the clubhouse room where we were speaking that night. Larry watched a crew cutting limbs to clear the driveway and suddenly said, "Lin, that's a Monterey Cedar. Great timber for boat building. If we could get the main part of the trunk home, we could cut it into wood for our boat! Sure hate to see it made into firewood." I used my best heel-dragging techniques, saying, "It must weigh a ton. We've got another eight-hundred miles to travel, can't get it up past the washouts. How are we going to cut it into usable timber without a mill?" Larry's enthusiasm, however, had gained him a dozen followers among the clean-up crew. "Come back on your way home," one said. "I'll get a chain hoist from the boat repair yard. Easy to lift it into your truck with that. You can stay at my place for the night."

A week later, at the end of our tour, we headed south with a tree trunk as big around as Bob Steele, but at least ten times heavier, bumping and thumping in our truck bed. A hundred miles before we reached Los Angeles, the first heavy rain in a week began to cascade over us. As dark settled in, I said, "Let's stop at my folks' place for the night. We'll never get up any of the back roads in this rain. Might as well get a good night's sleep." But Larry was impatient to go on, eager to be back at the work he enjoyed, especially since the radio report was for dry weather settling in by early morning. "You're worrying for nothing," he told me. "Road crew's probably been in and fixed the road by now." So we pressed on through the rain, slowing almost to a crawl as we were blinded by the heaviest downpours.

It was close to nine when we finally approached Elsinore. "Let's go into town and rent a motel room for the night," I suggested. "Then I can shop for groceries, you can get the mail."

"I want to sleep in my own bed tonight," Larry growled in the bullheaded tone I hate to hear. The determination that is his biggest strength, that makes him willing to take the first step toward a goal that lays four or five years of hard work away, is also at times his fatal flaw. Like an unthinking machine, he'll just keep shoving, not realizing a step back, a one-night pause, could let some obstacle move out of the way and smooth his path. Even when we turned off the highway onto the dirt of El Toro Road and immediately began to hit potholes and rain-washed ruts, he refused to reconsider. When, minutes later, we came to an impassable washout on the road leading into our canyon, Larry turned the truck around and said, "It's only been raining for a few hours. The Lindell route had a week to dry out before this rain came; there was only one swampy area on that route."

"What about the really steep part on Lindell? With that tree in the back it will be even harder to get up there!" I said in what I hoped was a gently persuasive tone. "Let's spend the money for a motel room; we just earned some extra the past week."

"That tree trunk will give us better traction," he retorted. "Besides, it's almost stopped raining." So we bumped and thumped back to the crossroads and began carefully picking our way along the remains of the private road leading onto the plateau to the west of our canyon.

The farmer at the top had an old road-grading machine he used to clear the five miles of private trail. We could see evidence that he'd been down the road recently. With no stream to rampage along its edges, with no dam bursts to contend with, the potholed, soggy track provided relatively easy going for about a mile. Then we started uphill. Eroding hillsides had dumped piles of debris onto the road. Our tires lost their grip as we tried to climb the first part of the steepest grade, a grade that often got our wheels spinning when it was completely dry. I held my breath as the truck ground to a halt. "What about going to a mo —", I started.

"WE ARE GOING HOME TONIGHT!!!" Larry growled as he backed downhill and got a running start at the steep incline. This time we hit that grade at speed. The truck bucked and jumped over the mud and rocks. *Thump, thump, crash, crash.* The noise seemed unimportant over the low-geared roaring of the engine. We swayed and rocked but kept moving. We both cheered when we braked to a stop at the top. Then I glanced back.

The truck bed was empty. I tapped Larry on the shoulder and pointed. He grabbed the flashlight from the glove compartment and climbed out into the light drizzle while I searched under a pile of luggage on the seat next to me, looking for what had come to be a symbol of Bull Canyon life, my high-topped rubber boots. Larry's cursing had died down a bit when I joined him to stare at the latest dent in the tailgate. We hiked downhill together in silence. A half-mile back, the tree trunk sat on a hump of mud, just clear of the track. "We'll leave the damn thing there. Might be able to borrow Bob's tractor and big chainsaw and slice it in half before I lift it back into the truck. No one but us would want it, so it's safe where it is for a few days."

We climbed back up the hill on foot more easily than the truck had, then drove on across the plateau. Two miles from the upper crossroads, just beyond the farm, a car sat mired in the middle of the road. Swampy ground spread twenty feet on either side; the fields beyond were still flooded. "Larry, let's turn back and get a motel room," I said as he got out to study the tracks of another vehicle.

"Someone else got in, so can we," was his only comment.

"But those are mud-tire tracks," I moaned.

The frustration of the last seven weeks seemed to well up in him until he erupted like a volcano. "WE ARE GOING HOME TONIGHT. WE ARE GOING TO GET SOMETHING DONE TOMORROW. WE'VE BEEN OUT HERE IN THIS DAMN CANYON FOR FIVE MONTHS AND I HAVE NOTHING TO SHOW FOR IT. I'M TIRED OF SCREWING AROUND WITH FLOODS AND HOUSES AND SHEDS. I WANT TO GET TO WORK AND BUILD MY GODDAMNED BOAT."

He slammed the truck into gear, hit the gas and we skidded into the muddy ruts, the wheels spinning as we passed the mired car. The truck began to slow, then stopped, its front bumper even with the mud, its rear wheels almost out of sight. I sat completely still in the almost solid-feeling silence. Larry turned to me and quietly said, "Some day I suppose we'll find something humorous in this whole stupid situation."

He looked so discouraged, so drained by frustration, that I forgot his outburst, his stubbornness, and only wanted to fix his hurt. "There's a light up ahead," I said. "I'll walk up and get some help. They'll probably have a tractor or something. You wait here in case someone comes along."

"Ya, sure, some other fool's going to be out here at ten o'clock at night," he sighed. "But go on, maybe you can convince someone to give a hand. I've sure done enough towing to ask for one myself. This will probably be more than a four-pointer before we've finished."

I marched away from the truck, boots chafing my nylon-clad ankles, mud spattering the hem of my going-to-town skirt as I slipped on wet places in the road. The moon was out now and the night bright as I started up the last few hundred yards of the dirt path that led to the light. It shone from a lean-to alongside an old trailer. "Hello, hello," I called. The light went out. The door opened and three mongrel dogs began running at me, howling and leaping. I stopped dead still. They, too, stopped, twenty feet from me, snapping and growling. "Hello, hello," I called again at the darkened trailer. The dogs began their racket again. I saw a flashlight go on. The door opened and a half-clad man stepped out. "Guess you won't go away. Who the hell are you and what the hell you doin' on my road so late?"

"We're stuck," I said, pointing.

"You're stuck, everyone keeps getting stuck. I'm sick and tired of jerking out stuck trucks. All I've been doing for weeks. Where the hell you headed?"

"We're trying to go home. We live in the stone cottage over in Bull Canyon."

"You must be the crazy boatbuilding people Steele told me about," he said, with a bit less anger in his voice. "Your man know how to ride a motorcycle?"

"Yes, why?" I asked.

"Tell him to take that one, keys in it. Go home, come back tomorrow and you can use Bob's tractor. He brought it over for the great stick. You can take it back to him. I'm tired of having it here. If it's gone, I won't have to tow people out anymore. Glad to be rid of it." He turned, shut the door, and yelled at his dogs to shut up, and then all was quiet and dark again.

I actually began to enjoy the situation now as we rode along the moonlit track on a tiny, off-road motorbike, me clutching Larry's waist with one arm, trying to hold a flashlight in front of us with the other. It was the only light we had to illuminate the worst bumps and ruts in the muddy road.

Halfway through this final stage of our saga, when we were both walking the motorcycle over a particularly rough patch of road, I happened to brush my hand against the back of my pampered, used only-for-dress-up wool pea coat. "Larry, is there some dirt on my coat?" I asked.

He took my flashlight and said, "Turn around." His burst of laughter told me what I had already come to suspect. There was no mudguard on that bike's rear wheel and now a wide strip of mud and gravel ran up my coat and into my hair.

"You look just like a chipmunk, a perfect stripe," Larry choked out between gulps of laughter. The sheer ridiculousness of the situation hit me just then. I looked around at the moonlight-washed, rocky hillsides. A glorious profusion of stars, undimmed by city lights, seemed to sparkle as if laughing with Larry. An owl hooted nearby. I began to laugh and like two overgrown kids we climbed back on to the motorbike to enjoy the last of our trek to the cottage.

"We must be the luckiest people in the world," Larry said as he held a match to the kindling I'd laid before we left. I set an oil lamp on the windowsill and began to boil some water for hot buttered rum.

"Uh-huh," I agreed as I searched the pantry for a snack. "Biggest problem we have in the whole world is a truck stuck in the mud and a coat that's got to go to the cleaners. You should have seen your face when the truck started to sink... you were so mad." And again we were off in gales of laughter.

Then we heard a shout. Marlys Steele came stomping into the kitchen, her whole body shaking with rage, her face livid. She pulled off her boots and plowed toward the fireplace sputtering, "He's an absolute bastard. I hate him."

Bob stood on our porch roaring with laughter. "Saw your light when we were walking down the hill. Had to tell you about Marlys' latest circus act! Just had to," he began.

I felt trapped between Marlys' obvious anger and the uncontrolled mirth that barely covered Bob's spiteful glee. But, as Bob began a replay of their evening's "fun and games in washout land," I couldn't help laughing and Marlys slowly lost her edge of anger as she sipped her rum. She was soon adding details to the story.

"Hadn't rained up here for five days," Bob went on. "So I took the truck out to get some provisions and went to have dinner where Marlys is staying. She started bitching about not having enough underwear. Kept complaining about crotch crawlers. Wanted me to bring her some special pants that she claimed stayed put. I told her — you want underpants, come home with me, and spend the night. I'll take you out in the morning. The road out hadn't been too bad — came the Lindell way. But damned if it didn't start to rain as soon as I suggested we go back in. It poured! Worst downfall since the dam burst. But, Marlys wanted those non-creep pants — well, I had to get out and dig twice on the way in and we got through to the top of the hill above the concrete spillway. The road down to the creek had turned to mush. I wasn't going to risk my truck going down that mudslide. So, I said 'You want your fancy pants, you are going to get them. Get out. We're walking in.'"

Marlys interjected, "I told him to forget the clothes. First time we stuck I said forget them, but he got madder and madder!"

Bob climbed out, he explained, and started down the hill on foot, ignoring Marlys' protests. So she pulled on her boots and started after him in the easing rain. "I took two steps past the truck," Marlys said, "and all of a sudden my feet were gone!"

"I heard a howl, a swoosh and a scream like a train whistle going by," Bob continued. "Marlys flew by me going downhill on her ass like she was on a polished slide. I heard a huge splash as she hit the spillway. Then silence. Thought she'd killed herself. But, when I got there this silly female was sittin' on her ass in the stream, crying. Got me furious. I grabbed her by the collar and marched her all the way up to our place..."

"Ya, he was like some crazy tyrant, kept muttering 'You want your goddamn pants, you are going to get 'em!'"

Trying to picture a soaking wet, mud-covered, sputtering Marlys made me laugh harder and harder. Now, she sat in fresh clothes she'd put on at their homestead, her bright red Afro drying by the fire, her well-groomed elegance in sharp contrast to Bob's rough work clothes, her anger slowly subsiding to lay just below the surface.

As Larry then told our evening's story, teasing me about "let's go to a motel room," I could see the marked difference that made our hassles into "adventures" while the same problems were nothing but a subtle torment to Marlys. As the two of them left to hike out to where Bob's truck waited four miles up the road, Marlys once again let it be known that living in the country, acting like a redneck, was Bob's dream, not hers. She called back, "I want out now so I can get to some place civilized before morning. Don't want to miss work. Don't want to be trapped up here in this damned canyon again."

Later, I climbed gratefully into the hot shower thinking that sharing a dream definitely made life flow more smoothly.

It was noon before Larry came thumping up the driveway the next morning. Our pickup truck a bit the worse for wear, our log nowhere in sight. "Where's the wood?" was my first question.

"Ya want to hear the best stick story of all?" Larry countered. "Jerry, the guy who loaned me the motorbike, told me about it while he was hauling me out of the swamp. It's a seventeen-pointer at least! The other farmer over on Lindell Road hired a well-drilling rig. The rig was on the back of a big flatbed truck, couldn't make it up that steep grade — the one where we had trouble last night. So he came and got Jerry. Jerry used the old tractor to add some power and traction. That thing's heavy — it's even got its wheels filled with water to add weight, but it wasn't enough. The rig kept sliding back when they got to the steep part of the hill. So they went and got two more friends. Finally,

ended up needing the tractor, two pickups and a four-wheel drive flatbed to get the rig up the road. They put long chains between each truck; whole train stretched almost a hundred yards. Things were going great until they reached that switchback at the top, the one that wraps around the really steep gully. Jerry couldn't hear anything over the noise of that tractor. Didn't hear the honking and yelling until too late. His tractor had more traction than the Chevy pickup that was in the middle of the train. Skidded that pickup right off the road. Ended up dangling upside down over the gully, held by a chain at either end. Its driver was scared shitless, hanging head down in his seatbelt. Finally, had to lower the truck into the gully on its top. Brand new Chevy, practically demolished it. The roof squashed right in, doors jammed; driver had to crawl out the window. What a riot. I'd love to have seen that one."

"What about the log?" I asked, as I, too, laughed.

"When Jerry got me out, I drove down to town. Took the long way in, only one that's passable. Got the groceries you needed, decided to call the county and see when they were going to do something about the road — I mean, seven weeks, that's getting to be a bit too much! Got through to the road department. They said 'No one told us El Toro Road was washed out.' Can you believe it? Here, the Army is still helicoptering in feed for the Hecks' horses and the National Guard is supposed to be co-coordinating the flood clean-up and no one's told the county about our road."

I guess in the grand scheme of things, a five-mile-long road that only serviced seven homes could be far more easily forgotten than the highways and thoroughfares that were still being rebuilt in the valley below us. But when I saw two official-looking men walking up the road in the late afternoon sunshine, I ran out to offer them coffee and encouragement. "Why didn't anyone tell me about this mess," the inspector said. "We'll get in as much of a crew as we can tomorrow. Probably be able to open the road enough so you can get safely in and out in a couple of days. Take a week or two to make it right."

An evening weather report of fine, clear skies for the next few weeks combined with the assurances of the men from the county, turned dinner into a party. Larry poured a glass of wine for each of us and we toasted the capriciousness of the weather gods and the crazy streak that seemed to be part of our lives together. Only we or Noah would choose to build a boat on top of a mountain in the desert and find ourselves in the middle of a flood.

"And what about the log, when are we going to get it?" I remembered to ask as I banked the fire for the night. "We're not," Larry murmured. "Farmer on the other side saw it, and said it looked like great firewood. Took a chainsaw to it before I got there. All I ended up with for all that work was a bunch of sawdust and a bashed-in tailgate. I guess we should have taken a motel room last night."

Chapter 8

Children of All Ages

I could hear nesting birds flitting around the eaves of the shed as we finally hauled the backbone timbers for the boat into an upright position. A dozen twig structures lined with soft feathers now graced the spaces between the open rafters and gave the boatyard a slightly ragged, but homey look. The first buds were forming on the sycamore trees, no green showing yet, just swelling brown bumps at the branch tips. "God, it's been a struggle," Larry sighed, as he secured the soaring stem timbers in place. "Sometimes I feel like this boat doesn't want to be born." As I looked at the graceful sweep Larry had carved from a square chunk of timber with tools that appeared little changed from those pictured on 2,500-year-old Phoenician and Greek vases, I agreed. "It's been a difficult pregnancy so far."

Pregnancy — everything in the hills around us preparing to give birth. Everything fertile and reproducing, creating the next generation. It wasn't the first time I'd been subtly reminded of our childless state. Usually the reminders seemed cause for rejoicing. I'd watched a close friend's relationship being torn apart as their teenage son came back from a gut-wrenching tour of duty in Vietnam laden with a crippling drug habit. We tried to offer what support we could as they mortgaged their home, their future, to defend the heroin-addicted son after he held up a liquor store with a loaded shogun. Other friends wept with regret for sixteen-year-old daughters who were pregnant and rushing into marriages that pulled two still-children out of school into low-paid, dead-end seeming existences.

So few of our friends seemed happy with the situations they faced as their children fumbled through their teens that we rarely questioned the decision we'd made years before. On our very first evening together, I had declared to Larry my desire to set off into adult life without children. I joked about the curse my mother had put on me. I'd been fifteen and frustrated in my search for independence, a search made more difficult because I had grown up surrounded by boys. Summer holidays were often spent with three families at a lakeside cottage, six boys ranging from a year younger than I to five years older, as my only playmates. When I'd cried about being left out of their rough and tumble games, my mother had yelled in frustration, "Either learn to keep up with them or learn to be more independent. Find interesting things to do so they'll want to do them, too. I'm not going to spend my life finding things to keep you busy!" So, I learned to run with the boys as best as my short legs would let me and they did include me, sympathizing when I was hobbled by "girl clothes," chiding me when I cried over skinned knees.

But my mother's tune changed when I turned thirteen. "Lin, you can't go running off all over the place with the boys. You're a young lady now; you've got a reputation to protect." Her reasoning made little sense to me and led to almost daily disagreements, and once again, I'd ended up in another of the screaming matches I couldn't seem to avoid when my mother questioned some action that made complete sense to me. After an hour of tears and yelling, her face turned menacing, her whole demeanor changed. She seemed to tower over me with her half-inch height advantage. She looked straight into my eyes and with her fists clenched and trembling pronounced, "May you have a daughter just like you." Then, like a biblical prophet, she turned and walked darkly away, leaving me drained and shaking.

Larry had laughed at my story that first night and pulled me more tightly into his web by saying, "Kind of feel like I already had a kid, my baby brother Marsh. He's 13 years younger than me and I did enough diapering and babysitting for him to know I didn't like it. I once read, 'leave fame and adventure for the childless' — don't know about the fame part, but I definitely want to do some adventuring."

I'd enthusiastically embraced his philosophy and together we'd gradually gathered stories of parental disillusionment, ignoring any that didn't reinforce our position as we adventured through the years. So now it came as a shock when something in my body, call it hormones, along with something in Larry's mind, possibly a sense of his own mortality, made us wonder about the decision we'd made long before. It might have started because we were being confronted by friends who, after their careers were well established, were having late families. They whispered their warnings in the loaded language of parenthood, "You'd better do it before it's too late, before you miss the boat."

Our mothers shook their heads and warned us, "You'll be lonely when you're old. It would be a pity to lose out. Now's your last chance." Their warnings came close to being lectures as they implied our childless state was a case of self-indulgence, that it was almost indecent to go through life unencumbered. Nor had it helped when my brother's eight- and ten-year-old daughters wanted to run off with us for country weekends. They'd loved our old truck, made the inside of the camper their private playroom, giggled outrageously as they bathed naked among the trees, showering with cold water drawn from the well. My mother came to take them home and was surprised to find we'd had such a good time with these two grand-daughters whom she saw as lazy, spoiled by suburban shopping-mall life. A week later, I received a letter from Mom. She described how she'd laughed when the girls' mother asked, "What did you do at Lin's house?"

"We had to sweep the whole house because company was coming for dinner," Cami said.

"You never do that here, even when I ask you," their mother replied.

"Yes, but when Aunty Lin says her house needs sweeping, it really does. Besides, she said she wouldn't feed us if we didn't."

"I've threatened the same thing," their mother retorted.

"Yes, but Aunty Lin really meant it!" both Michelle and Cami chorused earnestly.

My mother's letter concluded, "You really have a persuasive way with children. You've got the ability to teach them. You'd make great parents, lots to share with your kids. You've had your adventures, so you wouldn't feel you'd missed out..."

"Maybe we should think about kids," Larry said again that evening. "It would be a good time to do it. We'll be here for two or three years, so a youngster would be out of diapers before we set off sailing again. It would be fun to see what a kid of yours looked like."

"If they were all mine, they'd have big hazel eyes, lots of thick hair, short legs. Mix you in, they'd have big hands, pink complexions, have to watch the sun just like we do. Definitely wouldn't be tall and lanky," I joked to cover my confusion. Already pictures of the added complications of extra humans under my care crept into my mind. "I'd have to give up writing," I said.

"No, you wouldn't. I'd take care of the children in the mornings three or four days a week. You'd take care of them afternoons while I did the heavy work in the boatshop."

In the canyon, out of the canyon, any mention of the thoughts we were having seemed to open a floodgate of conflicting opinions. Bob and Marlys joined the debate. "I want a baby. Bob doesn't. Told him I go off the pill in six months. Then it's his problem. Either he gets a vasectomy or we get a baby," Marlys stated.

"I'll get a vasectomy, damn it, just can't take any time off right now," Bob retorted. "Too many kids in the world anyway."

"What about Bob and Marlys, think they'll have kids?" I asked Pete Shomler when he came by on his way home. He'd opened another can of Bud, then leaned against his car and laughed, "Na, Marlys will keep taking the pill and Bob'll keep talking about having a vasectomy. He's made a dozen appointments in the past four years, always chickens out. He's changed his mind so often, we call it his vascillectomy."

"What about you? What do you feel about having children?" I asked.

"Great for me," Pete answered as he climbed into his car to leave. "I get them to move rocks for the walls of the house. Sandy takes care of them. That's her job. Good place to raise kids. Lots of things they can do to help me."

The more people we talked with, the more confused we became until finally Larry said, "We've always liked to know exactly what we are letting ourselves into before we make long-term commitments. We tell friends, try sailing and cruising before you spend all your savings on a boat of your own, charter or borrow friends' boats. Thing about boats is, you can always sell them if you don't like them. Can't sell kids. Once we go for it, they'll be a real long-term commitment, twenty or thirty years the way I see it. Why don't we follow our own advice? Borrow some kids for a while, live with them, see how they affect us. I'm sure someone we know could use a few weeks off. Then, at least we'll know something about the practical adjustments we'd have to make."

I agreed. In the past this active approach to decision making had worked well for us. I mentioned it to my mother. "Wouldn't be the same," she said. "When you live through nine months of pregnancy, you're already in love with the creature you created. Having someone else's kids wouldn't prove anything."

Then, as we began our search for children to charter, we found that an amazing number of friends seemed eager to loan us their youngsters. They were so eager I began to wonder if their eulogies on the joys of parenthood were sincere, or an attempt to ensnare us in the myth and hide the realities of the day-to-day struggle of raising children, holding down jobs and still having time for each other.

Almost too soon we arranged to be co-caretakers of three-year-old Nathan and eleven-year-old Amy, children of a friend who dreamed of going off cruising with her boyfriend and her children for a year or two. Now she could test the waters, as we took care of the children, while she tried six weeks of life at sea in the confines of a small sailing boat. We'd try out parenthood for the first part of her absence, secure in the knowledge that a grandmother waited in the wings, ready to take over if the children didn't settle into our life in the country. The catch — a small-seeming one, since the children had already charmed us completely — the package included a 110-pound Great Dane and a two-pound hermit crab.

We brought them home and it was after midnight when we pulled to a stop as close to the kitchen door as we could. Two sleeping children, four duffel bags, sleeping bags, teddy bear, plus two fifty-pound sacks of dog food made a huge pile inside the back room. A fist-sized hermit crab scrambled against the sides of a sand-filled box on top of the mess. A sleepy three-year-old padded back outside. "Where's Lady? Can't sleep until she goes to bed near me."

"Stupid animal is too dumb to jump out of the pickup," Larry whispered. "It was bad enough lifting that dog into the truck; don't tell me I have to lift her out too!" Not only did he have to lift her out, he had to carry her across the kitchen. The hard, polished tile floor scared the ferocious-looking animal, who slipped and skittered over any smooth surface. (In fact, he had to lift her in and out or over something at least three times a day.) By the time two children, a dog, and hermit crab plus two weary adults were settled in that first night, Larry was sighing, "What have I let myself in for?"

Halfway through the next morning, I screamed the same words as Nathan ran into my office space for the tenth time in an hour to show me a special flower he had found.

"You've got to be tougher if you want to have children around and get something done. Just send them out to me, plenty to keep them busy around the boatyard."

The next morning I was more successful. I explained the rules again, "You stay outside until noon. Then, I'll take you into the village with me after lunch, and we'll go down by the lake." Twenty minutes later, I heard the patter of small feet. The door leading into the front room swung slowly open. I just looked up and pointed, never saying a word. The door slowly closed. I chuckled to myself as I tried to concentrate on my writing while pondering the relativity of time. To a three-year-old, twenty minutes probably *did* feel like a whole morning.

By the next morning, I was beginning to question my self-discipline. The children, urged on by Larry, were meticulous about following the rules. I'd hear them tiptoe when they came in to use the toilet, talk in whispers whenever they were close to the cottage. But I couldn't tune them out, nor suppress my own curiosity. I'd hear screams and laughter, go out the door to learn the cause. "We've got a rattlesnake. Come see the snake," Amy called from up the hill.

"Too early for snakes. They're still hibernating," Larry yelled across the yard "Go back to work, Lin."

But I couldn't. "Sorry, kids, snakes don't have legs," I explained, when I reached the spot on the hillside above the boatshed where a large lizard was trying to sun itself and ignore this invasion.

I walked back down the hill and boiled up a cup of tea. Then I tried to concentrate on describing a stormy night in the tempestuous waters off the Italian island of Sicily where the Sirens had lured Ulysses onto the rocks with their wondrous songs. Like Ulysses, like the lizard, I tried to ignore the invasion I'd let into my life, tried to resist the urge to forget my goals and devote my whole day to their games and explorations.

Evenings were wonderfully full with the children. I'd listen to screams and giggles as Larry wrestled with the two of them on the old beanbag chairs we used by the fireplace. We'd bargain over how much had to be eaten before dessert could be served. Then seconds after dinner finished, one of the children would rush for my guitar and hand it to me, saying, "Sing about the baby ducks or the big brass bed." I'd settle on the hearth and the two youngsters would snuggle into Larry's arms on the beanbags and sing along until yawns called the evening to an end.

◇◇

I was amazed at the secret telegraph system that seems to call children together. A man I'd never seen walked up the driveway two days after Amy and Nathan came to stay. "I've got a trailer on the far side of Lindell. Live there part of the year. These are my two kids from my first marriage—staying with me a few weeks. New wife's pregnant, kids tire her out. They want to know if they can play here." The eight- and nine-year-old were an easy addition, and almost every afternoon, I'd load all four kids into the back of the truck and bounce slowly through the canyon to show them the Indian paintings on

Amy and Nathan.

the hill opposite the cottage or the secluded waterfall two miles away where deer sometimes came to feed. The Great Dane would amble along behind us, her tongue almost dragging on the road. She would sag to the ground whenever we stopped and refuse to move until all the kids were in the truck again. Even though I made a staircase of wooden boxes to help her climb into the truck, Lady never got up the nerve to do it on her own. So our speed was dictated by her ever-diminishing progress until we often returned home at a crawl. But the kids, and eventually even I, hated to leave her behind.

Sandy's youngsters soon joined the afternoon play sessions. When the big earthmoving equipment began the final repairs of the rain-ravished road nearest our cottage, it was a common sight to see six youngsters hunkered down in a row by the side of the road, dreaming, I suppose, of driving those huge, powerful machines.

As each day passed, those youngsters seemed to entwine me in their spells. I did find that I no longer had many quiet moments with Larry. I couldn't use him as a sounding board for the stories I was writing — every time we'd start to talk about a project, Nathan would come charging in with a "special flower" or Amy would come in to ask for another Band-Aid or dog biscuit. But the trade-off was the pleasure I felt as I watched them learn a new skill under my direction. I was delighted when Amy lost her fear of using matches to light the fire — gradually, she learned to strike a light at the first go, then ignite the kindling matter-of-factly and store the matches safely away from any flames or sparks. I felt proud when she finally came to trust and depend on me to be responsible for her baby brother, so she could revert to being a curious child herself, racing on colt-like legs down the paths and along the course of the stream. Before a week had passed, I was in love with those children. Larry had fallen just as hard. He'd make up little chores to help them feel they were really an important part of his project. Each day, they'd clear out the shavings he made as he carved away at the big backbone timbers. I saw how much he was enjoying their company when he came in at coffee time to get me. "Come and see the kids at work." I quietly walked to the shed window to watch Nathan intently separating hundreds of tiny nails from the sawdust that had filled their container, while Amy dripped machine oil onto the threads of the three dozen clamps lining the wall rack, then conscientiously ran the screw on each one, in and out, in and out, to lubricate it.

"Wonder if our children would be as bright as Amy and Nathan? Wonder if we could figure out how to have our own and still work together part of each day?" he asked when we lay in bed listening to their quiet breathing in the next room.

As a farewell treat, I took all six children out to Riverside the last Saturday of our trial parenthood. *The Black Stallion* was playing, a movie about a boy's adventures, which begins when he is shipwrecked on a deserted island with an Arabian stallion. I had loved it when I'd gone to see it a month previously with Larry. Larry actually had tears in his eyes as that fun movie ended. I wasn't surprised to hear the children talking about it all the way home. The next morning, as I was packing their clothes, I heard hollering. Amy came running into the kitchen only a few steps ahead of Nathan, whose short legs worked double time in his climb up the hill next to the cottage. "There's a stallion loose, we need something to catch the stallion," Amy called.

"Stallion," I thought to myself. "Horse, who has a horse up here besides the Hecks. They're at a horse show this weekend." Then I remembered. Pete and Sandy kept a tiny Shetland pony at their place. "Here's a rope, Amy. Go get a carrot from the fridge. Catch the stallion," I told the youngsters. Twenty minutes later, Nathan proudly led the swaybacked red and white pony up the driveway. It stood only a hand-span higher than their Great Dane, but nothing could have dampened their pleasure as together we led the pony back up the hill to its proper home.

Though the house was quieter when we came back after returning the children, the Great Dane and the hermit crab back to their own family, it didn't seem empty at all. It felt like the scene of a long, fun-filled party, where every guest left feeling sated and content. "What did you think of having children in your life?" Larry asked.

"They sure are wondrous things. Wasn't it amazing the way they learn so quickly? They kept me thinking all the time," I said, as I prepared a salad and Larry sat on the counter stool spreading creamy feta cheese on a cracker for me to nibble as I worked. "Thanks for that. It's nice to have you back here in the kitchen with me. Funny but I kind of missed you while the kids were here. I almost felt a little jealous at times. You'd be out there playing while I cooked dinner. You'd be in the beanbag with them, cuddled up almost asleep while I fixed their beds. They had your attention and I had to take care of all of you."

"How do you think I felt?" Larry answered. "You'd go off in the truck having all sorts of adventures with half a dozen kids instead of working alongside me in the afternoons. Organizing everyone seemed to take all the time we usually spend planning and thinking together. Neither of us got near as much done the past few weeks, not that I expected we would. But I loved watching you teach the kids how to cook, how to make reed baskets. You'd make a great mother, you know."

"Do you think we'd figure out how to balance our life better if they were our own kids?" I asked Larry.

"We'd have to lower our expectations a bit, be less ambitious. We could do it," he replied.

We or he or me, I wondered over the next days, as gradually I stopped listening for the sound of giggling children, stopped thinking of games or songs I could have taught Amy and Nathan to fill the quiet evenings in front of the flickering fire.

"Are you going to have kids?" my sister asked next time we were together.

"Problem is, we fell in love with Amy and Nathan," I answered. "If we could have those two there wouldn't be any question at all. But after seeing how much time and attention they took we know we can't really afford kids until this project is finished. So plan is, I'm going to stop taking the Pill when the boat's almost finished, then let fate make the decision for us."

"You want kids, have them right now. You keep thinking about it, you'll keep finding reasons to put it off a little longer. You aren't getting any younger," Bonnie said echoing the words I heard in my own mind.

I paused for a moment to consider my next words. "Bonnie, I think there are some drawbacks to planning life as carefully as we do. Probably if we just went ahead and had kids right now, didn't think of all the pitfalls, we'd survive. The kids would survive."

"Are you going to have babies?" my nieces asked when they came to spend another weekend with us.

"Not for a while," Larry and I both answered, maybe a little too quickly.

"Good, you'll have time to borrow us more," Cami said, with such apparent satisfaction that I forgot the glimmers of lost opportunity, the twinges of hormonal guilt that would remain with me long after the possibility of having children of my own was gone.

◇◇

As spring advanced and the very first frames of our boat thrust their arms into the air, the rattlesnakes made their appearance. Like most city-bred people, snakes made me feel more than a little uncomfortable. As a Californian child I'd been taken on long hikes through the hills around Los Angeles where Mom and Dad warned, "Don't go scrambling over rocks without looking, might be a rattlesnake sunning himself on the other side. Its bite could kill you." I remember hearing the buzz that my brother and I were sure was the warning of a rattler one hot summer day. My unbounded ten-year-old's curiosity overcame my fears as I helped my brother search for that elusive

My nieces, Michelle and Cami.

Larry's mom, Beryl.

reptile. We poked through the weeds with long sticks for an hour, listening, poking, looking for tracks, yelling, "just exploring," when our parents called from our campsite to ask what we were up to.

Until that first spring in Bull Canyon, I'd always wondered why my brother and I had been unable to catch up with the snakes we'd heard rattling during our summer days together. Now, as sun warmed the rocks around us and began to wilt the less hardy of the desert flowers, I heard the unbridled hum of thousands of cicadas. I finally caught one so I could listen up close to the rattle-like sound this lima-bean-sized creature ground out like a constant dirge. Then one day, Larry called to me from the boatyard. "Come and see what I found under the woodpile," he yelled.

As I stood well back from the vibrating coil of the wrist-thick rattlesnake, I marveled at its warning. Only children, or the uninitiated, could confuse the benign buzz of a cicada for this. As I approached to within a dozen yards, this teeth-grating rattle overpowered all the buzz and twitter of the insects and birds swarming around the tree shaded yard. "Ominous" is a word too often used, yet it is the only one I can think of. Ominous described that square, darting head; ominous described that flickering, forked tongue; ominous described the slow undulations of its coiled body. Fear welled inside as I stared at it, yet I couldn't move away. As that snake quivered and held its ground, I slowly began to see the delicate pattern of its desert-colored scales, the diamond design along its back. I was startled when Larry picked up a long board and said, "Now you've seen it. I'll kill it."

I hadn't time to comment before its head was smashed and its rattle silenced. "Had to kill it — if it breeds around here we could lose Dog," Larry said with a sigh that held a real sense of sadness. He carried the snake gingerly down the driveway to the trees near the stream where he assured me coyotes would enjoy a feed. With the curiosity that I sometimes feel hasn't changed one bit since I was that ten-year-old co-explorer, I gingerly poked at the pale rings of the rattler's tail. The rattle sounded again, softly, like an echo of the warning the snake had given to say, "You are the intruders, leave me alone."

The memory of those long curving fangs made me think twice when my sister Bonnie brought her family up for the weekend.

Bonnie had appeared in my seven-year-old life like a living, breathing birthday gift. My brother and I seemed never to have one minute of jealousy or resentment at including this charming doll-like creature in our lives. My mother found our antics amusing at first. But by the time Bonnie was trying to walk, Mom could be heard yelling, "Put her down, she's got legs of her own." My baby sister grew up trying to please everyone, to fit in so Allen and I wouldn't tease her. She succeeded with Allen. But, probably because I always fell for my older brother's practical joking and could never seem to outsmart him, I took out my frustration by teasing Bonnie to the point of torment. Through the years, as I grew ever more at odds with my parents, she worked quietly in the background as a miniature diplomat trying to bring back the tranquility our home had experienced for the first six years of her life. She was ten years old when I stormed off in a huff, and only years later did Bonnie reveal how pleased she was when Mom turned to her for sympathy, for reassurance that she was a good mother and hadn't driven me out onto the streets and a life of crime and poverty.

Long after I left Bull Canyon, I realized that Bonnie and I really knew very little about each other. During my wandering years, she'd watched as my parents talk changed from, "Where did we go wrong with Lin?" to "Wonder what she's up to now?" to "Can't wait until they get closer to home so we can spend more time with Lin." Now, Bonnie and I were, for the first time, getting a chance to spend more than an hour or two together, and I enjoyed watching her complete comfort with children, listening to her stories of the work she did as a special educator with deaf students — when I could get her to talk about herself. But at the same time, I could feel a discomfort between us as she tried to resist "pleasing her big sister" and fought back against the jealousy she must have felt at the attention my parents gave to Larry and me at the expense of Bonnie's family. I probably aggravated her discomfort because I understood so little of the concerns of her life, a life I'd barely known.

Bonnie had married a city boy who, I think, wished he'd grown up in the country. Warm, full of good humor and an endless supply of jokes, Mike was often frustrated by the demands of a high-pressure advertising job that stole time he'd rather have spent enjoying his family, his toys and friends. Lanky, definitely attractive and well over six-feet-tall, his casual outward attitude toward people made him appear far more at home in our country place than we did, and definitely more at home than he was in his suburban tract house. Soon after they arrived, he dug into the back of his pickup truck for a shot gun, a skeet-shooting contraption, plus a big box full of black and green clay disks, then said, "I know, you want me far away from the cottage, so I don't scare away any of your pet birds." He started up the trail toward the well, his year-and-a-half-old son, Kurt, skittering along next to his tooled leather high-heeled boots. "No, Mike," I shouted. "Safer if you set up your throwing machine here. I don't want Kurt stumbling around in the rocks. Might be a rattlesnake. Its bite could kill him."

Bonnie and I kept an eye on Kurt as we lazed in the warm sun and watched the green and black disks fly through the clear air in a high-peaked arc, to be shattered by the blast from Mike's gun. "Want to take a few shots?" he called to Larry.

"Haven't had any practice for years," Larry answered. "Not since I went hunting with my dad back when I was in high school. I'd just waste your ammo. Go ahead. I've got some little jobs I want to do on the truck."

I turned our tiny porch into a water playground for Kurt by putting an old sprinkler fitting on the end of a hose, and turning it so a fine spray flew three feet into the air. Then I went over to hold a wrench for Larry as he adjusted something on the truck. "Does he have to mess up the place with those damned skeets?" Larry mumbled as we both worked under the hood of the engine. I, too, hated seeing the rocks and bushes of the hillside invaded by the glaringly unnatural litter of black and green pottery. "Bonnie told me they are made to melt away as soon as it rains. He's enjoying himself so much. He's always having to listen to rules. Let's not say anything. I like having the family come up here," I answered quietly.

Bonnie got up from her sunbathing spot and called to Mike, "Keep an eye on Kurt. I'll be in the house for a few minutes."

"Okay, sure," he called back as he pulled the skeet-launching line again and aimed his gun.

Larry repositioned his screwdriver and said softly, "Sure hope your sister's right, but means we have to look at the mess for the next five months, probably won't rain again 'til then. Wish you'd told him to go up the back road." I could see Larry tensing as each shot from Mike's gun shattered the still of the afternoon only fifty yards from where we worked. I could sense him wrestling with the desire to retain the magic natural feeling, the quietness and remoteness that surrounded us each day, yet share it with friends and family, who spent most of the year trapped in the confines of the city.

Bonnie came out of the house and called, "Mike, where's Kurt?"

I looked toward the porch, where two bright red and green hummingbirds darted in and out of the sparkling spray of water, undisturbed by any toddler, then toward Mike who slowly realized Kurt was nowhere in view. I could see the edge of terror creeping into Bonnie's eyes as she turned to scour the endless jumble of rocks surrounding our homestead. I felt terrified, too, as I thought of the snakes sunning behind rocks and ran toward the back of the house to search while Larry ran toward the timber-filled garage. I heard Mike bellowing, "Kurt, Kurt," anger and concern reflected in each call.

"What a responsibility. They move so fast, they're so curious," I thought. There had been a dozen times when I hadn't been able to spot young Nathan during his short stay with me. I'd felt instant panic, the feeling that not only was the child an easy prey to a dozen possible horrors, but I'd be utterly and completely vulnerable, and guilt-ridden for life if I failed as a caretaker. Any regret that still remained from our decision to remain childless disappeared as we searched.

Then, the sound of a child's laughter came clear and sweet from the boat shop. We all converged to find a sight I'll never forget. Instead of heading towards the rocks and bushes that hid so many potential dangers, including rattlesnakes like the one Larry had killed only a few weeks before, Kurt had wandered over to play next to Larry's band saw. He'd discovered the soft, fluffy, teak sawdust that lay in piles around its base. Now he was tossing the golden powder into the air and laughing with glee, as it stuck to his wet, nude body, until he looked exactly like breaded chicken. And, towering over him, Stetson in one hand, shotgun in the other, glancing first at his wayward son, then at his relieved but angry wife, stood a guilty-looking father, who I'm sure, at that moment and maybe others, wished he'd grown up to be a lonesome cowboy.

Chapter 9

Water

"Up and to the left," I called, my voice echoing inside the huge, empty water tank. The end of a galvanized bolt shoved its way through the ragged bullet hole. I threaded on washers and a nut, and then held a wrench while Larry tightened the assembly from outside the tank. "Okay, up two feet and almost directly in line," I guided Larry as I climbed onto the wooden stool I'd carried in with me.

We'd been working all morning to patch the holes riddling our main water storage tank. There had been a generous supply of big lead washers in the old storage shed, and black gobs of tar spotted around inside the galvanized iron tank showed where similar bolts and washers had been used years earlier for this same task.

"Wonder if we should paint the tank brush-green so it wouldn't make such a great target for hunters coming up the road?" I suggested to Larry when he lowered his ladder into the tank, and came inside to help me slather tar sealant on the newest patches.

"Green? Nope. Have to paint it brush-yellow or rock-pink to make it less obvious when summer comes," he answered. "Nothing will be green then. Our springs will probably slow up a lot, too. That's why I want to get this tank patched and the rest of the water system working really well. If we get it filled and keep it topped up, figure we could go for a month or two even if the well dried up."

"Bob Steele says our well has never gone dry. Ellie says we've got more water up here than anyone else in the canyon," I replied.

Water. This was the key to life in Bull Canyon. I'd spent much of my life depending on other people to assure me a constant supply of water, rarely giving a thought to how it reached my tap. Now, we had to take personal responsibility not only for finding it, but containing, preserving and conserving it. As summer approached, water seemed to have become an obsession with us and everyone in the canyon.

The first time we'd come to see the stone cottage, I'd lain on my stomach to look inside the old well just up the ravine from where we eventually built the boatshed. A dead snake floated on the reservoir of clear cool water. Larry found a rat-chewed dip net in the shed and scooped the carcass out. Then I'd used a flashlight for a more serious look inside. The top few feet of the well were lined with close-fitting stonework. Beneath this, the roots of bushes and trees could be seen, following the tracks made by rivulets of sweet water that meandered down the dirt walls. We'd measured the depth of that hand-dug pit, then I covered a sheet of paper with numbers as I rested in the sunshine. "There's 4000 gallons of water in there right now. If a normal California family uses 420 gallons of water a day, we'll probably use 150. So, if we fix the big tank and fill it..."

"Lin, where'd you get that figure? Seems like a hell of a lot of water for a family to go through in a day," Larry asked.

"Read it a few weeks ago, story about the L A water system."

"Sponge brain, how can you remember so many numbers when you can't remember anyone's name?" Larry teased.

He was right. I could forget my best friend's name, but numbers stuck. I catalogued them away for some unknown future use, and loved digging them out at odd moments as much as I loved playing the number games involved with computing how much water we could have if...

"Stop sittin' on your butt playing with numbers," Larry had said that day. "You need some exercise. Let's hike up the gully and see where the stream starts."

We'd fought uphill through shrubs and weeds for another eight hundred feet until we reached a stand of sycamore. Animal tracks converged into the shade of the trees, an eagle's nest hung in edge-of-collapse disarray in the branches of the tallest tree. Knee-high piles of leaves covered the ground, rustling softly as we explored the cool glade. A rock face formed the uphill side of the glade. Rivulets of water seeped out of fissures in the rock to gutter downward to a tiny pool that spread beneath the decaying leaves. Larry was like a ferret, almost in a frenzy as he raked through the leaves. "Look, 'ol man Payonessa's done some work up here a long time ago. Shows this spring's always been here. Do you know what that means?"

An artesian spring — in this dry, dusty country, it was like magic. My mind flew off to the melting snows and tumbling streams of the High Sierras as I thought of how long it must have taken for water to run from there through hundreds of miles of underground rivers to reach our hilltop spring when Larry insisted, "Lin, this is really important. If we dug a catchment area here it could give us gravity-fed water right to our tanks, no well-pumps, no motors to worry about." His mind was off in its world of building, engineering, and plumbing.

He went up to explore that trickle of water a dozen times before the rains came. He'd talked with Bob and Pete about his idea of controlling the spring right at its source.

"Heard rumors about that water," Bob said. "But it's not much use. Waste of time. If you want real water, you've got to get a drilling rig in, go down three hundred feet. That's where the good water is."

Pete just shrugged, "You going to lug concrete and gravel up that hill? You ain't got any kids to help. Not enough water to matter. Besides, if you trapped the water up there, the lower well would probably dry up. Forget it, use what you've got. Never heard of your lower well doing anything but slowing up a bit over a long summer."

But Larry wore his most determined look as he trudged up the hill carrying a shovel and pick a week later. Mariano clambered up behind him, humming a mariachi tune as he carried more digging weapons. The first evening Larry came down, muddy and happy. "Loads of water up there. Here's what I need from town tomorrow," he began, adding to my never-ending shopping list.

When I returned from town, I heard shouting and laughing from up the ravine. I grabbed the roll of heavy plastic Larry had asked for and climbed up the track which was now becoming quite distinct.

"Una piedra."

"Okay."

"Una piedra," I heard as Larry's muffled voice asked for a rock. Just before I reached the glade I heard him call again. "Una piedra."

Mariano's voice called back, "Okay, una piedra grande."

Silence.

Then roars of laughter interspersed with choking Spanish.

Then curses, angry curses from Larry.

I rushed to where a huge pit lay, trickles of water making a substantial puddle over the layers of old metal road signs that lined the bottom. Larry sat on a pile of rocks, looking up at Mariano, his anger slowly leaving his face. "I asked the bastard for another rock. He handed me a goddamned boulder, knocked me flat on my ass," Larry muttered.

I tried not to laugh as I thought of the language barrier that would always exist between our high school Spanish and the Spanish our helper used. In English, there must be half-a-dozen different words to describe the size of rocks, from pebble to stone to boulder. In Spanish, only one.

"I warned him," Mariano said to me in apology.

"Yes, I heard. But, next time it's an extra big one, make sure you have his attention. Say 'Mira, Mira, look, look up.'" I walked down the hill, chuckling at the thought of a typical Larry situation. Once again, he'd been so engrossed in planning his next move, he'd never looked up and he'd been oblivious to one word, the word grande, after piedra.

Both Bob and Pete came by to inspect Larry's catchment and filtering pit as he set a concrete standpipe in place, covered the whole area with enameled road signs we found in the shed, then with plastic and finally, to my surprise, a foot of dirt and leaves, so only the standpipe, capped with a big, flat rock, showed where three days work had gone.

"The dirt will keep animals from digging down to get to the water," he explained to all of us.

"Your siphon system will never work," Bob said. "It'll get an airlock and stop running as soon as the summer sun hits your black pipe."

Larry answered, "I'll start it tomorrow and see what happens."

"Soon's the creek's gone underground, animals will eat through your hose. Better to forget it, and do with what you've got," Pete said, shaking his head.

"So, I'll bury the hose," Larry answered.

But Mariano, who had grown up in the desert regions of Northern Mexico, where water was almost as scarce as money, had no doubts about Larry's system. He was in full agreement with Larry's feeling that gravity was far more dependable than motors and pumps and definitely less expensive.

The water that gushed through that long black pipe was cool and clear and wonderfully sweet. Friends from the city often brought empty jugs when they came to visit, carrying the artesian water back to homes where tap water was over-flavored by chemicals and the taste of old public pipes. Bob Steele asked about Larry's system a month later.

"It's working great, feeds right into our big tank, runs day and night. Had to shut it down a few weeks back, tank was over-flowing." I got the distinct feeling that Bob was disappointed when something he had disparaged was successful. It was almost as if, like a parent who sees their child make the first wise decision on its own and thus feels less needed, our neighbor resented Larry's growing comfort with the challenges that surrounded us.

But Bob and Pete had been partially right. As soon as the summer came and the last bits of green faded so only the trees along the ravine and in our hand-irrigated front yard showed cool against the desert colors, the trickle stopped. I walked uphill to see if our spring had gone dry. Halfway to the glade, a puddle spread to show where a small animal had gnawed a hole through the pipe. Mariano came back to trench in the line. "While he's here, let's put in a siphon starting line," Larry suggested. "Just in case Pete's right about airlocks." So another length of hose now led from a T next to the big tank, down to a patch of ground where in my optimistic way, I was trying to plant flowers to brighten the yard. I became fascinated with the mechanics of water, mechanics the Romans and Carthaginians had used to their advantage. I spent hours playing in my mind with the physics of forcing water to flow uphill, pulled by water flowing downhill somewhere further along the line. For the first time, I began to understand why the people of LosAngeles could afford to pipe water from rivers five or six hundred miles away, across three or four ranges of hills and mountains. I could commiserate with the people who lived along those far away watercourses as they worried that the growing demands of Los Angelenos would suck their lakes and rivers dry.

When Larry came in from the boatyard in an angry mood one day, my hours of musing paid off. "Generator can't handle this heat. If I run it for more than a half hour it shuts down." Soon after we'd moved to the canyon, Larry had located a big diesel generator we could afford. We'd bought it cheap from the San Diego harbor patrol fire-fighting boat. It needed some repairs, but Larry's earlier experience working on big logging equipment as a twenty-year-old made him feel confident he'd found a bargain. "It's a marine generator. We know lots of people in Newport who could use it if we ever get real electricity up here. Sell it for a good price. We've lots of water to cool it."

Normally, a marine generator has the whole ocean to run through its cooling system. Larry had made a substitute water supply by interconnecting four fifty-five gallon drums and filling them with water. During the cool weather this had worked okay. But the summer heat meant the water temperature in his barrels quickly reached the shut-off limit of the machine. "Got to come up with a better system," he groaned.

"What about using the lower well, run the water from it, through the engine and back into the well. Now we're using the artesian water. We rarely need that."

"Nice idea, Lin, but the motor's only got a small pump, not sure it could pull water all the way down and then back up the hill."

"But the siphon," I said. "Like from the top well. If the water siphoned down to the engine, the pump wouldn't have to work very hard."

Larry stared hard at the wall for a few minutes, "Just might work. Got lots of hose laying around. Worth a try."

Two days later Bob made his appearance to announce, "Marlys is making tacos, come on up." As we sat on dilapidated old couches in front of the Steele's hilltop trailer and watched the setting sun paint the far hills in evening colors, Larry said, "Lin had a great idea, cooling my generator with the well water. Can run it all day now, no problems."

Marlys sighed, "All I ever hear out here is talk of water now the rain's stopped and the roads staying put. I'm looking forward to the day when I can just turn on a tap and forget about where the stuff comes from. Bob's promised I won't even be able to hear the well-pump or generator when he gets the house finished. 'Course he's been saying that for five years now." Then she murmured quietly to me, "There are times I doubt I'll ever live in that house."

Bob gave her a sideways glance. "You seemed to enjoy all the funny stories about water tanks and wells when I first bought the place," he said. "Remember when Pete was trying to fix that old wooden tank at his place? It was still sitting empty a year after he bought the land. You could see light through the seams in it. He tightened up the bands, covered it with old burlap sacks and kept wetting them down. Then he kept trying to fill it. But no matter what he did there were still lots of tiny leaks. One day an old guy from up the road came around and told him to put fish in the tank — the leaks would stop. Pete ignored him until Ellie said she'd heard the same. So Pete got a dozen just-hatched catfish from catfish corners. A week later the leaks slowed down, then they stopped."

"Yeah, sure," I said.

"He's right, Lin," Marlys said excitedly. "Don't know how they did it, but the leaks stopped. Fish are still there. They eat the mosquito larva too. Pete's big tank always stays tight."

We walked down off the plateau late that evening, my flashlight catching occasional flashes of Dog's white-tipped tail as he sniffed among the dry crackly weeds at the roadside. "Maybe those fish are instinctively protecting their environment," Larry said contemplatively. "They probably sense they'll die if the water keeps running out."

"Sure, I can imagine a committee of fish planning their action," I said. "What would they use to plug the holes?"

"Think about it, Lin, they could gather up algae, bits of twigs. Beavers build dams, birds build nests, why can't fish build plugs?"

I never did decide if the fish story was true. No one else we met had a wooden water tank to test the idea. But I did see the fish in Pete's old tank. I did see its bone dry sides bleached white by the desert sun while inside it held crystal clear water. And Marlys, she never seemed to exaggerate or put people on...

I stepped on something soft and squishy as we walked up the driveway. I ignored it. I heard rustling noises in the brush. Then my light caught a strange glimpse of Dog. He was leaping straight into the air in a stiff-legged stance. I flashed the light around the front yard. The driveway, the porch, the weed-patch yard, all were covered with walnut-sized frogs. They bounced and jumped in every direction. Dog would prowl up to smell one. It would leap away from the feline's threatening nose. Dog would jump, a startled expression on his whiskered face. "It's like the plagues," Larry groaned. "First floods, then mud, then frogs, then flies, my boatyard's alive with tiny flies — can barely work unless there's a good breeze to blow them away. I spent half my time brushing them out of my eyes. What next?"

I got the broom from the boatyard to sweep the miniature frogs away so we could open the door without a total massacre. Water, an overabundance of water in a normally dry land — that is what had caused all of these plagues.

◇◇

Eight months after we moved to the canyon, we began to feel the intensity of the desert summer. The scorching dry heat began to bronze even the hardiest bushes and shrubs unless their roots were close to the course of the streams and springs that blessed our homestead. Early morning dew glistened momentarily, to evaporate the minute the sun crept over the edge of the hill. By noon, an almost overpowering aroma of sage blew through every open window. Then by early afternoon the winds began, blowing down through the canyon strong enough so my desk became adorned with rocks to prevent papers from flying across the room.

Larry welcomed the wind that whistled through the slits between the eaves and walls of his shed. Then the radio predicted yet another ninety-eight-degree day.

I heard the sound of loud hammering, the snarl of a Skilsaw, then a loud crash. I ran to the kitchen window to see a panel of plywood fall off the building. By noon, when the breeze began to build from a whisper to a whistle, Larry had an open air shed, the walls only shoulder-high around most of the buildings.

"What about winter? It will be hard to work when it's cold and rainy," I stated, as perspiration formed while I mixed a salad to take out for lunch under the shade of the trees.

"We'll worry about that later," Larry answered, as he slugged back another tumbler full of iced lemonade. "It's sure better in the shed right now."

But as much of a blessing as that afternoon wind was, it was also the cause of yet another plague. Dust. Clouds of dust. I'd close the uphill-facing windows the minute I left my desk each day, but still dust crept in. Each morning, I'd lift my notebook and see its outline drawn perfectly by rose-colored dust. I'd sweep the kitchen floor every evening, but still each step we took left a foot print outlined with dust. The green leaves in our tree-shaded yard turned beige with their coating of dust. I gave up wearing white clothes since within minutes I'd brush up against something and have a rose-colored smudge on a previously clean shirt.

"All day I face the barren waste, without a taste of water, cool clear water..."

I'd hear Larry sing from his dusty, bone-dry boatyard, as he too had to sweep layers of blowing dust clear of his band saw table ten times a day.

Dean Wixom, a favorite boatbuilding friend, drove in one Saturday morning just when the summer heat reached its zenith. He laughed at my apologies for the grit that defied the three-times-a-day wiping of the kitchen counter. "Take the day off. I'll show you something that is close by but not the least bit dusty."

"We'll go change our clothes, be right back," I said, eager to be away from the dry desert colors that glowed so vibrantly at dusk and dawn but turned a monotonous, washed-out yellow in the harsh glare of the relentless mid day sun.

"Forget changing, just get a towel. You really don't need one thing more," he said.

Dean refused to tell us where we were headed as we drove out of the canyon and onto the two-lane highway. Then, only eight miles beyond Elsinore, he directed us onto a narrow road marked simply, "Glen Eden, members only please." We headed toward softly rounded foothills nestled against the sheer coastal mountains and made a final turn into an extensive woodland, shaded by ancient California oaks. A guard post blocked the road, and beyond a sign reading "Nudist Camps of America" we could see inviting green lawns, well-tended gardens.

We drove into an almost full parking lot, shaded from the outside world by shrubs and trees, and I watched our host comfortably slip off his clothes, fold them and lay them on the car seat, then pick up a picnic basket and stroll toward the entry building with an air of assumed sophistication. I followed. The sense of freedom I always feel when I pull off the binding elastic band of my shorts, the clinging, sweat-inducing fabric of my summer shirt, was there to overlay my slight feeling of self-consciousness. I tried not to stare as I walked past dozens of people enjoying the Olympic-sized indoor swimming pool, shower rooms, café. Dean lead us out into the thick green grass beyond the buildings and within minutes, staring changed to appreciation of the crowd that swam in the even larger outdoor pool or played tennis, volleyball and tetherball clad only in sun hats and sporting shoes.

Dean and Larry disappeared into the welcoming waters of the swimming pool, while I slid into a nearby Jacuzzi. Bodies of every shape and size crossed my view, unhindered and relaxed without the social structuring, the class labeling of clothes. A woman who must have been past seventy strolled by, a huge white straw hat shading a heavily lined face, lace-trimmed white socks and immaculate tennis shoes accenting the deep tan that covered her age-sculpted body. Her buoyant carriage caught my eye, then she passed and I saw a gold and blue butterfly tattooed on her left buttock. "I'll bet she was a real swinger in her day," I thought as the bubbling water soaked away the last vestiges of desert dust.

An exceptionally handsome, middle-aged man walked by, deep in conversation with a long-haired, smart-looking woman. His arm rested comfortably around her waist. A line of surgical stitching scars crossed the woman's chest, the only sign that previously, a normal, full, round breast had matched the one that remained. The big C, breast cancer, a fear which always lay in a hidden corner of my mind leapt to the fore. On the very day I was born, my grandmother had died of the dreaded disease, afraid to tell anyone of the lump slowly growing in her breast, afraid of living in a mutilated body that might be seen as hideous by the man who shared her life. Yet, in the bright sunlight, this woman laid to rest any fears I had. I saw no deformity, just a misfortune overcome, a person as attractive as and possibly more interesting than many of the nymph-like teenagers who cavorted with their friends nearby.

As I strolled back toward the quiet shaded spot where our blanket lay, I passed a heavily muscled man in his late twenties lying absolutely prone and statue-like, eyes closed and covered by tiny plastic discs, sun-bleached hair carefully combed to be clear of every inch of his face. A thin string led in a straight taut line from a loop around his neck down his chest to another loop that held his penis so its tip pointed directly at his chin. I tried to suppress my curiosity and walk on by, but the comfortable open atmosphere added audacity to my curiosity. "Excuse me, but what's the string for?" I asked casually.

"Makes sure my tan's even all over," the sunbather replied, just as casually.

The sound of water surrounded me as I lay back in the dust-free, sweet-smelling grass, the splash of swimmers in the pool, the bubbling gurgle from the Jacuzzi, then the rhythmic sigh of the lawn sprinklers urging the grass to richer greenness. This verdant oasis in the desert of Southern California lulled my senses yet left me feeling uneasy as the afternoon sun blazed down to bleach and suck the last bits of moisture out of the hills beyond the carefully delineated hedges.

Later that evening, as Larry and I worked together opening each of the windows in the stone cottage to catch the cool breezes that always funneled up the canyon a few hours after sunset, I learned he, too, had felt uneasy as he played amidst that abundance of water. We stood quietly in the sun porch listening to the call of the owl that nested near our front gate. Larry began to hum.

"Old Dan and I, with throats burned dry and souls that cry for water..."

"You thinking the same thing I am?" I asked. "Just how much water is there? The way the population in the valley is growing, the way all of California is growing, will there be enough water to keep our springs going out here?

"We've got the big tank topped up, the wells full, the spring's still running," Larry murmured. "Don't think you have anything to worry about. I feel like we've finally got things under control."

But as I blew out each of the oil lamps in the front room my mind seemed to overflow with numbers: 450 gallons for every family every day, 1000 for the spas and pools at Glen Eden, 150 gallons for me, 50 for my trees... I couldn't stop wondering, how long would the water keep flowing from our precious spring?

Chapter 10

Interlude

Our leisure life had fallen into a soul-refreshing routine. Once the rains were over, our landlords Jimmie and Barbara would drive up the canyon on alternate weekends to see how the two of us were getting along with our boat building, well digging and book writing. We'd invite the Steeles over for a laughter-filled dinner and a bit too much wine. Barbara and Jimmie would spend the night in the back room, which they had adopted and filled with furniture to fit their desired comfort level, including flannel-lined baskets for their two German shepherds. The next morning we'd all be up with the first cackle of quail. I'd show Larry the premade meals I'd left for him, then shove my way past the dogs into the back of the crew cab of Jimmie and Barb's work truck to ride down canyon, over the hills and mountains to the moist cool air of the California coastline. We'd arrive in Newport Beach where I'd leap out and wave Jimmie and Barbara along their way to their latest construction site. Then, before the first joggers were up and about, I'd have my seven-foot dinghy launched and be on my way out to where *Seraffyn* sat looking neglected and fettered after so many years of swinging freely to her anchor in exotic coves and faraway places

This was one more part of the master plan we'd dreamed up as we crossed the North Pacific two years before. During that long stormy passage, we'd filled the dreary, uncomfortable hours by scheming about the token effort we should make toward being responsible, creating some capital to "protect us in our old age." We knew it was time to do some serious planning, since, as Larry topped the forty mark and I trailed by only five years, we still had nothing in any Social Security plan, nor had we saved a penny more than the initial $5,000 nest egg we'd held onto since we first set off sailing together.

"Here's how I think it could all make sense," Larry had said, as we fought yet another gale four hundred miles south of the Aleutian Islands. "We find a safe, inexpensive place to keep *Seraffyn* while we build the new boat. You take a day or two off every second week to keep her in good condition and ready to use. That will give you a break from taking care of me, some space to think about your writing and yourself. Then I'll stop working for a couple of days, we'll go sailing, see some of our seaside friends. It'll be sort of like having a holiday cottage, a real change, a reminder of why we're working so hard. Then we'll go back and work ten days straight. If we keep *Seraffyn* and earn the money to build the new boat, when it is time to sell her, we'll end up with a real nest egg. Might even find a piece of land somewhere in Southern California, not far from Newport or Balboa, something in the path of future development. We could buy that land on time, get a second hand trailer home to live in, build a boatshed, fix the place up while we build the boat. Then when the new boat is a reality, we could sell *Seraffyn* and pay off the land. That would set us up."

His ideas had given me something to mull over as I lay battling seasickness in the confines of a narrow, lee-cloth-shielded bunk, trying to ignore the screeching wind and growling waves that washed past our tiny, hove-to, storm tossed yacht.

Now, as I enjoyed one of my waterfront weekends away from the canyon, I had time to savor the results of our scheming. Although Larry's idea of a trailer on our own piece of land had been supplanted by the advent of the old stone cottage, the rest of "the plan" had more or less worked as we'd hoped. Visualization became the pop-psychology term for the scheming Larry and I often indulged in. As I looked up the harbor to see sails on several boats we recognized, I recalled the dozens of times when our dreams had turned to schemes that eventually did work out almost as we had planned. This morning was one more time when the pieces were fitting together. I had come to cherish the relaxing time I had completely to myself on the boat.

I did spend long but leisurely hours scrubbing the decks, sanding and re-varnishing hatches, or washing oil from the paint work and topsides, indulgently using gallons and gallons of the water *Seraffyn* sat in. But what surprised me most is that on those days when I was on my own, I rarely sought out any of the friends we had around the waterfront. Instead, I'd reach the goal I'd set for my day, then row ashore and walk to the local shops to buy some special treats, fresh blueberries, creamy Stilton cheese, french-style patés, glistening fillets of fish fresh from the local boats, all treats that were abundant here amidst the homes of millionaires and seashore holiday makers but unavailable in far less affluent Elsinore. Then I'd carry them back on board where I'd sing along to opera tapes turned at volumes that would have been painful to Larry. I'd dig out jazz cassettes by the Nylons that just didn't suit Larry's tastes but made me want to dance like a dervish in the tiny confines of my dust-free, rat-free floating cabin. I'd eat totally unbalanced dinners of giant, cake-like chocolate chip cookies followed by tomato and green pepper salads and fresh raspberries, go for midnight rows around the bay or sit on deck reading to the light of an oil lamp until my eyes drooped. I sometimes paused to wonder at this change from my younger days when I lived in dread of spending more than an hour or two by myself and had wanted the reassurance of a constantly ringing phone to feel "popular."

Larry's arrival on Saturday morning would put an end to the quiet. Although he thrived on hours, days or even weeks of solitude as he ground away with single-minded attention to whatever his current project might be, once he could look back and say, "projects coming along well, we need a break," he loved to fill that break with people — old friends, new friends, family — the more the better.

"Let's get out some fenders. That's Jimmie and Barb's boat," he said one late summer morning, pointing toward a gleaming red racing yacht that emerged from around the end of the island. As they tied alongside, their teasing and scheming expanded our world far beyond the rocky walls of our weekday canyon.

This couple held a special place in our gypsy-like lives. They represented history, a sharing that went back almost as far as Larry and I did. In 1966, only a year after the two of us met, a charter-yacht skipper walked into the shed where we were living and building our first boat and called, "Hey you guys, I've found two other people just as nutty as you." He introduced Jimmie and Barbara and their shaggy German shepherd, then showed them the framework of what we hoped would become our future cruising home. At just under six feet in height, slim, with bouncy blonde shoulder-length hair, Barbara had a wild streak she never tried very hard to hide. Jimmie, brown-eyed, curly-haired, stood 5'9," just like Larry, and had strong, wide shoulders, a washboard stomach, slim hips and legs that should have been inches longer. With his devilish and quick sense of humor, Jimmie had a tendency to encourage Barbara's craziest stunts.

When we met, they were living happily on a 23-foot-long Herreshoff sloop. The three of them (which included the 85-pound dog) shared a space little larger than a small shoreside toilet while Barbara worked as an accounting clerk and Jimmie painted docks and apprenticed to the local house builder. They had just arrived in Southern California and discovered sailing. "Cost us less to buy this boat on time than to rent a apartment. Money we save lets us fix the boat up," Barbara said a few days after we met. She showed me the storage locker she rented on shore, every inch filled with expensive elegant suits and dresses from a previous life. Then we set off from the dock on *Squall*, their handsome, but cramped little craft and within minutes cemented a friendship that came to feel like the best family life could offer. As we built *Seraffyn*, Jimmie and Barbara's *Squall* became our main source of recreation. She was also a reminder that we were on the right track. If the four of us and the dog could go out for four- or five-day cruises and find it fun, then Larry and I would easily be able to live on 24'4" long *Seraffyn*.

By the time we launched *Seraffyn*, did some perfunctory sea trials, and set off for Mexico in 1969, Jimmie was a full-fledged house carpenter, Barbara a well-paid office manager. They forwarded our mail to us during the next eleven years as we wandered around on our boat. We followed their exploits through the letters they included with each package. The two of them began filling their spare time rebuilding old houses together. The profits went toward buying undeveloped lots in the exclusive hills of Laguna Beach, lots considered too difficult to build on by others with less vision. Jimmie would design and frame up houses uniquely fitted to their site. Barbara thought little of sneaking out to hidden canyons late at night and using her amazing lifting power to load up their truck with river stones which she set into magnificent walls and fireplaces on homes that sold even before they were completed. "Sweat equity," Jimmie called it, as they strove toward their American Dream.

After sailing completely around the world, we returned to find them even more full of mischief and eager to share their hard-earned, but slightly unexpected wealth, not only by loaning us the stone cottage but with a very gracious win/win eating arrangement. Barbara absolutely hated cooking, so the two of them ate every meal in restaurants. Jimmie loved and missed home cooking so we traded straight across, no guilt at all as they sported us to meals at their favorite waterfront eateries during our weekends at the beach and I fed them spreads of fresh baked bread, hearty lasagnas and stews and garden fresh salads during their country weekends with us.

Now as Jimmie secured their latest forty-foot race boat alongside, he said, "Gingerlee has invited all of us over for dinner. Let's go out for a sail as soon as the wind comes up, then tie in front of her place."

"First coffee and news about your canyon capers," Barb insisted. They both chuckled as Larry described his latest water-gathering schemes. "You guys lived for years using only the forty-five gallons of fresh water in your boat tanks," Barbara stated. "You bragged about being able to survive on a gallon per person per day. Why do you need another 6000-gallon tank out there in the canyon?"

"Didn't need to flush toilets with fresh water, didn't need to water trees or wash dishes for dinner parties," I retorted, ticking off the water uses on my fingers. "Never needed long hot showers to get rid of the dust or mud. Now we've found that artesian spring, I can forget about conserving water, forget about measuring the water level in each tank and just use it."

"Remember, nothing is ever as good as it looks or as bad as it seems," Jimmie stated with a wink and a chuckle. Then talk of the canyon, fresh water, dust and boat building fell by the wayside as the wind filled in. We uncovered *Seraffyn*'s sails, and followed our friends' boat out into the open waters beyond the bay.

Jimmie's words came back to haunt me a few months later. We'd taken a break from our boat building/writing routine to have a sailing/working holiday. We'd spent ten days earning extra boatbuilding funds by sharing sailing stories and putting on slide shows in New England for those who dreamed of sailing off in their own boats. Then we rewarded ourselves with ten days sailing around Halifax and the Bras d'Or Lakes in Nova Scotia, courtesy of friends we'd met in Finland during our wandering years. On our return we'd driven up the canyon, our pockets laden with an infusion of cash, feeling refreshed and eager to get on with our projects. I commented to Larry, "Can't wait to see how my trees made it through the heat. Bob promised to turn on the water for an hour every other day. I got my trench dug perfectly so every tree gets a good wetting without having to move the hose. Wonder if any of the bulbs I stuck in the ground have come up."

Larry didn't comment as he was concentrated on keeping the truck on the smoothest parts of the road to quiet the teeth-jarring juddering as we bumped over the corrugations that appeared like evil curses toward the end of every dry season. Most days I readily accepted this corrugation-forced snails' pace, but now I felt impatient as, for the first time, I wondered if we'd been wise to go off for so long. "Don't expect too much," Larry finally answered. "Steele gets pretty busy. He said the place would be fine on its own. Said he'd drop in every day to feed the cat. Hard for him to take care of your trees, too — he's lost a couple hundred of his own because he didn't remember to water them."

Dog must have sensed our arrival. We found her pacing back and forth in front of the old swing gate under our street number signpost. She purred and rubbed up against my leg as I unlocked the gate, then strutted proudly ahead as we ascended to an amazing spread of new growth. Bright green leaves sprouted on the black locust, silk oak, peach and lemon tree I'd planted to try to continue old man Payonessa's tradition. Well-defined rings of wet earth proved Larry's concerns unfounded, but I refrained from gloating as we jumped from the truck to survey our domains, me to the house, Larry to the boatshed.

My country world looked just as I'd left it, neat and organized. Time and again during our years together Larry had teased me as I went about a thorough house cleaning just before we left on any trip longer than a day. I'd retort, "My mom always used to tell me, leave it clean, and it's a pleasure to come home." And as I wet a sponge to wipe the layer of dust from the long kitchen counters, I appreciated once more the wisdom of her words.

Larry's angry yell, ringing across the yard, broke my reverie. My anger more than matched his when I learned every power tool he'd owned was gone — drills, skilsaw, hand-held power planer. "Should never have listened to Bob. Should never have gone — what a waste," Larry moaned. I ran back to search the house and noticed the key that usually lived on a hook under the eaves now lay on the gravel near the front porch. I opened the pantry — there hidden in among the bottles of soft drinks sat our portable short-wave radio in the spot where I'd put it for safekeeping. Nothing in the cottage appeared to have been moved, except our easily-spotted, easily-fenced spare cameras, which were now missing.

Bob Steele drove in as Larry was laying out each of his handmade chisels, his carefully collected smoothing planes and specialized boat-building tools on his long work bench to inventory them.

"Really, really sorry about this. Happened three days back," were Bob's first words. "Came down and found the lock on the boatshed door open, back door of the house open, couldn't find your spare keys. Could have been one of those dirtbags from Sandy's place. She had some of her old friends up there for a stay. Didn't mean for anyone to know you were gone, but Newhouse asked Pete if you were ready to do that welding work. Pete asked me to give you the message. Guess she overheard me saying you wouldn't be back for another week. She must've mentioned it to one of her friends. Easy for them to sneak over here on their way out the canyon. If you'd had a dog up here like I said before, would have kept them away. I did a good job of keeping your trees growing, Lin," Bob said, trying his hardest to turn the conversation onto a more comfortable track.

"I wish he'd let my trees die and kept his mouth shut instead," I griped to Larry, as I glumly set out dinner later. Larry didn't seem to be listening as he wrote down the tools he'd lost, putting a check-mark next to those he needed to replace immediately.

"It's not quite as bad as it seemed at first," Larry murmured. "None of my really valuable tools are missing. He didn't take the hammer you bought me when we first met, or Charley Weckman's ships carpenter tools and then there's the adz Art Clark gave me. Those are truly irreplaceable. Some of them were used on square-riggers a hundred years ago! We can buy all new power tools in one day of shopping."

I looked over his list, made a quick mental price tally and shook my head. "Not bad? That's $1,500 worth of tools, half of the money we earned for all the talks we gave. That's half our savings down the drain."

"Lin, it's only money," Larry insisted as he had often before during our lives together. "I can always go out to the beach, live on *Seraffyn*, and find some boatbuilding work if we run short. But maybe we do need that dog."

I couldn't dismiss the burglary as easily. Cost was not my only concern. Sleep wouldn't come as I lay thinking about the insecurity that had forced its way into our secluded life. "We both agreed, no pets," I whispered just in case Larry had managed to fall asleep.

"Not a pet," he answered, "a working part of the place. An alarm system. Look in the free ads tomorrow when you go to town. We want a big, loud, watchdog."

"We'll fall in love with it and be heartbroken when it's time to leave. You're already worrying about that cat. She was just a freebie — a working part of the place. Can't take pets with us on the boat," I countered.

"Be at least two years before we have to worry about that," were his last words before I heard gentle snoring.

"Be lots of time for us to fall in love with it," were my thoughts as I tossed and turned through half the night.

Excellent watch dog
Pretty
Shepherd mix, 1-½ years.
Good with kids
Neutered, free to good home.

I read the ad, then phoned. "Why are you giving away this paragon of virtue?"

"Got any chickens? Close neighbors got any chickens? She's a chicken killer," answered the farmer's wife.

Cindy definitely was big enough, loud enough, and eagerly aggressive when we drove into the farm yard. Standing almost as high as my waist, ears more like a jackrabbit than a dog, legs of an Afghan hound, body of a shepherd, thick gold hair that was silky to the touch. And in the throes of her car sickness, Cindy turned into a whimpering coward as she made the cab of the truck we all shared into a smelly mess.

From the day of her arrival we noticed every one of our visitors honked as they drove in. They'd stop right where Cindy stood her ground at the top of our driveway, growling, hair bristling with defiance, teeth bared in warning. They'd wait inside the car until one of us snapped her lead chain in place. Even Bob Steele, who came by frequently to remind us Cindy was his idea, never realized that lead chain was part of an elaborate charade played by two animals and two reluctant owners. For Cindy was a real pussy cat. She was completely cowed by Dog, aka Shadow Cat, and would roll over and wave her legs in the air if anyone told her to. It took only a few days before Larry insisted I bring her a biscuit each time I carried morning coffee out to the boatshed to admire the newest teak plank he'd laid in place as our next boat slowly changed from a skeleton to a hull.

Although the break-in left me with serious concerns about continuing our twice a month forays to the ocean, I knew we both needed the change of pace, the different perspective that let us think through what we'd gotten done, what we planned to do next. Even more, I needed the physical reminders *Seraffyn* gave me as I outlined yet another chapter to tell of the adventures we'd shared gliding among the islands that had inspired Homer's Odysseus, or accidentally sailing into a secret submarine base in the Dalmatian Islands of the Yugoslavian Union of Communist countries, which we learned was held together only by the strong personality of Tito. Each time I hauled on a halyard to raise our sails, sea-shanties sprang into my mind,

Way haul away,
We'll haul away together.
Way Haul away,
We'll haul away home.

Then I'd look aft to where Larry stood tiller in hand, sparkling blue eyes taking in the set of the sails, the lift of the tell-tales, and feel his contentment at being in his real element.

Unfortunately, now each time we settled *Seraffyn* onto her mooring, then rowed ashore to begin our trek back to the canyon, a slight feeling of entrapment flitted through my mind. What would we find when we reached our hilltop boatyard? Had we made a mistake in trading the freedom of our sailing life for the constraints that now molded our days and months?

Then I'd think of the warm greeting that lay up that dirt road, the eager barking and bouncing of a dog named Cindy, the purring, strutting welcome of a cat named Dog, and the break-in began to fit into Jimmie's reminder that not only is nothing as good as it looks, but nothing is as bad as it seems. Without that distressing incident we might never have broken down and added these pleasures to our lives.

Chapter 11

Shaping a New Home, a New Confidence

"That was a good week," I commented as we lingered over iced drinks just before dusk one Saturday afternoon. Summer was drawing to a close. Both of us felt fresh after a cool shower. My long heavy hair dried quickly in the warm breeze that rustled through the trees of the front yard. The desert blue jays waking from their heat-induced lethargy cackled at the smaller birds searching for bugs among the red and yellow blooms of the acacia bushes. "Come on over and look at the frames I got set up," Larry suggested. "Bring your drink with you."

I followed him and lazed on the newly completed backbone of the boat, seeing it as a growing thing instead of the looming work object it appeared to be on other days. It felt good to look back over the week's work, to contemplate small steps we'd taken toward each of our goals, to see our lives and home settling into a sort of logical unity.

I'd spent the mornings finishing another chapter, which brought my project close to its halfway mark. Our weekly mail had brought an unexpected check for a story I'd sent off to England. The extra funds meant one more month when Larry could keep working full-time on the boat. But more important, that check was further proof that I could earn the funds to support us both, proof that I was not dependent on Larry's earning power to sustain my accustomed standard of living, even if someday I ended up on my own.

As a teenager, I'd listened to my dates going on about how they wanted their wives to be smart enough to be able to talk to their clients, but how they wouldn't want that wife to earn more than they did. Then, when some of my female friends stretched toward "professional careers," the popular wisdom seemed to be, "Have to be careful about who they date, the man has to be someone who can earn more than they do." But, inwardly, I doubted my girlfriends wanted a career once they married and had babies. After all, in 1963, there were fewer than six thousand women lawyers in the whole United States, and fewer than fifteen thousand women with medical degrees. Even after Larry and I began working together and decided to try for a permanent relationship, he had mentioned his concern about the pressures that could be exerted on a man's ego by earning less than his wife.

I'd never had to worry about earning too much. Larry's woodworking abilities easily eclipsed my bookkeeping skills. Even when we formed a small business partnership, and later when we worked as a delivery team, it was Larry's skills that we marketed, with me as the back-up crew. Larry, with a sensitivity I came to admire, assured me that he'd never have been able to demand such high wages without my back-up. But there were times when I felt slightly unnerved, even trapped, by Larry's ability to earn respectable amounts wherever we happened to be while I was paid far less to tidy up behind him. Even though I kept track of our finances, and was never in the awkward position of asking for money that some women found themselves in, the constant publicity of the growing feminist movement began to cause me some soul-searching and confusion — because I loved the life we were leading.

In fact, I was, at times, more comfortable with the economics we practiced to remain debt free and maintain our non-traditional lifestyle than Larry was. But questions still nagged at me. What if there came a day when I wanted to get out of our partnership? What if there came a time when Larry didn't feel like being responsible for earning our cruising funds? Sure, we had enough put away to survive for three or four months, but what about the long term? Larry had tried to downplay my concerns saying, "With your imagination, you'd find some way to earn what you need." But, all I could imagine was the drudgery of a daily commute to a monotonous desk job far from the ocean. Then, soon after I tried writing about sailing which, at that time, was a man's subject, soon after my third or fourth check arrived from the magazine editor, Larry said, "See, I told you. If you figure out how many hours you actually spent writing that story, you probably earned more per hour than I do."

During the next seven years, even as Larry began to write technical articles, which I edited and typed for him, our combined writing earnings were only frosting on the cake, extra funds that seemed to float into, then out of, our lives, adding small luxuries but never sustaining us. But now, ten months into our new writing and boatbuilding projects, our plan was beginning to work. Instead of writing on rainy days or during night watches as we had when we were living a wandering life, I forced myself into a more disciplined routine in hopes of earning enough to pay for this far more expensive life we were now leading. I accepted an advance and committed myself to a book contract. That in turn, meant deadlines. And now, the old-fashioned fears I'd had as a teenager came back as concentrated writing began to produce financial rewards. Though I felt a sense of personal triumph, I tried not to let other people know my income was supporting both of us. I didn't want Larry to feel pressured, so I rarely mentioned our finances other than to give him a twice-monthly summation of our situation. But, that unexpected check showed me how much Larry's thinking had changed through the years. "It's really neat to see you keeping ahead of all our expenses," Larry had said when I showed him the banking receipt on my return from my day in the village. Then, after he'd helped me carry in groceries plus a bag full of mail, and we were sitting at the counter reading each letter, I finally brought up the concerns I'd been harboring. "Does it bug you to have me supporting you?"

"Hell, no," he'd answered. "I think it's a great division of labor, really efficient. It would take us years longer to get this boat built if I tried to do it in my spare time. I wouldn't enjoy the work near as much, wouldn't be able to concentrate my energies. You're doing what you do best and enjoying it. I'm doing the same. We end up with a new floating home, free and clear. When we sell *Seraffyn*, we'll have a real nice nest egg in the bank. And, to top it all, I feel more secure, knowing you could support both of us if something serious happened to me."

A couple we had recently met came for dinner one Friday night, Shearlane and Robert Duke. Shearlane, an editor at the *Los Angeles Times* and a feisty women's liberation advocate stated, "It's time we women became more independent." In 1981, it had become apparent that the Equal Rights Amendment was doomed to failure, and all over America other women were shouting similar chants. Larry quelled my last concerns by countering, "I think semantics might be causing a lot of hard feelings against the women's movement. Lin is taking care of the here and now financially, I'm taking care of the longer term. Good to feel we're both self-sufficient people. We rely on each other, but we're definitely not independent. Independence seems such an aggressive word. Sounds like women want to be separatists, like guerrillas, cut off from men. I'd rather hear about people pooling their skills, working together toward a goal."

Shearlane glossed over Larry's comment, saying something about breaking tradition, fighting the system, winning each skirmish. Militant was definitely the tone that rang through the feminist movement of those days. I could look at my own life and see why this anger developed. When, as a first-year college student, I chose to try my hand at the male bastion of education, the structural engineering department, I'd been told to expect a failing grade by a professor who strongly felt women belonged in the schools of education, nursing or music. I could have gone to a local junior college to take the required course and thereby circumvent this professor's prejudice, but easier choices were open to me, and I took them without fighting. Other women did fight, and a few years later, I'd have had recourse against that professor as public education institutions were forced to prune down the barriers of sex discrimination. I remembered needing a father's or husband's permission to take out loans or to get a credit card. This too had been changed by hard-working women's rights advocates.

There were still, fifteen years later, inequalities, and probably always would be. But, I had begun to wonder if there actually was a conspiracy to protect male dominance. Maybe some women, like me when I was back in college, were using the inequalities as an excuse for their own lack of initiative, their own lack of direction. I now saw younger women graduating into professions and skills previously closed to any but the most determined. I saw women my age returning to colleges or trade schools to take up new careers we'd never dreamed of twenty years before. I had come to worry about those women who were full-time mothers and homemakers by choice. Did other, more career-minded women have the right to devalue them, saying they were copping out, only appendages to the men who were their partners? Maybe it was time to slow down and look at the role restrictions imposed not only on women but the men around them, to search for the balance that could promote self-sufficiency as Larry said, instead of the independence Shearlane proclaimed.

These questions drifted through my mind as we talked that night, leaving me as confused by the goals of my female friends as I had been by the complete acceptance of the chattel-like role I had seen among the majority of Islamic women we'd met in our travels. I heard Larry's words that night, even if my guests didn't. This added to my sense that logic and order were growing in my life in the canyon, if not in the fast changing world outside.

If my mornings in the office corner of our front room made me feel financially and emotionally more confident, the four afternoons each week I spent working with Larry in the boatyard gave me lessons in mechanical confidence. As Larry had been building his shed, then cutting and shaping backbone timbers, I'd been kept busy securing supplies and building materials or cleaning up the shop. I'd enjoyed the contrast between my desk-bound morning and the physical work of the afternoon: raking, moving wood, holding the ends of boards as they turned from rough sawn, scraggy timber into smooth satiny wood on their journey through our antique thickness planer. My day had a good division — office mornings, boatyard afternoons, domestic homemaker evenings, all within two hundred yards of each other. But by early summer our first year in the canyon, I'd tired of just being a helper, learning little, seeing nothing long-lasting developing directly from my afternoon's effort. "Okay," Larry suggested. "You want to build something, I'll make you the official millwright. You be in charge of the shop gear and machines. I need six more sawhorses. Take a look at that one, it's the best of the lot. Buy materials when you're shopping tomorrow and build us some."

Around this time, Bob Steele began working almost full-time outside the canyon with his D8 Caterpillar. We'd hear his pickup truck come down

the hillside road early each morning as he headed off into the far reaches of Riverside County. He'd converted his truck to carry a huge tank for diesel to fuel his Cat. Every two weeks, he came by to fill up the diesel drum in our generator shed. "What are you pounding on, Lin?" he asked as he prowled around the shed to assess Larry's progress and note any changes around the place.

"I'm trying to get these blankety-blank nails to drive in the right direction," I grumbled as I pulled out another bent one.

"Here, let me bang 'em in," Bob offered, reaching for my hammer. "Hey, Larry, where's a real hammer?" he yelled. "This thing's just a toy."

Larry came out from transferring diesel and said, "Lin's doing just fine. Come see the shelf she put up in here."

I was kind of glad Bob had gone and left me to my struggle with the two-inch-long nails. Each time I hit one fair and square, and watched it sink in a bit deeper without bending, I felt good. But I tried to time my hammer blows so I could listen for his comments when he saw my shelf. I knew that shelf sagged in the middle. Next time I'd put the supports closer together. But either Larry had coached Bob, or Bob's crueler teasing was reserved for Marlys and other men because he came out and said, "Sure making that shed a more useful place. You'll get better at pounding nails. Got a cool drink around?"

The three of us sat on a pile of timber drinking lemonade and Bob said, "If you want life to be easier this winter, you really need to get a double truckload of gravel up here, cover the driveway and yard in front of the kitchen. It'll only cost about two hundred bucks. It'll keep the mud down when the rains come. Might even cut down some of the dust."

"You going to do it up at your trailer for Marlys?" Larry asked.

"Naw, waste of time. Trailer's only temporary. Besides, Marlys is used to country life. Doesn't spend her whole day out here anyway. Doesn't spend any time at all here if she can help it. She's usually sittin' around all prissy in an air conditioned, carpeted office."

Just before the sun crept behind the hill across the canyon, I proudly set a plank across two sawhorses. I was covered with sawdust, one thumb was tender from mis-aimed hammer blows, two fingernails were snagged. "Not bad for a first attempt," Larry said, even though the horses wiggled when he put his weight on them. "Here, if we put an extra brace across each leg they'll work just fine." I held the sticks he cut as he drove each nail in with two sharp hammer blows. "You'll catch on. Takes time. Tomorrow I'll show you how to service and grease the big bandsaw. If you take care of the machinery — the plant, so to speak — I can keep making frames. You can't do the boat

building, but you sure can be helpful keeping the shop up to date. Come on, it's too late for you to cook dinner. Let's take a shower and run down to the village for a bite."

I came to love working around the shop. Sometimes, while I was taking a pause from sanding or varnishing or greasing machinery, I'd sit back and marvel at the way Larry made woodwork appear so easy. I watched him stare at a piece of knotty, scruffy wood, then turn it over and around in a slow, almost mesmerized way that sometimes made me wonder if he was daydreaming. All of a sudden, he'd lay a pattern on the board, pencil around it, make a swift saw-cut, give it a few deliberate strokes with a hand plane, a brush with the belt sander then he'd hand me a beautifully finished part, not a flaw left, the wood grain flowing in a logical pattern, corners rounded and smooth to the touch, and the shape perfect to nestle into its assigned place in the grand scheme that was laid out on seventeen pages of blueprints.

I wasn't the only one amazed at the shapes Larry was building. Each frame soared in graceful curves above the floor brackets made from wooden patterns Larry had designed, built, then sent out to the foundry to be cast in solid bronze. The castings were connected to the frames, then to the sweep of the backbone timbers, so that by the end of summer, anyone driving up through our gate was met by a majestic-looking skeleton that towered almost twice a man's height to fill the huge doorway of the open-air boatshed.

The local sheriff had driven up to see us soon after we moved in. "Have to patrol over 1,400 miles of dirt roads. Good to know the people in these isolated areas in case we need their help." He'd been reticent and polite, but I could sense his curiosity, his concern that somehow we might cause him problems, maybe growing marijuana, fencing stolen goods or being involved in any of a hundred less than lawful schemes where isolation could serve as a cover. Only four officers worked to patrol an area three times as large as New York City with a population only slightly larger than found in most New York apartment buildings. Dave had become a frequent visitor since that first visit, stopping whenever he drove through the hills to check for stolen vehicles, runaway kids or to ask if anyone had seen strangers when a prisoner escaped from the Chino jail, forty miles to the north. Each time a new deputy joined the local force, Dave would delight in winning the wager he made just before he turned up our driveway. "You tell me what they're building in that big shed, I'll pay for drinks after work."

It was Dave who solved one of our biggest problems during a visit early that week. "Only outside traffic I see in these canyons that doesn't make me curious is the UPS truck," he said.

"Didn't know they delivered up here. The post office won't," I said.

"They'll go any place that has an address," Dave answered.

"We haven't got an address," I said. "But, it sure would be nice to be able to get things brought direct. Right now, anything we order from the industrial supply house gets sent to the music shop. If the package arrives just after I leave town it means sometimes I have to wait almost two weeks."

I called the United Parcel Service office during my next day in town. The manager said, "No address? Got a road name? Then make up a number. We sometimes deliver packages to an auto-mechanic who lives at the fork of Lindell and El Toro. His number is 15000 or something, add 1000 for every mile and choose a number. I'll tell Chuck where to look for your sign."

I painted a big number sign, 26201, and Larry nailed it to a tree at the base of our driveway, and by the end of the week one more Riversider began to wonder at the shapes Larry built so deftly. Chuck, the driver who cheerfully jumped down from the seat of his brown and gold box of a truck about twice a week, claimed he had never been near the sea. The boat bits and pieces scattered around our shop brought comments like, "Make a good lamp base for that seafood restaurant they're building down the highway from Corona." He never saw Larry actually building the frames for the boat since we always heard his truck long before it reached our drive at mid-afternoon, and used this as an excuse to take a break and share a cold lemonade to drown the dust of the hot summer days. I think Chuck must have been waiting to ask the question for weeks, because he seemed embarrassed when he finally blurted out, "Where do you get all those pretty shaped pieces of wood?"

With an absolutely straight face, Larry said, "Sears and Roebuck."

"Never seen them in the big store in Riverside," Chuck answered, shaking his head.

"That's where farmers and ranchers shop. These come from the catalogue sales at the Sears near the coast," Larry replied with a little smile, and a wink in my direction.

A week later Chuck was back with more packages. He looked at the last set of frames we'd lifted in place outlining the transom of the boat. "Really pretty," he said, "but how come you're the only people I deliver packages to on the north side of any road in this county whose address ends in an odd number? Did you get your number from Sears and Roebuck, too?"

We never did change the number. Eventually, three more of our neighbors began having Chuck deliver things they ordered from shops in the city, and they, too, made up numbers following the sequence we chose. Nine years later this caused some confusion when the county and the U.S. Post Office finally got around to trying to organize the inhabitants of Bull Canyon.

Pete Shomler dropped in late one Sunday afternoon to ask if Larry could re-saw some large pieces of timber he'd found at Pedlars Village. Pete wanted to use the wood as roof beams in the stone monolith that was slowly growing in front of his trailer.

"How's Sandy? Where are the kids?" I asked when the noise of the saw, backed by the growl of the diesel generator, finally shut down.

"They're mending holes in the garden fence. Got another couple hundred feet to go. Gophers been getting in underneath. Go right through the broken glass I put in a trench under the wire netting. Takes full-time work to grow any real amount of food out here. Lost half the garden to deer last month."

As with every newcomer to the country, the sight of all that empty earth, the lure of the fresh succulent produce pictured on seed pouches next to the checkout stand at the grocery store, the wilted store-bought lettuce that lined the lower shelf of my refrigerator halfway through each week, began to work like subliminal advertising on me. Instead of leafing through sailing or news magazines, if I had a spare minute at the drugstore, I began leafing through gardening digests. The long, even furrows of newly budding green in hundred-acre tracts along the highway caught and held my eye. The farmer at the local fruit and vegetable stand became a patient target for my questions about soil, compost, potassium, magnesium, iron, manure.

Sandy looked at the bare land in back of our cottage where even weeds had a hard time growing. "Save you lots of money if you get a garden growing. Isn't much flat space for you, but better than nothin'. Pete fenced over an acre for me and the kids to plant. Takes a lot of water and lots of work, but I can really grow enough to make it worthwhile. Could sell some stuff next season and buy fancy trim for the dresses I'm making."

Pete was more than eager to prepare me for the trials and tribulations of farming in the canyon. He described the rampaging army of squirrels, gophers, rats, deer and birds as if they were all waiting, poised to descend on any bit of green that dared poke its head out of the ground in an organized way. "Garden's good for my kids, keeps them busy when they're off school," Pete stated. "It'll keep you busy, too, help fill up your time. Good place for some of your wood chips, but remember, first dig a two-foot deep trench around the edges, put wire netting down, then put broken glass in the trench. Saves taking the bottles to the junk yard, discourages the gophers. Then..."

Larry reminded me, "You're pretty busy already, Lin. We seem to eat well enough. Forget it. How much money will you save anyway, after you buy fertilizer, seeds?"

I was a bit frustrated by Larry's disinterest. This was the same man who would go out of his way to save any seedling tree he saw. He'd goad me into working with him to transplant each eucalyptus that seeded itself and shot up between his timber piles, so now a dozen new shoulder-high trees lined our driveway and a future grove bravely waved its young leaves along the course of the stream below us.

Larry had decided he had to leave a gift in exchange for the use of the cottage, and to him a gift meant living, growing trees. He never begrudged the time I spent pampering and watering the dozen specialized trees we chose with such care at the nursery in the valley below us. I sometimes teased him, saying that he was trying to guarantee that there would be timber for the boats he wanted to build when he was eighty. But he answered, "Every time I sit out under these trees I think of Old Man Payonessa. Ellie says for five years he came up here every day during the summer and used a bucket to carry water from the well to keep each of these trees alive. He did that until he finished the first part of the house and came to live here. And what would this place be without his trees, just another desolate piece of sagebrush covered hillside, no place for birds to nest, no shade for wildflowers. Might not even be much of a spring up the hill — the trees keep the spring water from drying up as soon as it reaches the surface. His wife's flowers and gardens didn't change a thing, but his trees did." Every time I looked around at the hundred trees that made our yard such an inviting oasis, I had to agree.

But somehow the efficiency of picking a few dozen leaves of lettuce for a salad, right when I needed them, appealed to my sense of organization, my desire to have things around me tidily arranged and under control. Soon I had several little trays of rich, black, store-bought soil lining the wide window sills of the kitchen. I watered them each evening and checked each morning, hoping to see the very first bit of green poke its head into the light of day.

Bob Steele and Marlys sat at the counter one afternoon and watched me rearrange my array of trays as we waited for the coffee to perk. "I had Mariano clear Marlys a garden space, even had him dig up the ground and mix in the fertilizer, lots of mulch, some ashes. He got it perfect for Marlys and what does she do?" Bob asked in an exasperated tone. "Hell, she grabs handsful of seed and goes out and sows it like it's a damn wheat field. Radish, tomatoes, lettuce, cabbage. Now there's bits and pieces growing everywhere and she claims she can't tell a weed from a plant."

"Wasn't my idea to have a garden," Marlys snapped back. "Besides you made it too big. I didn't want to spend all day Saturday down on my knees sticking little seeds two inches apart for a mile. It will be more exciting to see what grows this way. Sort of like a grab bag. And, who wants to pull weeds every spare minute? I'd rather drive to Riverside and visit my sister. Then I can buy some good fresh stuff from Tom's Farm on the way home. His lettuce is already washed. There's no bugs hidden inside. Forget it, Lin. Gardening's not much fun."

But then Lee Newhouse came by to service his beehives and disagreed. "Gardening is easy. Just plant twice what ya need, let the animals have some and use the rest. It's good soil out here, never been used before. Just needs some care. That pile of wood shavings you've got there. Planning to use 'em?"

Larry shook his head. "No, I was just going to put them in the truck, so Lin can take them to the dump."

Lee appeared scandalized at that thought. "They're too good to be wasted. I'll come and clean up for you, put them under the chickens. A month or two from now I'll bring a couple buckets back for your garden — chicken manure aged in shavings makes a real good combination for the ground out here. But, remember summer's coming, you'll have to water a lot then, so don't get too big. Ma's happy with a ten-by-twenty patch. Don't want her working too hard. Not like when I was a kid. We don't need to put up vegetables for the winter, we can grow 'em all year round out here."

By the time Lee Newhouse came back with a wide shovel to scoop up the shavings around our planer later that day, I'd marked out an area the size of two cars by dragging my foot through the dust in back of the house. Then I began to dig. Rock-hard ground stopped me after two inches. Two hours of work had only a tiny trench five feet long nicked into the outline.

"Forget it, Lin. You've got better things to do with your time," was Larry's response to my complaints at dinner time. But I was determined — determined to prove I had some pioneering blood in me, determined to prove Pete's pessimism wrong. So I flooded my little trench and left the hose dripping all night. For an hour or two each evening before dinner, I dug, then soaked the ground to soften it for the next evening's digging. Each evening, I lined up my little trays of seedlings in front of Larry on the kitchen counter. "See, that's red lettuce starting in that one, spinach in this," I told him, restraining myself from touching the tiny new leaves lest I accidentally crush them. Larry's complete lack of interest in my gardening foray didn't dent my enthusiasm as I bought a three-pound book on the subject and read from it before we blew out the oil lamps each evening. Only when he helped unload a bag of compost and wire netting after the next shopping day, did he ask, "Sure you got enough wire for a ten-foot-by-twenty-foot enclosure? Doesn't look like enough to me." I shamefacedly took him out in back of the house to where a five-foot-square of ground was dug to a depth of about a foot. "The digging's really hard," I explained. "Thought I'd start small. My book says I can have thirty lettuce and twenty strawberry plants in this area. Next winter I can make it bigger."

"You've put this much time into it," Larry said. "You'd better be sure the animals can't get under your fence. I'd put a layer of wire along the bottom, before you put the dirt back in. Might as well put that pail of broken glass around the edges, too." His sudden interest in gardening took away some of the sting at my defeat. But it only lasted long enough for him to help wire the bottom and sides of the netting together. When it was time to start mixing manure and ashes, wood shavings and dirt together, Larry disappeared. Even the appearance of the first tidy row of carrot and radish tops couldn't lure him around the back of the house. My excitement at the line of proud little lettuce leaves, the first blossoms on three dozen strawberry plants, left him cold. But the sight of tears tracking down my cheeks at breakfast a month after my garden plot began showing its first neat rows of green, got him concerned enough to follow me out back. "Where's your garden gone?" he asked, as he stared at the moist, wire-surrounded patch of dirt sitting like a lady's handkerchief in the middle of the otherwise barren yard.

"Deer, see the hoof prints? Deer snuck in here during the night." Though we almost never saw the deer that sheltered in the more isolated corners of the canyon, we knew they were there. Every time someone moved dirt to fix the road, trench in a hose, or as I had, to plant a garden, sometime during the dark of night, deer would arrive and dance and prance in the fresh turned soil leaving hundreds of tiny half-moon shaped prints as testimony to their nocturnal capers.

My pot garden, upper right. The vegetable garden, lower right.

"Guess you'll have to cover the top of your garden, too," Larry said as he tried to keep from laughing at the sight of the tiny, trampled plot.

The new wire cover he helped install kept the deer out and made my entry so difficult that at times I began to wonder if fresh salad greens really mattered. Yet, each time I'd falter in my greening reserves, Marlys would show up. "I told Bob, if he'd think in less grandiose scale, I'd have fun with a garden." It wasn't too long before she came down to offer me a fresh, rosy tomato from the ten-by-ten-foot plot she'd laid out for their full-time Mexican helper to prepare in front of her trailer. "Pete and Sandy say it looks as silly as yours, but who cares? I can keep things in control in my garden."

She might have been able to. But mine didn't have the extra protection of two dogs, three cats and Mexican assistants. When the local coyotes decided to use our yard as a fighting ground, and Larry made one more pilgrimage to the back of the cottage to see the broken uprights, trampled strawberry and lettuce plants, the carrot tops wilted by the urine of those howling scavengers, he laughed out loud. "I guess if it was easy, everyone would be doing it, Lin. So don't give up. Try it my way. Take that old galvanized wash bucket from in back of the generator shed and fill it with the good dirt you've got here. Plant the lettuce that didn't get ruined in that and I'll lift it onto the stone wall here." He pointed to the foundation that formed a square behind the cottage. Its flat-topped wall stood waist-high so the top of the tub would place my garden just below shoulder-level, above the reach of gophers, rabbits, deer, coyote — in fact, ninety percent of the "enemy." Better yet, I could watch the new shoots shyly emerge into my world right from my office window.

But one pot — how small it seemed once it was filled and planted. I didn't look forward to the teasing I'd get when Bob next came to fill our diesel tanks. "Go talk to the junk man behind Pedlars Village next time you're in town," Larry suggested. "He'll have some old tubs, we'll punch drain holes in them."

I was unable to imagine anyone other than Larry or my Bull Canyon neighbors holding on to misshapen, rusty, outdated washtubs. But old Bernie came out of his swaybacked house trailer as soon as I braked to a stop. His huge, cracked bare feet seemed immune to the bits of old metal, wire and decaying building demolition materials he stepped over and around as we walked the length of his railway-bounded yard. "Junk, ain't got any junk, only second-hand supplies. Can't call nothin' junk 'til it's rusted away back into the ground," he mumbled as he pushed old rolls of fencing wire out of the way. He pulled out a stack of battered washtubs. "Some got holes in 'em, but you said you don't really care. Take what you want, two bits each. Like I told you, nothin's junk 'til it's rust on the ground. 'Til then someone might just find a use for it."

I laughed as I drove up the canyon road, my seven well-used wash tubs clattering in the back, a roadrunner keeping pace half-way up the hill. Larry often joked, "One man can live on what three throw away." Bernie seemed to be doing just that. I began to wonder about the acres and acres of trash I saw being mangled by huge machines when I took bi-monthly trips to the county dump. I wondered how many re-usable treasures were being buried there each day while guards made sure no one picked up anything to carry away from the crushing blades of the giant bulldozers.

That row of eight tubs gained a grudging nod of approval from Bob Steele, who said, "I'll have to dig out all the old tubs behind the shed for Marlys. Knowing her, she'll probably want to plant flowers in them, rose bushes, tulips, or something dumb."

I forgot my garden problems then, enjoying the limit the tubs put on my green thumb scheme and feeling completely in control of one more aspect of my country life. I'd planted the first of my autumn lettuce when I happened to run into the sheriff as I walked out of the post office. Instead of calling a cheerful hello, Dave fell into step beside me. He coughed, started to say something, stopped. I couldn't imagine what his problem was, what could be of concern to the long arm of the law as we knew it in Bull Canyon. Then, after three false starts, Dave blurted out, "I've heard rumors and you can't stop the deputies from dropping in on your place. It's pretty interesting up there."

"We enjoy their visits," I said. "They're a nice break for us. Good to know someone's keeping an eye on the place."

Dave interrupted, "But the word's going to spread and we have to stick to the law."

"The law?" I asked.

"Well, ya, the stuff you're growing... Don't want to get you into trouble but..."

"Me? Growing? My garden's so small it's a joke," I replied.

"Look, Lin," Dave said, stopping well away from anyone who could overhear him. "I heard about your pot garden. Stuff's illegal as hell, even one plant's illegal and I can't risk protecting you."

I laughed, so hard tears began to run down my face. "Please come see my pot garden next time you're out our way," I finally managed to choke out.

I savored that conversation all during the time I spent bringing in the first kindling of the season. Larry was elated by the cooler days, the crisp evenings, the glowing autumn color as the leaves of liquid amber and sycamore trees began to turn from green to maroon to rust before falling to the earth to fertilize the next year's growth. I saved that tidbit for the special time we spent mesmerized by the flickering flames that warmed us from the big stone fireplace before we settled in to eat our dinner. Larry burst into roars of laughter as I told him about my brush with the law. Then, suddenly he said, "It's Steele. It's just like him to pull a stunt like that. It could have been a real hoot if it worked. Can you imagine being raided by the narcs? Helicopters, patrol cars, paddy wagons. They'd have been as embarrassed as H by your 'pot garden.' With his luck, Bob would have managed to be sitting on his hill watching the whole damn folly."

Chapter 12

Fire

"Nada, nada, limpio," I heard Larry calling to Mariano as the two of them worked along the hill in back of the cottage. "I don't want one twig, one leaf, left on the ground from here right over to there."

I wasn't too happy about this latest project — the cost, the ugly scar it would leave all the way around our little niche in the wilderness. Bob Steele had just trucked his big bulldozer in from Riverside to clear a fire break completely around his home site. "You guys had better do the same," he warned, pointing at the thick parched brush that surrounded our cottage.

The heavy rainfall of the previous winter had encouraged the brush and weeds to grow twice as thick as it had been when we first arrived. After six rainless months the desert heat had burned every bit of green out of the hills around us. The earth wore a thick, shaggy carpet of absolutely dry kindling: grass, leaves, twigs.

The mid-October mornings were now crisp and dewy. Without the blasting heat of summer, I'd have thought the fire dangers were past. But Bob was insistent. "If you're broke, I'll pay Mariano and you can pay me back later. When the Santa Ana winds start to blow, the ratbags who come out here are dumb enough to throw burning cigarette butts out their car windows. You won't have a chance if one starts a fire down canyon from here." He pointed at the towering eucalyptus that provided the desperately needed shade for Larry's work area. "Those trees will explode if a fire gets within a hundred yards of them, turn into a time bomb unless you clear a good wide break."

In the year we'd known him, Bob's homesteading advice had rarely been wrong. "Cheap insurance," Jimmie Moore agreed. "If these trees burned down, this place wouldn't be worth much to anyone. I'll pay half as long as it's a real good firebreak."

As the machetes and rakes cleared a forty-foot wide swath around the buildings, I realized that Larry and I, in our naiveté, hadn't considered the possibility of brush fires when we fell so hard for this sheltered-feeling canyon. Now I had one more reason to feel trapped. In fact, I felt slightly guilty.

I'd grown up in Southern California. I should have remembered sitting on our rooftop as a youngster and staring in wonder as the desert winds of late autumn fanned huge fires in the mountains surrounding us. The flames dancing along those distant mountain tops held a strange fascination as they slashed through the black of the night. By daylight, the dirty brown of the smoke-filled skies, the ashes that blew for dozens of miles to lay a greasy black film on clothes and cars, destroyed any sense of beauty. After each major fire, my father would take us to see if our favorite secret canyon glades had been spared. The miles and miles of black desolation I'd seen now came back to haunt me. How could I have forgotten? How could I have encouraged Larry, a rain-soaked Canadian, to build a wooden boat, a wooden shed under oil-laden eucalyptus trees in a dry, brush-filled canyon? Damn it, I thought, the nearest fire department was probably thirty minutes away and we had no telephone to call them.

One morning, soon after the hill-defacing firebreak was completed, when the sky to the east turned crystal clear and the mountains to the west seemed miles closer, I felt the tingle of energy I remembered from years ago. My hair crackled as my brush ran through it. The skin of my hands and face demanded oil as the humidity dropped. Before I turned on the radio I knew the first Santa Ana wind was coming and by late afternoon would be gusting at tree-limb-breaking force. As a youngster, I'd loved that wind. I'd held my jacket open like a sail to propel me along and turn my leaps off any curb into the sensation of flying. I'd marveled at its ability to sweep the skies of the huge city, the hills, mountains and ocean waters that surrounded it clear of smog to expose a breathtaking beauty. On the evening of the first Santa Ana wind of each year, my father would drive me up to Mulholland Drive to overlook the valley, so we could survey the millions of star-like lights spread in a carpet beneath us.

But now I waited for the wind with dread and rearranged my schedule to drive into the village for another reel of garden hose. The first exploratory gusts of the easterly wind sent white fingers of foam streaking across the lake as I drove on to the post office. All three of the town's fire engines stood outside their shed, gleaming in chrome and red, and the complete uniformed team of firefighters, augmented by a dozen volunteers, waited under big walnut trees at the normally complacent-seeming fire department. I was irresistibly drawn to talk to the fire truck driver who was busy polishing a non-existent spot off his hose encrusted pumper-truck. "What's the chance of fires right now?" I asked, praying for reassurance.

"Highest risk I've seen in my whole career," he sighed. "This here baby is going to be pretty busy, I reckon, especially if this wind gets up like it sometimes does."

"We're out in the canyon. Just cleared a fire break," I said. "Think that will help us?"

"Depends," he said as he polished. "Haven't lost a building in those hills in the five years I've been in this district. But never had brush as heavy as this before."

By the time I headed back up the canyon, cold gusts of wind began to slam against the side of the pickup truck with enough force to make me grip the steering wheel harder. Instead of slowing down to savor the sight of the roadrunner that joined me at the washout below the narrows, I rushed homeward, my mind in wind-blown turmoil. I tried to be logical about the fear that was growing inside me, but almost everything we owned was in that wooden shed; thousands of dollars worth of nearly irreplaceable timber, tools that were like old friends to Larry, a year of our labor. And, in the house, the stone walls could hold back the heat of a fire, but what if the wooden rafters caught? What about the hundreds of photos, the papers, the three-quarters completed manuscript? We hadn't bothered to insure the cottage or its contents. Not only would the cost have cut too deeply into our budget, but also, the things we found the most valuable in our lives were uninsurable, irreplaceable. I was already fatalistically accepting the life we'd restructure after everything was burned out, thinking how we'd started with less money in the bank when we first met, so we could always start again. Besides, I assured myself, we still would have the little boat that had served as our home for all those years. It sat safely fifty miles away from this tinderbox, almost forgotten, except for alternate weekends.

The single towering palm tree on Ellie's ranch swayed and shook its tousled head as I rounded into the open air of the upper canyon. On impulse, I turned down the driveway leading past the pond and slowed to miss the shambling pack of German shepherds that pretended to stand guard along the approaches.

"Come on in, have a drink. Get out, you mangy hound, let Lin in," Ellie barked as she shoved one of five dogs out the door. "Devils hate this wind. Keep trying to sneak inside, place is messy enough without all their hair. Look at the dust this wind's blowing in."

Ellie retreated to the back of her house as soon as she'd poured me a cool drink and returned a few minutes later with every hair back in place, fresh lipstick gleaming fire red. "This wind's horrid for my skin. Makes me want my facelift sooner, wrinkles show so bad."

"Ellie, you've been out here longest. What about fires? Bob's got me worried," I finally interjected.

"He's got good reason. Hasn't been a fire on this side of the road in years. Probably need one, brush's getting dangerous." She pointed across the canyon. "That side burned three years ago. Fire moved really fast. Started up above the crossroads. I remember old Jo Caphart trying to out-drive it. Fire had already passed her house before she'd gone a mile. Fire department just came and had a coffee break at her place while it burned by. I think one of them told me they put half-dozen little blazes out, ones that started inside her cleared area. Then they came down here and we had a good chat while it burned clear to the firebreak at Green Valley road. Fire chief claimed a smoker started it," Ellie said as she lit another of her endless chain of cigarettes. "But, confidentially, I heard the fire department did it on purpose. Kept them busy so they could get some overtime pay. Weren't many fires that year. Rain came early. Brush wasn't very high. But don't you worry too much. Fires don't like going downhill. Your house is well clear of the brush. Your shed is in that draw. Look around and you'll see the bottom of the draws are rarely burned out. But just to be safe, make sure someone knows you're away if you go out during these winds. Then one of us will keep an eye open for smoke up your way."

For the first time I really noticed the difference between the brush on opposite sides of the road. Piles of rosy boulders and rocks stood in bold relief above a light covering of sage and tumbleweeds on the far side, with the charred remains of older bushes poking skyward as a reminder of the fire that had rushed through. But on our side, where no one remembered any tales of a fire in dozens of years, only occasional rock tops showed through the tangled brush and creeping vines. And now the firebreak surrounding our buildings looked more like a well-ironed, neatly settled shirt collar than the brutal scar I'd seen only a few hours before. Pete Shomler's little truck was sitting at the cottage door. I burst in. "Pete, do you think the fire department started the blaze that burned across the road? Ellie says they did it to earn more overtime."

"Earn money!" He laughed as he opened up the Bud beer Larry kept in the fridge for his occasional visits. "Not smart enough for that. Dumb fucks were out joy-riding in their truck after a false alarm. Decided to turn around on a narrow spot up at Lindell. Backed into the brush and a spark from their exhaust lit the whole damn canyon. Kept them good and busy for a while, but cleared our side of the road. After the fire passed Jo's place, crew just came and sat at the big clearing below our place while it burned through here. I drove down and told them things were fine up top. Didn't want any officious assholes up there nosing around. Besides, Sandy and the kids were keeping ahead of everything. That fire really did move. Things got so hot we all jumped inside the water tank to keep cool while it rushed past. Lost a few of our small trees. Burned up a lot of the trash I'd been meaning to take to the dump myself. Lots of soot around, but Sandy cleaned it all up. She's good at that. Our side's pretty clear now. Not much to worry about even if a fire does start — nothing to keep it going. But your side's pretty thick. Good thing there's not too many houses out here. If ever there is, things are going to get dangerous. Fire department can only watch a few places at a time. Sure you don't want to cut those eucs out? I've seen them explode when a fire got within a hundred yards. Dumb trees anyway. Make a real mess and can't use them for nothing."

I looked at the eucalyptus trees that towered far above our boatshed. Instead of seeing the shade-producing, bird-nest-laden friends of summer, I saw menacing enemies shaking their fists above the assembly of timbers that was starting to assume major proportions in our life as the Santa Ana wind gusted to seventy miles an hour and the soaring hawks fought to gain even an inch against its power.

The gusty wind was so powerful and unnerving that Larry was glad to work inside the house the next day, editing each sentence I'd written and chasing the typographical errors that seemed to pepper my pages. Ever since I'd begun writing, I'd looked forward to discussing the story ideas with Larry, jotting down his suggestions, thinking them over and working up an outline to share before I set off into my own mental world. Then a few days later, I'd offer Larry the rough-typed pages to read, hoping he'd be full of praise, ecstatic over the prose that remained between cross-outs, changes and bad spelling. If he chuckled as he read, I'd glow. If he suggested a better word, I'd think about it and usually agree. But if he said, "This isn't really clear," I'd have to step back and remind myself that his suggestions usually made sense, instead of retorting, "Any other fool would understand it!" If I was calm and thought for a few minutes, I generally came up with something that made both of us feel better about the offending sentence. Yet, every once in a while he'd hit me wrong, shaking me off my perch by saying, "You're pretty long-winded here," or "Do you really need all this, you already said it once before." I'd leave the room to avoid snapping at him. My whole body would tense and if all else was normal in our lives, I'd keep from flaring up by saying, "Put a question mark next to it, and I'll think about it later." Then I'd remind myself that I'd asked for his opinion. I didn't have to take it as gospel. Unfortunately, logic sometimes deserted me completely and I'd flare up, only to aggravate Larry who'd yell, "Okay, don't ask for my help if you don't want it." Then I'd feel guilty, remembering times when he'd caught errors that would have embarrassed me had they ever been printed, times when he'd suggested a change that led me off on one of the wondrous tangents that make a story sing.

That windy morning, I seemed to forget all the advantages of having an in-house editor. Maybe it was the insistent, howling wind that sent tumbleweeds rolling down the canyon and broken branches scudding against the house. Maybe it was the radio reports of a blaze out of control fifty miles to the north. Maybe it was, as some psychologists suggested, the overactive ions caused by the extremely low humidity and high barometric pressure. But I flared up every time Larry suggested any error had crept in among my precious words. After the third flare-up, Larry snapped, "I'll look at this when you're in a better mood." Then he stomped out, slamming the door so hard that a pile of books slid off their shelf.

I sat glumly behind my desk, angry at Larry, angry at the book-cluttered floor, angry at the realization that I had been the sole cause of the whole mess. I looked at the offending paragraphs and soon found a simple way to combine Larry's suggestions with my train of thought. I grabbed a jacket and ran out, paper in hand, to read him the new words and encourage him to return. I was halfway across the yard when my knees seemed to wobble. I yelled and my voice carried with the gusting winds. Larry ran out from under the spreading framework of the boat, then turned and watched with awe as it began to rise and fall in the premature rhythm of the sea. The earth beneath us rose again and subsided. I watched the boatshed sway, then heard a cracking sound from the stone cottage. Within seconds, the earth grew steady beneath my feet. I ran into the house and kicked aside chunks of plaster that had fallen from the crack that now ran up the wall from the door frame to the ceiling, and turned on the radio. Reports filtered

in, reminding me that we were within thirty miles of the San Andreas Fault, one of the biggest earthquake faults in the world, the epicenter of quakes that had been known to tumble buildings and freeway overpasses. Now I had something more to worry about.

"Worry if you want," Larry teased me when he finished adding more supports to the boat, then came in to suggest we again try some editing. "The wind is dropping, the whole spread survived a real good quake. Floods, frogs, bugs, rats, earthquakes... Maybe we'll be spared fire."

As the winds dropped, I did try to look more logically at the odds. Just because there hadn't been a fire on our side of the road in living memory, this didn't mean there'd be one while we lived there. "Besides," I teased Larry as we lay in bed and watched the moonlight flow through the branches of trees that now stood serene and still, "we're protected by the goose alarm. Ellie told me last time there was a fire out here, the Newhouses heard their geese cackling madly well before the sun came up. Got up to take a look. The geese were all facing up-canyon, really making a racket. Lee went outside and smelled smoke. Got in his car, drove to the swapmeet, called for help. Seems someone else on the far side of the fire called the fire squad in Perris. Within twenty minutes, engines from Elsinore were headed up the canyon. Unfortunately, fire trucks from Perris came in over the back road. Lead car from each company had a head-on collision right at the fire. No real damage, got the fire under control in a few minutes, because there wasn't any wind. Wonder why those geese made such a fuss. The fire must have been two miles away from them."

"Simple," Larry answered. "They smelled smoke and knew it meant danger. Wanted someone ready to let them out of their pen."

"But how did they know the difference between smoke from someone's fireplace and a brush fire?" I asked as I nestled into his arms.

"Survival instinct, all animals have it. They need it," he said sleepily. "Nice to know there are two fire departments ready to come up the canyon. The road's in good shape, they can move fast on it, but that crash was a warning. Would pay to stay off the roads if any fires are burning."

Survival instinct, I thought as I lay there. The animals might have it, but did I?

◇◇

Sooner or later, I knew we'd have to take the step that forced its way into our lives later that week. Though we reveled in having *Seraffyn* waiting for us down at the beach, her replacement in the canyon was beginning to take on a life of its own as Larry finished securing all the frames in place then added bulkheads inside the basket of timber to define our future home into forepeak, main cabin and lazzarette. With each passing month *Seraffyn* became more like a favorite scrapbook, full of memories to be fondled, then set aside. We knew she had become an unjustifiable luxury, a drag on our resources, yet we were reluctant to put a "For Sale" sign on the vessel that represented freedom. "We'll sell her when this boat is planked up," Larry said. "Then we'll be halfway finished so we won't feel like we're cut off from sailing for long." I'd agreed with him and eagerly planned for the holiday cruise we'd take, three hundred miles south to Mexico, the next spring.

But when I drove up from town to see the boatshed silent, a strange car in front of the kitchen, I sensed change in the air. "Man in there wants our boat," Larry said as he came out at the sound of the truck horn. "Told him she's not for sale yet, but you come meet him."

There is nothing I like less than changing what Larry jokingly calls my, "tidy little plans" once I've made them. But the life I'd chosen seemed to be in direct conflict with tidy plans. For a week the two of us took turns trying to put off the inevitable, listing the pros and cons of changing the plans we'd laid out long before we even moved to the canyon. If we sold *Seraffyn* we'd have a surprisingly generous supply of money in the bank, in fact far more than we had expected as the man who wanted her had made an extremely generous offer. But without her we could no longer think of putting everything on hold if the urge struck to run away to sea for two or four or ten months. No longer would we have our options well spread, and as Larry reminded me, "We'd have all our eggs in one basket, all right here in this canyon."

"One basket might be a lot easier to carry than two," I'd countered, thinking of the constant carrying of food and clothes back and forth between the cottage and the boat. There had also been my concerns about *Seraffyn* laying unattended on her mooring when winter gales swept through the distant harbor, the worry about Cindy and Dog, theft and now fire, each time we left the canyon to use her.

"Yes, but if your eggs are all in one basket, you really have to take care of that basket," he sighed as once again we went over every aspect of the choice we had to make within ten days.

Bob wasn't due to come by to deliver fuel for three or four days. Neither the Newhouses nor Ellie were at home when we drove down canyon headed for Newport Beach. The weather forecast was for the kind of autumn day that we loved best: cool, but sunny with light winds to help us enjoy the long sailing weekend we had planned. We didn't think of driving up to the Shomlers to say we'd be away — we'd often been gone for two or three days before. Besides, our minds were preoccupied with the pros and cons of selling the boat that had been the center of the last fifteen years of our life.

As I scrubbed two weeks of accumulated bird droppings from the boat, my hands seemed to linger over each curve of wood, every battle scar that represented one more bit of the history we'd shared. It was midday when we finally cast off our mooring line and reached out onto a slowly undulating sea. "Let's sail to Long Beach, I'll take you ashore for dinner. You deserve an evening out," Larry suggested. "Then tomorrow we can have a better slant on the wind for Catalina Island. Looking forward to seeing Shearlane and Robert's new boat. Be nice to anchor in Cherry Cove, it's been years since I saw it."

I remember looking at the sky to the east after rowing back from the promised shoreside restaurant meal that night. Something was making me more edgy than the still unfinished decision we'd tossed back and forth all evening. By morning that something had a name. "Morning, calm seas, light westerly breezes. Santa Ana winds expected by afternoon, gusting to 50 knots," the radio announcer intoned in a bored voice.

"We've got to get home," I said as soon as I heard the words.

"Yup," Larry agreed, pulling on his jacket to go on deck. "Catalina would be a lousy place in a Santa Ana wind, so no one would expect us there. Let's get going before the wind fills in. No one in the canyon knows we're out."

Neither of us had patience for the work of keeping the boat sailing, work we usually enjoyed. A fitful wind carried us slowly south toward the place where our truck waited. I left the radio playing softly, listening for any update as the late October day warmed to almost summer-like temperatures and the air began to lose its soft ocean feeling. Then I heard what I'd subconsciously been expecting. "Brush fire fanned by gale-force winds threatens six hundred homes near the University of San Bernardino, arson suspected." The first whisper of the scorching desert wind heeled *Seraffyn* and sent her scudding away from Long Beach. "Better tuck in a reef," Larry called down. "Get on your foul-weather gear. Looks like our last sail's going to be one to remember."

Storm-force winds soon fanned the seas ahead of us, flattening the swells that normally roll across the Pacific to spend their energy on this sandy coastline. We were roaring through almost smooth water, close in to the shore as salt spray flung itself across the decks and almost blotted out the view I tried to ignore, the words I tried to pretend I didn't hear. For now the skies to the east were black with smoke. The tiny scraps of sail that shoved the boat forward turned flamingo pink and glowing orange in the premature colors of a smoke-created midday sunset. I turned the radio to full volume as the station delivered news of canyon fires out of control and the homes of two thousand people up in smoke. As each new fire area was described, I'd try to locate it on my mental map of the desert communities to the east of our secluded stone cottage. "Sunnyvale, that's south of us," I said ticking off another arson-set blaze that threatened someone else's home and treasures, but not mine.

The boat moved at its top speed, roaring through waves that marched away from the shore. That speed had seemed wondrous when it carried us toward adventures in foreign lands, then homeward toward the schemes we were now involved in. But as flakes of soot began to settle against the spray-wet sails, the seven miles an hour we were moving seemed impossibly slow. "Our last sail," I said to myself as I thought of our boatshed, our cottage, the beautiful trees that stood unprotected from the lunacy of any match-wielding misfit. As the huge oil-drilling platforms, midway between Long Beach and Newport Beach, loomed in the smoke haze that rolled like a cloud across the sea, the radio blared, "New fire reported to the west of Santa Rosa Mine Road, near Perris, hard-pressed fire crews calling for National Guard assistance. Arsonist appears to have started fifteen blazes, highway patrol on alert."

"Larry, we're in trouble," I said, as I tried to cover my fear, my frustration with being at sea instead of protecting our home.

"Not much we can do other than pray fires really do burn slower downhill," Larry sighed as he leaned into the gusty winds and steered to gain every bit of speed. "Hope our firebreak does its job. There is one other good break between us and Santa Rosa, that's at Lindell. The fire crew's probably there right now. We've got two hours of sailing ahead of us, might as well enjoy it. Pretty glorious, isn't it?"

Yes, I had to agree that there was an unbeatable thrill about being in storm winds without huge ocean swells to contend with. Yes, there was still an intense tingle of satisfaction in knowing the boat beneath us was one we'd built, one that could carry us through winds as strong as this. The sky blackened, though, and grew more ominous, interfering with any pleasure I felt. Underlying everything was the growing knowledge that this was the last time I'd feel the almost living creature that surged and scudded beneath my feet.

As Larry had sensed that morning, this was to be our last sail on the tiny ship that was the link we had with the beginning of our relationship, the one constant we had besides each other in an ever-changing life. I, too, saw those smoke-filled skies as a sign that we could no longer divide our life, that to gain something worthwhile you usually have to give up something else.

Then the protecting stone breakwaters of Newport Beach reached out to enfold us as we performed the almost automatic moves required to force a sailboat into the teeth of the wind. "Savor each tack," I said to Larry. "Like you said, this is our farewell to *Seraffyn*."

There was an irony about those last few tacks. *Seraffyn*, with her old-world look, had become a well-known sight at the yacht club on shore. Our almost anachronistic practice of using only sail power to maneuver in a world where the reliability of cars and motor-driven boats made most people distrust this centuries-old skill also attracted attention. So we weren't surprised to see the verandah of the club filled with binocular-toting spectators, especially as the howling winds had discouraged everyone except a few wild-eyed windsurfers from going out on the water. Everyone, that is, but the two of us, who were sailing as hard as we could to rush to the aid of our threatened, canyon-bound child. Our eagerness to secure the boat may have been part of our problem, the constantly changing velocity and direction of the stormy wind as it charged down through houses and buildings and around the islands of the bay definitely contributed, but by the time we had missed the mooring three times in a row, we came to feel *Seraffyn* was the cause. She didn't want to be discarded from our lives quite so easily. Even on the fourth attempt, when we did hook the mooring pennant as we tacked closely between the dozens of boats that bucked and twisted on their moorings around her, we had to struggle to haul *Seraffyn* to the mooring strop and wrap it around the smooth familiar feeling mooring bitts for the very last time.

The smoke-filled skies and roaring winds denied us any chance to linger over the last moves of settling the boat onto her mooring and folding away her sailing gear. Instead, we rushed for our truck and began the long drive past hills blackened by fires that still smoldered on each side of the six-lane freeway. Twenty major blazes had overtaxed the firefighting resources of three counties, and the announcer's words barely filtered through as I thought of the magnificent skeleton of our future adventures standing unprotected and far too isolated in the path of the flames. Half of a university was reduced to rubble during the time it took us to drive toward the lonely stone cottage. Fire engines and low-bed trucks loaded with heavy digging equipment rushed in both directions past us. A road block manned by the local sheriff stopped us at the bottom of Bull Canyon. "Only residents allowed in," the officer said as I looked toward the smoke towering over the hills to the east. "The boat place, yup. I know that one. Get goin', only two companies up there. They'll be spread pretty thin. Fire over in Cleveland forest has all the other companies tied up."

Bull Canyon seemed strangely benign as we wound through the narrows, honking at each curve. I felt desperate to rush onward, yet fearful not only of a collision, but of the sight we might see around the next corner.

The Lone Palm Ranch came into view; the air was heavy with the smell of smoke, the sky full of drifting ash flakes. The harsh winds of the past twelve hours were dying and the single palm tree waved sedately over the green of Ellie's pond, undisturbed by any of our deep-set concerns. The up-stretched arms of our future boat seemed poised in welcome at the top of our driveway when we reached it. After Cindy's tumultuous greeting and Dog's purred insistent leg rubbing, all was absolutely calm in our yard. Nothing looked different, other than the cloak of ash that dusted everything in grey and black and swirled ahead of the last puffs of wind to almost cover the huge tire marks that now patterned our front yard. Those tire marks seemed to glare at me as I climbed out of our truck. Their ruts and ridges stood as a silent memorial to the men who had covered for us during our absence, an absence which now seemed neglectfully careless.

The silence of the canyon seemed almost overwhelming as we looked for any other signs of the threat that had prompted our headlong dash from the shoreside. Smoke still drifted over the hills above us to draw us onward even though the cool of evening made the protecting stone walls of the cottage a tempting refuge. Together we climbed upward past the artesian well and its spread of autumn stripped sycamore trees. I felt emotionally exhausted, almost let down at finding everything unscathed. I sensed Larry felt the same and expected him to say something like, "See, you were worrying for nothing again." Then we reached the crest of the steep hill, less than a thousand feet from our hand-cleared firebreak. The sight before us made me grip Larry's hand more tightly. As far as we could see, to the north and east, not a bush or tree stood unscathed. Bare, blackened limbs of desert sage reached toward the brown-stained sky and soot-stained piles of previously hidden rocks now stood clear above the fired earth. A few clumps of sycamore still stood, but their limbs, too, were scorched. Just below us, we could see the fresh scar of a hastily cut fire road that had broken the advance of the consuming flames before it reached the crest of our hill, then plunged downward into the narrow ravine where the boatshed lay. And even now, in the last light of evening, we could see dozens of tired men loading equipment back onto soot and dirt-covered trucks a half mile below us.

I wasn't surprised to see Bob Steele's truck waiting when we climbed wearily down the hill. As I arranged the kindling and lit a fire to warm the house and try to dispel the chill that seemed to have crept over my whole body, I listened to Bob's commentary with only half an ear.

"Fire inspector says it was arson for sure," Bob said as he settled himself carefully into the one chair he trusted to hold his weight. "Talked to him when I saw the crew up here. Firebreak you cleared made them feel safe leaving their cars and equipment in the yard when it looked like the fire would come down this canyon. That arsonist did you a favor. Now that the break at Lindell's cleared even wider and there is no fuel left on the back of these hills, your side of the road's pretty protected. Besides, there's rain coming this week. Fire danger will lie right down. But next time you leave to go off sailing, tell someone."

"Won't be going off sailing anymore. We decided to sell our boat today," I said as the heat began to dispel the chill in my body if not in my mind.

"Lin and I have decided to stop playing around and get to work. I can't live out here forever worrying about the next fire season. It's going to be two more years, no matter how you slice it. So now we'll be more inclined to stick to the job at hand," Larry said as he offered Bob a drink of rum, then came to sit in front of the fire.

"You guys seem really spooked by this fire," Bob said. "Hell, it's just part of life out here. Never lost a home in these hills, the inspector told me."

Bob stretched stocking feet toward the well-confined blaze. "Thought you really liked the canyon, now you're talking about moving on."

"Not yet," Larry answered. "Got this project to finish. I'm enjoying working on it and I do like the canyon. But I can't feel completely comfortable about putting my fate in the hands of the fire department that might not arrive in time. Look what happened over in San Bernardino, crews got there too late to save the university."

"But that's just because they were fighting to save homes instead," Bob said. "Big difference over there — it's all built up, surrounded by big trees, buildings right next to each other. Out here we've got lots of space, not too many buildings. Not too many crazies either. Bet the arsonist came over from Riverside, some city kid."

As soon as Bob left, I turned the radio on to listen to reports of fires being brought under control as the wind died, of refuge being sought for families who had lost their homes. The accumulating costs of businesses lost, reports of millions of trees destroyed, which exposed the mountain sides to the eroding forces of the winter rains. The numbers rolled off the announcers' tongues, only to be lost amid advertisements for used cars and insurance companies. But my mind couldn't dismiss the damages and disruptions so easily. What kind of person could have such a wicked fascination with fire that they could cause all this turmoil? Who could care so little about their friends, the people around them, I wondered?

Four days later Bob drove in with Pete Shomler in the seat beside him. "Your worries are over, just come back from the fire department," Pete called out. "That fire was set on purpose. The thirteen-year-old up beyond Lindell got mad at her folks. Wants to move into town so she can be near her friends, wants to play with them after school. Her folks were out at a horse show. She listened to all the reports about arsonists and bingo! Bright idea! Fire got one of their old barns, wasn't much of a barn. Crews got there before it touched the house. Like I said before, she probably did us all a favor, not much brush left uphill of us now."

"What about the girl?" I asked.

"They'll keep her in a county home for a few weeks," Pete said. "Then she'll be right back where she was before, a screwed up juvenile waiting for the next excuse to burn someone out."

"Ah, come on, Pete, she's not a bad kid. Kind of lonely for a youngster out here," Bob said. "Don't think we'll have to worry about her anymore. Can't say the same for the nutter who started those big blazes over in the national forest."

As the first rains of the year drifted lightly down on the canyon, I breathed a mental sigh of relief and tried to ignore the very first pangs of restlessness I'd felt since we'd decided to stop wandering for a while. "You know, being a gypsy makes you less vulnerable to crazies like the kid up the canyon," I said to Larry one day. "I mean, if we didn't like a situation or didn't trust someone, we could just lift our anchor and move on."

Larry poured some rum into his glass and reminded me, "Even gypsies have their problems. Remember being stuck in Gibraltar because we had to earn some money? We didn't particularly like it there — dirty, crowded. And remember waiting for our passage down the Suez Canal, we were stuck in Port Said for weeks, hot, bombed-out city, almost no food in the markets."

I sighed. "I really like it out here most of the time, but at least in those places, I didn't have to worry about someone taking revenge with a single match."

"Every place you live has some disadvantages," Larry said, as he came around the counter to hug me close. "You weren't any more interested in living in the city while we built this boat than I was. So worrying about the chance of fire for a month each year is the trade-off for living almost rent free in a place that's different. You're the one who hates normalcy. This canyon's

sure not normal. No druggies shooting each other, no drunk drivers shoving you off the edge of the freeway, no neighbors having a shouting match next to your bedroom window. Look at the odds. This cottage has stood here for sixty years and not a fire scar on it. Relax and enjoy it all. Not much to worry about now it's raining."

Though I had to agree, I still felt a sense of unease. So much had changed since the first Santa Ana winds arrived to herald the fire season only three short weeks before. Now my sanctuary had two flaws — each year I'd have to worry about the Southern Californian's fifth weather season, fire season, and until three days ago, when we'd reluctantly signed the papers that transferred *Seraffyn* to her new owner, I'd known in the back of my mind that if things went terribly wrong in the canyon, we could sail away with a few days notice. We could leave any fears or frustrations behind and rejoin a life that had worked before. Now we had that elusive thing — a chunk of money in the bank — a $40,000 cash nest egg we'd often wished for as we wandered. But was that enough to compensate for the freedom I'd given up? Logic said it was. We had a plan, a goal that was definitely obtainable if we both worked hard. Life was going well. But, as I listened to the tinkling of windchimes in the chinaberry tree outside my window, I got very little sleep that night.

Chapter 13

California Dreaming

"If it's just earning bank interest, you're wasting it," Jimmie Moore warned Larry as the winter rain pattered against the roof for the third day in a row. "Money has to keep working or inflation will eat it up. Now you've got some, put the smallest down payment you can on land that looks useless to everyone else. Make a deal that lets you pay interest only with a balloon payoff four or five years down the line. Then mold and shape that land so it looks romantic, desirable, and sell it. If you work it right you can make a profit before you ever have to pay for the place."

I'd heard this conversation before and was glad to be occupied in the kitchen. I welcomed the roar of Marlys' red Pontiac as it climbed the driveway. I tried to catch a glimpse of her reaction to the thick layer of gravel that now covered every inch of dirt from the kitchen door to the edge of the boatyard. "Sure nice to walk inside a place without having to take your shoes off," Marlys said pointedly as she dried her knee-high leather boots on the mat at the door. "Of course, in our place you can't tell the floor from the mud outside so doesn't matter if you take your boots off, as long as you don't climb between the sheets with them."

Bob Steele stamped past her toward the female-free haven near the fireplace. Jimmie Moore turned to him and said, "I was telling Larry he should buy land around Elsinore right now. Prices are rock bottom. Soon's the mess made by last winter's rain is cleared up and the freeway comes all the way out here, things will start to take off." He tossed another lump of timber into the fire and continued. "Larry, you could make deals on three or four places with the cash you got from selling *Seraffyn*. It's going to waste in the bank."

Bob agreed. "Larry knows my feelings. I've got my 260 acres almost ready to divide up so I can start building houses. Folks in Orange County are going to need space real soon. Offer them ten acres where they can build a sprawling house, a barn for some horses, all for less than they pay for a tract house on a crowded street, and they'll flock out here. I've got my lakes so they'll hold water, got roads to ten different sites. Come spring I'll start cutting building pads."

"What about cutting walls for our house," Marlys snapped from the kitchen, "or even cutting some flat space so I can have gravel around the trailer. Lin's got that and her roof doesn't leak. Bob, I promise you, if it rains like it did last year, I'm moving a bed into my office at Rancho California."

As I stoked the kitchen range and listened to Marlys' stories of office politics, I tried to block out the conversation going on in front of the big fire. But snippets about Jimmie's land development successes kept filtering through: "...got the fire road easement removed, instantly tripled the value... Barb got a job with the county, infiltrated their records and found a way around the hillside building code, made a bundle..."

Land. With an overabundance of both sunshine and open space, with a flood of people from the north and east of the country looking for both, Californians seemed to be elevating land speculation to an art form. Bookstores had racks filled with titles like *Make Your Fortune in Real Estate*. Radio and newspaper ads urged listeners to join three-day seminars with land development specialists, or with self-made millionaires who bought their first piece of land with no money down. The ads said, "You too can cash in on the riches, reap the benefits of the population boom."

California dreaming, that's what I called it. Old friends, who like me, had been products of the era when communes and kibbutzes seemed far more interesting than suburban homes, were now talking of the bargain fixer-uppers they were going to upgrade and sell at obscene profits. The same friends who had questioned the morality of time payments, who said loans were the shackles of modern slavery and banks were trying to suck them into the system, now talked of mortgage points, penalty clauses, fixed versus floating rates. Hippies who had carried Thoreau's books like a bible and blithely quoted "Use the land but own it not," were now proudly leading us through their latest "hedge against inflation."

I could feel Larry being lured into the shimmering web those two men were weaving. We'd both been fascinated by Jimmie and Barbara's land dealings. Over the past ten years, they'd transformed themselves from renters living on apprentice carpenter's wages to owners of two magnificent hilltop homes in Laguna Beach plus this land, cars, trucks, a nice yacht. As soon as everyone left that evening, Larry said, "Jimmie reckons he and Barb are worth about eight million now. So, his advice can't be completely wrong."

"But that's Jimmie's game. It's how he makes his living and it's a real hassle. He spends half his time running around looking for financing, or land to build on, dealing with construction crews, building inspectors, buyers, real estate people. Besides, I'd bet if he cashed out tomorrow, he wouldn't be worth two million. It's all financed to the hilt. Could you imagine owing what he does? Barb says they spend over $10,000 a month on interest payments," I said as I threw a protective web around the nest egg of cash I fondled in my mind like a precious jewel.

"You always see the hassles. Barbara says they get almost ten grand a month from the second trusts they hold on the houses they've sold. And what about the beautiful homes Jimmie's built. The land he's made more useful. Like this place. It would have all been bulldozed into a heap of stones if Jimmie hadn't bought it."

I glanced around at the stone and pine walls as the fire bathed them in bronze and golden lights. "It's a magic place, isn't it? It seems to respond to every little thing we do. If I have any spare time this winter, I want to line the edge of the gravel with stones, make some definite paths and boundaries for the flower beds."

"How'd you feel if it was partially ours?" Larry asked.

"It is," I answered. "The agreement we wrote up guarantees us another two years to enjoy it. Jimmie and Barbara won't worry if we need it an extra month or two. Sure appreciate having a place where we don't have to pay rent. I'm going to call the electric people again when I'm in town. See if they know any more about getting power up here. I'll try the phone company again too. Sure would make Jimmie happy, but I doubt if phones or electricity could get here in time to help us much."

Larry was quiet as we climbed into bed. Then he said, "Jimmie's got a good idea. We all have fun up here when we're together. He thinks maybe we should become partners. He's willing to sell us a half-share of the house and the 25-acre parcel it sits on. Then, after we've used it, he and Barb would use if for a few years while they sell off some of the other parcels they own around it. They would fix the house up some more. By that time we could sell it for a real profit. Really set ourselves up for the future."

I listened in silence, thinking of ways to stymie this overt attack on my cash stash while Larry outlined, "a really good deal. Only give Jimmie $10,000 now. Pay him interest on the rest twice a year. Then in four years we owe the balance. Lets us keep the majority of our money intact. We only pay 10% interest to him, the rest of our money is earning 15% in CDs, interest rates could go up higher, and we'd earn even more. Anything could happen in four years, and if worse came to worse, we'd use the rest of our money to pay him off and be free and clear and we'd own half of twenty-five acres and half of this house. Jimmie says we could realign the boundaries and end up with twelve acres separate to sell in a year or two."

"Sounds to me like Jimmie's got an interest payment to make this month and needs the cash," I said as I blew out the lamp and tried to block out the growing knowledge that we were being offered a bargain, a deal. I couldn't sleep until I finally mentioned, "I guess Jimmie sees it as a way to encourage us to push for electricity and phones. It would double the value of the rest of his land. If we owned half the house and got the power in, we'd make more in one stroke than we could from two books. But do we really want to get involved? I've never in my life owed any money, never paid interest. I like it that way."

"No risk, no glory," Larry snapped.

"Is there any glory in land speculation?" I asked.

"We're not speculating if we buy half this place. We're improving something, fixing something up, creating a lovely place for someone to live where very little existed before. Someone has to do it. We've got a bit more spare time now *Seraffyn* is gone. Think about it for a week," he said as he drew me into his arms beneath the down-filled quilt.

◇◇

"Your GMC for sale? Its exactly the model I'm looking for, a real classic," the man at the oil depot asked as he rolled a fifty-gallon drum of kerosene into the back of *Old Gold*. He wasn't the first to ask. I really liked driving around in that 1969 pickup. I liked knowing it was a real truck, not a car souped up with a trendy body to look like a cowboy carry-all. At first, I thought I was somewhat alone in my fondness for pickup trucks, trucks that had seats high above the normal traffic. I liked knowing I was surrounded by a substantial barrier of metal that could protect me from rampaging Honda and Suzuki sub-compacts as I drove the crowded streets of downtown Riverside and Orange County, liked waving to other pickup truck owners who somehow looked more contented, less rushed, than people in normal sedans. The latest Glen Campbell song, "I Love My Truck", rang through my mind as I roamed the valley crossing things off my shopping list.

I learned that there is no vehicle quite so useful, yet light-hearted, as the American half-ton pickup truck. Load it with a cooler, a mattress, and some sleeping bags and it became an instant Oklahoma RV, ready for a trip to the Calico Country Music Festival, where we could lay in its bed above the insect-laden earth and listen while late-night revelers sang of lonesome dreams beside campfires that sent ribbons of smoke across the desert stars. Load it with yelling kids and dogs, and it became an ice cream express, bumping down the rutted road and across the glistening streams. Throw a camper onto the back and it became a home-away-from-home, an instant guest room for the children of friends who came to visit, or a place to take a quiet nap when a day of shopping in the city grew tedious and tiring. But, best of all, the big empty bed of that old truck could carry anything and often did. I could overload it with trash, timber, tools, groceries, and drive it onto the roughest back road, knowing a dent or two didn't matter too much now the floods of the previous winter had knocked a few bruises into the fading factory paint job.

The winter rains were falling in a more normal pattern our second year in the canyon. A day or two of stormy weather each month was soon forgotten during the sunny days and crisp nights that followed. March, with its warm days and lengthening twilight hours, was drawing to a close as we headed up the rain-rutted road after a weekend down at Jimmie and Barbara's Laguna Beach house. The back of the truck was piled high with groceries, building supplies, a dozen pieces of wood left over from Jimmie's last construction job, and another old, but lovely desk we'd found in a second-hand shop to provide Larry with his own writing space. We slowed down to rumble into the knee-high waters of the big washout below the narrows and laughed together as I recalled the beginnings of the past year's floods and the day when Larry charged too boldly across the same spot. We'd hit a submerged rock that tore the spare tire loose from its rack beneath the bed of the truck. Larry had leapt out of the cab and rushed downstream after that bumping, jumping, water-borne wheel. Now the spare reposed in obvious splendor, bolted onto a rack at the side of the truck bed, just like I'd seen in the trucks rodeo cowboys drove. Now we, too, had lots of clearance beneath our truck so we could charge up rutted roads and across rock-laden streams.

Memories of the mini-adventures we'd driven through with this old pickup provided a welcome break from the overwhelming topic of the past six days. That conversation had been laden with constant lists of the pros and cons of "buying into the dream," of joining the California game, doing something "concrete" toward assuring our future security.

I was still uncomfortable with the whole idea. But Larry seemed so infected with the "dream" that even my frequent reminders of the fires that had roared so close to destroying all we had didn't dent his enthusiasm. "With that firebreak cut, all we have to do is keep close to the place for a few months each year," he said in rejoinder. "Look at the odds of a fire coming that close again. Remember, everyone in California lives with the same threat and manages to thrive. Once the boat's out of there we won't have so much to lose. Lin, you just hate switching gears. I know you've got the next five years neatly laid out in your mind. But think about it, it's a chance of a lifetime."

I was tired of twisting the idea around in my mind, of trying to convince Larry that we were better suited to maintaining our gypsy freedoms by avoiding debt, ownership, the ties of normalcy. Logic fought against the lure of that stone and timber magnet. I was off in my own world, while we rumbled through the dark toward the narrows then around the first tight bend in the canyon. Larry slammed on the brakes and almost threw me against the dashboard.

"Shh, quiet," he whispered, pointing along the path of our headlight beam. There on the road, head held proudly aloft, huge brown eyes glowing with concern, white chest bright against a golden coat, stood a doe, momentarily mesmerized by the light. Larry flicked off the light switch and she lowered her head to continue grazing by the roadside. Two small fawns stood alertly, close by her heels, the spots of youth showing clearly in the moonlight.

Larry took my hand in his as we sat in the quiet truck and watched, "Lin, this place is magic. I guess I want to feel we're really part of it, not just visitors. It may sound egotistical but change is going to happen up here and I'd like to feel we can help shape it a bit, make it a nicer place in the long term, keep it from being trashed like some of the other canyons."

The three animals moved off the road to drink at the stream and as we drove slowly past, the mother glanced over her shoulders to look me straight in the eye. For that short second something inside me yelled, "Run, now, while you're still free." Before I could put my thoughts into words Larry gave my hand a small squeeze. I hesitated and as I let my eyes roam the familiar-feeling canyon walls, the senuous curves of the road leading us toward the cottage, I saw he was right. We had become part of this place. I did want to help mold it's future. Then I laughed at my fears and began scheming along with Larry, outlining the research I'd start the next time I went to town on a quest not only for groceries, but for the information that could lead to the electricity, to telephones, to increased property values. We were in.

From the moment we became landowners, we began noticing a marked difference in the attitudes of the people who used the land in the canyon. There were the renters, people like Dolly and Bob who'd parked a secondhand trailer on forty acres owned by his brother at the very top of the canyon. To them, land was only a temporary stopping place, a plateau on the way to someplace that would hopefully be better. So an open pit at the lower part of their land received the refuse from their toilet. The rotting remains of their first trailer blocked the view from the road to where their slightly newer but still sway-backed accommodations sat amid piles of trash scattered about by a pack of mongrel dogs. When I happened to mention the idea of electricity to Dolly during a chance meeting at the market she lifted an untidy youngster onto her hip, found the pacifier the infant in her cart had momentarily misplaced, then snapped, "Couldn't afford it unless the welfare people paid. Besides, we'd probably be shoved out if Bob's brother thought he could make any money by selling the place. Says he doesn't know why he bought it anyway. Got no use for it. No one wants it the way it is. That's why we're there."

Then there were people like the Newhouses, owners of a single, ten-acre block of land that held their dream of space, of independence. "Doubt you'll ever convince the power company to come up here, not enough money in it. We all get on pretty well as it is. My old generator does its job real cheap, why try to change things? Not saying I'd stand in the way of it," Lee said as he looked around inside the old wheel-less bus that served as his machine shop. "Just that I don't have any money spare and I'm not sure I want all those officials coming up here, poking around." He started his wheezy old generator and welded up the drill bit Larry had brought along for his expert attention. Then he snapped back the shield on his welders mask and sighed, "If it ever happens, I'll hook in for Ma's sake, easier for her to take care of us with electricity. But sure hate to see too many people come out here. City folks start complaining about everything. They'll want to get rid of the dirt road, want piped in water, piped in gas, drive the taxes up, drive us out..."

I could see logic in Lee's concerns. Once we had a proprietary interest in the canyon, the three old cars that lay dying on his square of land alongside the stream, the old bedsteads and piles of scrap metal Lee continuously hauled home for safekeeping and dumped just off the road in what he called his "Okie bank account," became more than a momentary eyesore each time we drove up-canyon — they became an embarrassment, almost an affront. "They're really sweet people," we'd say to visitors who commented on the unsightly mess. "You should see how lovely their garden is, up by their cottage." Soon, we, like other neighbors who owned land that could some day be divided and sold off in ten-acre parcels, wished the Newhouses would plant hedges to hide the mess, so it wouldn't lower the tone of the whole canyon, wouldn't hurt the property values that were the basis of the California dream.

By far the largest number of landowners in the canyon fell into this last group — people like Jimmie Moore, Bob Steele, and Pete Shomler, who owned large parcels of land that could someday be sub-divided into smaller, more re-saleable lots. "Guy up at the top has had a couple of thousand dollars deposited with the electric company for six years," Pete said as soon as he heard we'd become landowners. "He wants to sell off a couple of sections so he can get the money together to build out here. He's been arguing with the electric company all that time, but they keep saying, 'no right-of-ways to bring the lines across from Santa Rosa Mine Road.' I know they already have them, friend at Riverside jail told me he heard from his brother-in-law, who has a cousin at the county assessor's office whose sister works for the electric company, that they just don't want to spend the money to bring the lines this far. I'm not going to play kiss ass to some soft-fingered patsy in a carpeted office just to get power. But sure would be good to have it. Sell off the bottom ten acres for some real money."

Even Ellie, who I'd always thought of as utterly comfortable with the canyon and reluctant to see it change, said, "Just needs some organizing to see it happen. That guy up top has never tried very hard, just paid his money and calls them once every month or two. Been doing the same for six years and never gets anything out of anyone. Would take a real concentrated effort to get power out here and I'll tell you, if it does come in, I'm going to sub-divide the place into four sections, sell off the bottom three, then build a real house on that ridge up there. Couldn't make enough to cover survey costs right now, but with power, telephones — you guys get everyone together and let's have a barbecue up here. Get lots of people to sign a petition, only way to do it is to get organized. I'll make deviled eggs; I've got mixers and lots of ice. Get Shomler and Steele over here tomorrow, let's talk about it over drinks."

Within two days Bob Steele and I became cohorts, as together we scoured county records and pasted together maps to form a mosaic of properties that covered the hills around us. Together we sorted through piles of tomes to find out where old easements led, to trace telephone line rights-of-way, electric power lines, even easements for roads dreamed up years before, but never built. I was completely foxed by the new Bob Steele I saw waiting outside my door in a freshly washed truck, hair trimmed, beard brushed to lay smoothly over a designer tie and ironed shirt, a silk and wool sport coat neatly folded on the seat beside him. I listened in amazement as he dominated the meeting we'd arranged with representatives of Southern California Edison, the largest electricity company in the United States, the local telephone company, the Public Utilities Commission representative. Gone was the gentle, but rough-edged bulldozer driver I knew. The soft-spoken, hard-hitting businessman beside me kept demanding facts, reasons, promises, as we traced rights-of-way we'd found. On paper the right-of-ways did appear to connect up with the power supplies enjoyed by people living five miles away on the far side of the hills.

"That was quite a meeting," I said, as Bob maneuvered his truck out of the parking lot. "I don't think they want to bring phones and power out to us, but they'll have to if we get them all the signatures they asked for. The PUC guy said they were bound by contract to supply us."

Bob's booming laugh shook the cab. "We'll get them their signatures. They're over a barrel because they took that $6,000 deposit six years back. They made a promise to supply that power, now they've got to do it. But the telephones — that's another story. We've got to keep the pressure on, form a community association, get formal-looking stationery, make the canyon sound like the really up-market place it's going to be. Then they'll see money in these hills. Right now we look like a handful of country bumpkins who couldn't even scrape up the money to pay a power bill. Those desk jockeys couldn't imagine living out here, so they can't imagine anyone else would ever want to. It's the usual bullshit. They don't want to put the electricity in until there are enough people using it to pay for it. Won't be people coming out here to use the place until the electricity gets here. That's why there's a public utilities commission. Keeps a monopoly like the power company from plucking all the plums and ignoring all the rest. You heard the man; they're obligated to extend lines to anyone who's willing to pay the proscribed amount, even if they do lose money on it. They make plenty putting power in where there's lots of people. But like I said, if we convince them we're a real up-market community, they'll be a lot more interested."

Just before we hit the first washout Bob screeched to a stop. "We'll start right here. We'll erect a big wooden sign, mount it on stone pillars, 'Welcome to Bull Canyon.' Have someone carve a raging bull on it. Make it look like this place is special," Bob spread his arms to encompass a scraggly looking stand of leafless sycamore trees surrounding by sparse, low lying weeds next to the rock cluttered washout.

I chuckled and said, "We'd better have any meetings with the officials right next to that sign. Wouldn't want to disillusion them by inviting them up to your trailer."

"What happened at the meeting?" Larry asked as he shook wood shavings from his jacket. I was more interested in the newest plank he'd added to enclose the hull of my eventual escape machine. I felt exhausted by the days of paperwork that had led up to a meeting for something that still seemed like a disturbing tangent to the reality of our life.

"It seems like I spend all my time pushing papers around. If it's not petitions for the utilities, it's writing letters that get no answers, trying to get editors to make decisions, never seeing anything concrete for my work. I wish I could be like you. You can actually see what you get done in a day, actually show me your progress. Me? I feel like there was nothing but words flying around today, no concrete promises on paper, no power poles."

"Come on, Lin, you're really good at paper work, and besides, you can't bend a plank onto a boat. If you get the electricity out here, you'll be a hero. So what happened?" Larry prompted.

"Well, we're going to have a big barbecue in a few weeks. Ellie's even going to get some friends who play country music to add some entertainment. That way the folks who own properties but don't use them will want to come to the party. We'll try to get everyone to donate fifty dollars to start it all, pay for meetings, mail. With eighty-six property owners, that would really help set up a good kitty. But we have to convince Ellie we don't need two cases of booze for the barbecue, just some beer and wine. If we don't get enough signatures at the party we'll at least have the ball rolling, get a community association that can apply some pressure. Bob's got some good ideas, I've got lots of letters to do up, maps to draw. Then there's the sign."

"Good old Steele," Larry laughed as I described Bob's latest idea. "A raging bull. With his nerve, he'll probably have the carver put great big balls on it."

The more the push for power became a routine (though often frustrating) part of my working day, and the more I worked with Bob to visit and map out the places where people indicated they wanted to build homes, the more I came to admire thought processes of the Old Man Payonessa who had been the first person to build a permanent home in this isolated canyon. He had taken time to get to know the canyon in all its seasons and moods before he chose the site for the stone cottage.

The contrast between Payonessa's site and the site chosen by the latest canyon dweller couldn't have been greater. Bob and I drove up the steep, winding, newly-bulldozed track on the property just beyond Ellie's to talk to Thomas T. Howard as he paced off the foundation markings of the hilltop house he was having a local contractor build for him. "What do you think of this view? Spectacular, isn't it?" he said as soon as we arrived. He spread his arms as if to embrace the ranks of hills, the distant lake, and the mountains to the west. "Told my wife someday we'd have a home where we would see the whole world, not just the neighbor's fence. And now we're going to have it. Electricity will get here before too long and I'll have my house while I can still afford it, before views like this cost a fortune. I've already decided — no trees near the house. I've seen your stone place. Can't figure out why anyone would come out here and hide behind the hills and block the view with all those trees."

Bob shook his head as we skidded down Tom's steep track. "Give him one summer up there and he'll do anything to get electricity, he'll never live on that site without it. No well-driller could get his rig up there, so they'll have to drill down here on the flat. Then Tom'll need a hell of a pump to push water up that hill, probably need two pumps to get the lift. How's he going to heat the place? In winter, it's going to be like living in a wind-blasted freezer. You'd think the guy would have asked around before he had a bulldozer trucked up from the valley. Look at his driveway. It'll melt away in the first heavy rains."

I took Bob's words as mostly sour grapes that day. Tom had hired a digger operator from outside the canyon so Bob's bulldozer sat idle beside his half-filled lakes while a rival not only earned money, but more importantly, got a chance to know this newcomer to the canyon. Instead of acting as adviser and confidante, instead of being able to steer jobs to his friends, Bob watched contractors he didn't know quickly reshape the top of the hill and build a stucco house. He was left with no excuse to stop by and add Tom's life story to his collection of canyon gossip.

But sour grapes or not, I soon could see how the desire for an eagle's nest, a place where he could be above his neighbors, was costing Tom dearly. Each and every item he and his wife needed had to be dragged up that hill no matter what the weather. Soon a parking shelter appeared at the bottom of his drive and we watched as each arrival meant unloading packages from the city car into the old four-wheel-drive Jeep that would spend its life going up and down the same track within the boundary of the same ten acres. During winter we'd see Tom carrying in desperately needed firewood for half of each day. And, when the first heat of summer came, Tom and Gail temporarily abandoned their dream to retreat to an air conditioned inner city bungalow. "Soon as there is electricity out here we'll be full-time neighbors," he told me as he came to pick up yet another set of papers we needed signed and notarized for the SoCal Edison Company. "We can't retire for another two years anyway. By that time you guys will have it all fixed up and we can put in real air conditioning. Can't stand the noise of our generator."

Each time I drove up-canyon, I'd glance at the empty black-roofed house that stood stark and unprotected by any trees other than two slow-growing cypresses that showed boldly against the yellow desert brush. Then a few minutes later, I'd nose the truck into the green tunnel of rugged pines, silky oak and acacia trees that shaded the drive leading up to the house Old Man Payonessa built. Sometimes I'd stop right there to listen to the chorus of birds, the whisper of breeze-rustled leaves, the ring of Larry's hammer, and if I was lucky I'd hear him singing along to his favorite country song of the week.

Then I'd drive up and park under the chinaberry trees that spread like umbrellas in front of the old stone house and wonder if we were accidentally going to destroy the tranquillity that blessed this secluded spot. How would I feel if someday soon I looked out at a view filtered by the trees and instead of open, brush-covered hills saw a marching maze of electric lines and hilltops bulldozed into submission, so bright-colored stucco houses could sit on top to command the view? How would I feel if instead of the quiet, winding wilderness-like dirt road, I saw a black ribbon of pavement filled with cars driven by people I didn't even know? But I had come to accept that change is a constant, and as Larry reminded me, "Since it's going to happen, you might as well be in there trying to guide it along, trying to keep it from destroying what you like most about the place." So I'd get out the ever-growing folder of documents that commanded most of my spare time and again work toward the electricity that was part of the scheme that would move us along the path of the California dream.

Chapter 14

Company in the Country

"How about putting wood plugs in the bulkhead?" Larry suggested as we finished eating lunch and headed out to the boatshed together. I eagerly agreed. Nothing could have suited me better this sparkling spring afternoon. I'd had a productive morning. Now I would be working where I could look through the frames of the boat, out past the open-sided boatshed and see the profusion of flowers coloring the hills around us. Larry and I would be within a few feet of each other so we could talk about our schemes and dreams. But best of all, I'd be using my hands to do something tactile and concrete, in direct contrast to the abstract processes of trying to dream up readable, saleable stories.

Over the past few days, Larry had fitted and screwed pieces of teak tongue and groove in place. My job was to cover each screw using the teak plugs I'd cut from scraps and off-cuts of the same wood with grain to match the vertical strakes. Once I'd put all the plugs in place, I'd trim each one using the chisel Larry had bought and sharpened just for me, then sand the bulkheads until they felt absolutely smooth beneath my hand. If all went well, I could cap my afternoon's contribution to our future home by applying the first of six coats of varnish to the woodwork that divided our boat into distinct areas: an area up forward for a stateroom, a main cabin for living and a lazzerette at the stern for a work bench and storage area.

We were halfway through our second year in the canyon, the plagues of mice, frogs, flies, floods and fires behind us and almost forgotten as the buzz of carpenter bees and the hum of cicadas added to my feeling that we'd chosen the right place to be during this part of our lives. Our conversation wandered as aimlessly as the hawk I could see grabbing each updraft to search for the mice that scurried among the bushes but avoided my cat-patrolled patch of earth.

"Did you enjoy biking up to the springs with Dean and Mary as much as I did?" Larry asked.

"I loved every bit of the weekend, seemed to rush by too quickly," I answered, relishing thoughts not only of Mary and Dean, but of other visitors who, during the past few months, had joined us for a leisurely break from the pressures of the city. Each gave us an important outside perspective of our country life. Then I recalled Ma Newhouse's warning the first month we moved into the cottage. "One thing I can tell ya about movin' to the country, gonna get lots of company. People ya barely know gonna drive out to see ya," she had said as she led my brother's kids, Cami and Michelle, over to the small fenced-in yard in front of her barn-shaped house. At her approach, three pair of pet geese clomped over to waddle and dance in a parody of excited puppies. I laughed as I watched the children overcome their shyness at these strange-seeming pets. "Yup," Ma went on. "For the first year your place will be full every weekend, every holiday. Be busy baking, cooking. Enjoy it, 'cause it won't last long. Soon's they figure out ya don't have TV, don't have a phone, they'll stop comin'. Too quiet out here after dark, nothing to do. My kids used to come and stay. Now the only time we see them's when they're broke or in trouble."

I glimpsed what she was talking about the winter before we actually moved to the canyon. Any time we mentioned we were driving out to work on the cottage, family, friends, even new acquaintances would say, "Mind if we come along? Nice to go some place quiet for a few days." Then we moved to the stone house on a permanent basis and that first Thanksgiving gathering seemed to turn on a stream of visitors. By the time the first warmth of spring filled the desert around us with flowers, that stream turned to a torrent. I came to expect weekends to bring two, three or even a dozen surprise visitors. I learned to keep extra food in the pantry. This helped overcome the confusion of city guests who'd say, "Know you weren't expecting us — I'll zip out and get something extra for dinner."

"Market's closed for the weekend," I'd explain, as I rummaged for additions to the salad or stew or pasta dish I planned to serve that evening.

"Don't worry, Lin will put an extra cuppa' water in the soup," Larry would say, a satisfied smile lighting his face as he offered them a glass of "Chateau Cardboard" from the stock of box wine we kept in the pantry.

At first, I'd loved greeting these unexpected visitors. They made our choice of a country boatbuilding yard seem more noteworthy, different. I'd loved showing them my favorite trails; the owl who lived in the hole in the ancient-looking olive tree at the foot of the driveway, the hidden waterfall two miles up the canyon, Bob Steele's latest bulldozing projects. They'd inspect our boat building and remind both Larry and me that we were making progress, even though at times we couldn't see it. The stone cottage rang with laughter and song as my guitar got passed from one strummer to the next. I'd sometimes look for an excuse to walk outside into the black night, untinged by the glow of any city lights. I'd revel in the sense of control I seemed to have over my private world as the call of a coyote echoed across the hills. I'd inhale the fragrance of the wood-burning fireplace as it mingled with the night-blooming jasmine. A blanket of smugness, almost superiority, would creep over me for those few minutes. I'd feel like I had created this whole picture, dreamt up its outlines, colored in the details, animated its characters. Then I'd walk slowly in to join the warm hubbub inside, picking

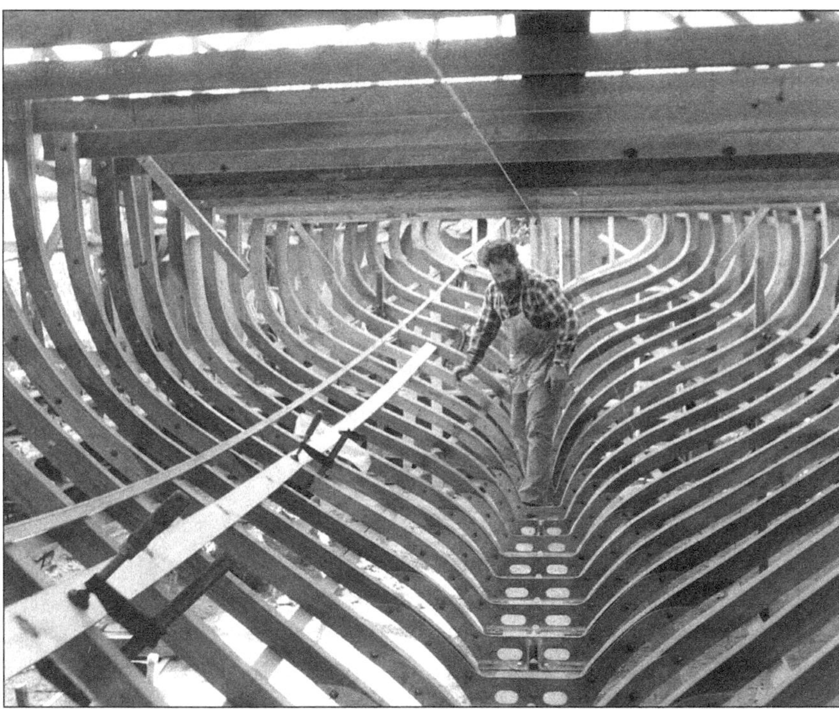

up an armful of firewood as I went, and Ma Newhouse's words would come back, "They'll soon stop comin'."

Larry, too, had enjoyed these weekends with friends who had to drive seventy or a hundred miles to visit. But, as the first spring wore on, the stream of visitors began to flood over into weekdays too. Then the third "friend of a friend" arrived during the same week and drove up to the boatshed just before lunch to announce, "Hi, Larry, had a day to kill. Thought I'd ride out and see what you two are doing. How's the boat building going?" By the time we waved goodbye to this pleasant visitor six hours later, I could sense an explosion building inside Larry. I, too, was feeling put upon. Now I'd lost my writing time, dirty dishes littered the kitchen and I hadn't scratched one item off my to-do list. As I watched our visitor's car disappear behind the first bend in the road, I sensed we'd get very little done during the few hours of daylight that remained.

Larry had stomped toward the kitchen and I heard the liquor cabinet opening. When I reached the cottage, he was already sitting glumly staring at the smoldering remains of the morning fire. "Had a day to kill, so he comes out and kills mine, too!" he'd muttered. "He and just about everyone else in Orange County can call in sick and get paid to take the day off. I lose a day of my life, no one's paying me. Our work doesn't get done. It's a real pain in the ass."

I'd been expecting a reaction like this. I'd felt some of this same frustration. My progress had almost ground to a halt over the past three months. Our weekends, and the majority of our weekdays, had been full of drop-ins, family, old friends, friends of friends, all curious to meet "those crazies imitating Noah out on a California desert mountain." Then there were people who had read our first two books and came by to ask questions because they too were hoping to sample the freedom we had enjoyed so much. Individually, we came to like almost every one of them, but...

"Those people wouldn't walk into a friend's work place and expect them to stop and talk all afternoon. They'd know it would get their friend fired. Can't they see we are working, too?" Larry had groaned as he poured a second shot of rum. "I mean, if they came by in the evenings it would be great."

"I guess anyone who works at home has the same problems," I said softly. "It's a pretty nice ride out here. Not surprising folks come during daylight; it's really hard to find this place at night. Besides, *you* always invite them in for coffee or lunch. Then they feel all relaxed, comfortable, see no reason to go."

"Don't lay it all on me," Larry snapped. "I figure I need lunch so I might as well stop. Figure they'll take the hint and leave as soon as it's over. But they don't. They hang around; seem to think we're lonely out here. I'm ready to barricade the damn driveway from Sunday night to Friday night so we can get some work done — we've only got a three-year lease on this cottage, already used up six months. Can you imagine the hassle it would be to move a half-finished boat and all this gear to another place?"

"Couldn't you just say, 'sorry, too busy to talk. Come back at five'?" I asked, remembering Ma Newhouse's wistful look as she related how her flow of company dried up. The distinct difference between Larry and me, one that probably worked as an important balance in our life together, was that Larry had always compartmentalized his life. To him, friends were like ice cream, to be enjoyed as a treat after a hard-working day or week. I could see the reason as I watched him entertain any guest we had invited. Just like with his projects, he gave them undivided attention. The minute they walked in, he'd stop whatever he was doing and hand them a glass of wine or a rum and coke. He'd plan special outings to interest them, encourage me to cook up interesting dishes to tempt them, make sure they were — to my mind — overly fed, overly wined. He'd put everything else in his world on hold while guests were with us.

I, on the other hand, am a social animal. I love company. But my idea of entertaining people when they did arrive was to invite them in and chat as I continued bustling around finishing whatever chores I had started. More often than not my guests would be handed a towel, a chopping knife or a gardening trowel and end up helping. That is, until Larry walked in to say, "Lin, why haven't you offered Jean something to drink yet?"

Our contrasting attitudes had occasionally led to some of the few real conflicts in our marriage and made me think Larry was, at times, his own worst enemy. "Make them feel welcome! Stop what you are doing and offer them a drink the moment they walk in. Don't put them to work," he would say.

"They're friends. I don't want them to feel like they are interrupting my day. Asked them to help me out so I could finish sooner. I got them drinks as soon as we finished clearing the weeds."

Through the years we had come to a comfortable compromise, Larry accepting that people didn't mind my relaxed attitude toward entertaining, me learning to shelter him as much as possible from what he saw as an invasion of his mental space by organizing people's visits around his boat work. But the flow of unexpected visitors grew into a torrent that first spring in Bull Canyon until I felt almost like a traffic warden. I began to feel the pressure of trying to support us with my writing as each interruption left another dozen pages unwritten. I felt Larry trying to crawl back into his almost hermit-like isolation and knew we had to come up with a solution. "Let us put a sign up like they have at Bill Lee's Santa Cruz boatyard," I suggested.

If you come after five, we hand you a beer,
If you come before five, we hand you a piece of sandpaper.
Lee's Boatyard.

Then I added, "But you wouldn't hand them a job, isn't in you."

"It's not like cutting firewood, weeding a garden or doing dishes, Lin. I'd have to supervise everything they did, then I'd get nothing done. Not many jobs for two people, and I can't concentrate if someone's talking to me when I cut timber or chisel things. If I screw up and cut a piece of teak too short it's fifty or a hundred bucks down the drain. Just lock the damn gate and make it look like we're not here."

"But what if they hear us? It would be rude to ignore them if they came walking up the hill. Besides, what if Chuck had something for us on his UPS truck?"

We finally reached a compromise. By late spring the gate was closed and chained loosely. Larry secured a sign board to the gate post. On it was a pad of paper with a pencil attached by a string and above this was a typed sheet of paper protected by plastic. The last lines read: "Please help us get our boat built. We can not have visitors on weekdays. Please come back after 5:30 or leave a note with your address and phone number on the attached pad. We'll include you in the Sunday wine and cheese afternoon we have every six or seven weeks."

I felt awkward the first time I heard a car pull to a stop. Then, I heard footsteps on the driveway. "Hey, Larry, don't stop working. I read your sign. Just want to say we'll be back at six and bring some steaks for all of us. Need anything else?" I could have run out and kissed Don Chillcott, but I refrained as I heard Larry yell, "Great, I'll look forward to it." And we both did. The day seemed to flow like smooth cream. The evening reunion with sailing friends we'd last seen in Spain five years before left us feeling comfortably sated and eager to continue working five and a half days a week.

It took me a few weeks to learn to ignore the sound of cars stopping, and then driving off. It was almost a month before I got over the desire to sneak out and see who'd left a note. Sometimes the notes were a bit peevish. A few drop-ins would leave none at all and didn't return later, but the flow of guests grew more logical and the closed gate slid to the back of my mind.

Then one day just before the blasting heat of summer filled in, my mother burst into the cottage unexpectedly. "Hi," she called, as she deposited a bag full of fresh vegetables and a pot of my favorite homemade chopped chicken liver on the counter. "Had a couple sick leave days coming to me. Decided to use them for a drive out here. Keep you company, help around the place today. Then tomorrow afternoon, we can all drive out to Hemet and visit my friend Ida. She really admires you. Help me store this food away. Larry and your Dad will want some coffee. Then we can start cleaning up your front yard."

I stood in stunned silence as one hundred pounds of vibrant, energetic motherhood managed to have the impact of a five-ton bulldozer. "But Mom, we're working," I managed to squeak out.

"Know you are, came to help. Get twice as much done so you can take tomorrow off," my mother said, as she grabbed the broom to begin shaping my kitchen into her concept of order.

I went out to hug Dad, torn between the pleasure of seeing two people I loved and the resentment at losing two mid-week days when we already had a weekend full of friends planned. Though Larry was the picture of politeness, as soon as we had a moment alone he hissed, "Tell your folks they can't stay."

"I can't just say 'go away.' Can't you find something you and Dad can work on together today?" I whispered. "Then I'll make a real nice dinner and we'll explain the problem tonight?"

"What about you?" he asked. "How you going to get any writing done? Tell your folks you've got a book to finish within the next two months, an outline to write for the next one. We're counting on the advance for the second one. It's the key to us being able to live out here. We can't treat them any different from any of our friends."

"They're my folks, not just friends, not just some new acquaintance we might or might not see again. So let me handle it my way. Mom and Dad are really reasonable if you don't push them too hard. I'll get Mom to edit the chapter I just typed. You mill up all that timber. Dad can help you with that instead of me," I said turning to leave before he could comment.

Mom didn't show her most reasonable side when I found a quiet minute to tell her we couldn't have any more company during the week. "I'm not company, I'm your mother," she stated. "Whoever heard of parents being told they weren't welcome in their children's home? Only saw you four or five times during the eleven years you were away. Now we can actually drop by, try to make you feel like part of the family and you get touchy. What's the big deal? We only get out this way once every month or so."

"But Mom, it's not just our house; it's our office, our work place. You wouldn't walk into Bonnie's classroom and expect her to stop teaching. Did you read the sign we set up at the gate? Last two months we have had over one hundred visitors — I figure unexpected visitors used up fifteen working days. It's getting desperate. We want to get something done or we'll never go sailing again."

"So? What's your rush?" Dad said in his quiet way as he brushed wood-shavings off his shoulders. "We like having you around."

"That's the problem, " Larry sighed late that night as we tossed and turned in the back room and my parents could be heard tossing and turning in the big brass bed. "No one really cares if we get anything done. They aren't keen on us leaving. We're cheap entertainment. They wouldn't mind if it took us ten years to build this boat."

"Mom and Dad are going on to Hemet in the morning. Let's get some sleep. I told you they were reasonable," I murmured, trying to shut out the memory of my father's rejected look.

"They may be leaving, but your Mom's not happy and now you feel guilty," were Larry's last words as he turned away to leave me staring at the ceiling and trying to reconcile the conflicting demands of a determined boat-building husband, my work and daughterhood.

"It's your life, you've got to make your own choices," Mom stated as she and Dad prepared to drive off even before I could offer them breakfast the next morning.

"Don't worry," Dad whispered, as he gave me a perfunctory hug, "we'll get over this."

The push to finish and submit the final manuscript pages of *Seraffyn's Mediterranean Adventures*, the relief of receiving that final advance payment, the seemingly rapid progress on the boat now that we'd organized our working time to be free of interruptions all gave me excuses to ignore the paucity of contact with my folks. A few months later, after our heat-induced midday siesta, I began working with Larry on a truly exciting project. I hauled on the block and tackle line as Larry guided each pair of rib-like frames he'd built into place, then trued them up. Now that I could plainly see the beautiful sweeping lines of our eventual boat, I realized the growth I participated in each afternoon in the boatyard provided ample reward for the hard choices that had obviously reeked of selfishness to some.

When autumn began its quiet approach and the intense heat of summer lost its grip I found an envelope from my mother in my post office box. Guilt flooded back as I slowly opened it. "I know it is an imposition, but I have visitors coming from England. They'd like to meet you; they're sailors and have read your stuff. Only time I can bring them out is on Thursday," Mom had written.

"Let's drive into town and get an ice cream this evening," Larry suggested without any hint of annoyance. "Then you can call and invite them all to stay the night. We aren't planning on going sailing this weekend, so we can put in some extra time over the next few days, then relax and enjoy your folks visit. I really like them, you know."

"What a change," Mom said as she gave me a quick hug and introduced her visitors. "You guys have really worked hard. Heard from your publisher yet? They're satisfied? Edith, come on out, and let me show you why they live out here."

I braced myself for the confrontation that I expected lay ahead when, free of the constraints of her visitors, my mother would castigate me for my cold-heartedness. But as I sorted out the staggering pile of food she'd brought and saw Mom pause just outside the kitchen window to point out the fruit trees I was trying to nurture, I overheard, "Sure am proud of these two. They are the most determined kids. Not everyone's willing to make hard decisions like they do." Knowing Mom, I am sure she meant for me to hear these words and they rang rich with understanding and forgiveness. The tension drained out of me as she and Edith headed over to the boatshed.

◇◇

With a far more gentle fire season behind us, a winter spiced but not overloaded with family and friends, the final decisions and gradual acceptance of owning this land and the old stone cottage behind me and warmth of this April day reminding us of approaching summer, the hours now flowed smoothly along. By late afternoon, the golden varnish flowed just as smoothly under my brush to highlight the ebony and tawny swirls of the teak I'd sanded. "I'll get some lemonade and my notebook. Think of anything you need to add to the shopping list," I said as I climbed clear of the boat. When I came back to join Larry, he was seated on a timber pile, Cindy leaning against his leg in anticipation of the dog biscuit she'd come to expect whenever I brought refreshments out to the shed. "Only a watchdog, not a pet," I teased as Larry stroked the dog's silky hair.

"You're the one who takes her running most afternoons and buys her treats," he replied. "But let's get serious. Help me think of what I'll need from the city." Pencil in hand, I prepared for the bombardment of items to add to my ever-present list.

Larry was ready to build the heavy-duty, specially shaped box that would serve as a mold for the lead ballast keel. The next morning, he added still more to the list. "Okay, two sheets of AC plywood, about 200 cheap 2-inch screws, some bondo putty... can't think of anything else right now... wish we had a phone so you could call and check back for things I forgot," he said as I prepared to drive off for a two-day tour that would take me from the dock-lands of Long Beach to the shopping malls of Orange County. "Say hi to Grant for me and drive careful, and get off the freeway if the traffic gets bad."

My last stop before heading back toward the canyon two days later, added a 40-pound ball of fluff to the load. Rommel, a Keeshond of impeccable breeding, was owned by the doctor who had looked after us for years. Grant Gould embodied the essence of sophistication. A physician, professional magician and pianist, he had little interest in sailing or boats. But for some reason, a friendship had blossomed between us as we'd built our first voyaging yacht. We'd kept in touch during our wandering years, and now he was a frequent visitor when we had get-togethers, be they wine and cheese Sundays or big family gatherings in Bull Canyon. "Thanks for taking care of Rommel. I hate the idea of putting him in a kennel for three weeks," Grant said. "I'm looking forward to seeing your progress when I get back. I'll drive out right from the airport.'

"Why not wait and pick him up the Sunday after you return? Larry's going to pour our lead keel that weekend. It'll mean a couple days extra without your dog, but –"

"Something I've never seen, wouldn't miss it."

"You did what?" Larry said as he patted Cindy to restrain and reassure her as Rommel strutted regally in to settle on the beanbag chair near the front room hearth.

"I invited Grant, and while I was staying with Jimmie and Barb, I told them to come along — Barb's bringing a roast turkey, and my folks, Mom's going to bring lots of her eggplant caviar, and of course I told Doug Schmuck, and I mentioned it to the lady who works in the chandlery. I'll get the fixings for hot buttered rum, we can keep it warm with the lead melting fires...Cindy, don't you dare come in this house, get outside where you belong," I snapped, as Larry came into the kitchen with the last bag of groceries and Cindy tried to follow.

"Lin, you can't make a party of everything. Lead pouring is hot, dirty, boring work. You're adding complications –"

"Larry, be sensible. We've got to keep two fires burning and move three and a half tons of lead into the melting tubs. That's a lot of work. Then, there's the fire risk. What if something goes wrong? I want a few people around just in case. Doug already offered to bring two spare fire extinguishers. That means four in all, so we need four people, plus stokers. Besides, everyone's fascinated by the idea, like pouring lead Cowboys and Indians when we were kids. Grant's eyes really lit up when I told him.'

Larry shrugged his shoulders and relaxed. "Hope you aren't planning on feeding everyone. You'll have to scout up more firewood if we run short."

Larry dug a deep trough into the boatyard floor, only an armspan away from the slowly growing wooden hull, then settled the shaped plywood box into place level with the earth around it. Rommel, our apartment-raised, single-parent-pampered guest, established his position of supremacy over both Cindy and Dog. Meanwhile, I had the new challenge of organizing all of the how-to and practical seamanship articles the two of us had written over the previous ten years into a sensible book manuscript. Our editor from Norton, Eric Swenson, was a keen sailor himself, and had been more eager than I about this compilation. I wanted to write the next volume of my *Seraffyn* series, to daydream of our past sailing adventures instead of being so hard-core practical. But pressure from ever-practical Larry, plus the promise of a larger advance from Eric swayed me. All of the final advance money we'd received when the previous manuscript had been accepted was now invested in lead, so the $5000 meant two things — the next several months were financially secure, and I'd become a real writer as now I'd reached the advance figure considered "professional" in *The Writer* magazine. Mornings began stretching into mid-afternoon when I'd force myself to quit so I could gather firewood for the big day. Then I'd put on my boots and take all three animals to rummage along the banks of the gurgling stream for the sycamore limbs shorn off in the winter winds.

That day, Cindy and Rommel played tag and ferret-out-the-rabbit games while I dragged branches to the waiting truck. Then the two pretended to torment Dog, while I unloaded the firewood next to a Volkswagen-sized stack of scrap lead that looked far too big to ever fit into the cavity in the boatshed floor. I laughed out loud as the two dogs went from silly-puppy-mode to watchdog-mode the moment Bob Steele drove up with his monthly tankfull of diesel for our generator. The cat immediately strutted over to wrap itself around Bob's ankles while I snapped a lead chain onto Cindy's collar in an attempt to keep up the ferocious watchdog charade. Rommel looked on the whole affair with disdain, marching off to pick up a well-gnawed bone and carry it into the kitchen.

"Not much of a watchdog, Lin. Looks like some kind of foot-warmer you'd find in a city apartment, something Marlys would probably like," Bob stated. "Whatever you do, don't rave about it to her. How you going to keep the burrs out of that shaggy coat?"

"No worry, just baby-sitting," I answered, as he and Larry took turns pumping fuel. "Come on by this weekend and meet its owner. We'll be melting all this lead down."

"Rather do that than dress up like a monkey to visit Marlys's folks," Bob grumbled. "But I promised. Told her, it's the last time. They want to see us, they can come out here! Bunch of pansies, complain it's not air conditioned. Only reason I'm going, her cousin does real good sign-work. Got to take him the drawings. Have a look — they're in the front seat."

The professional looking drawings Bob had created showed one more interesting facet of our bigger-than-life neighbor. Elegant stone pillars supported a well-proportioned, generous-sized wooden sign:

Welcome to Bull Canyon
No Hunting

The outline of a stomping, head-flinging rampant bull adorned the corner, big and bold as Bob himself.

"Looks great," Larry stated. "You buy some six-inch cedar or redwood; I'll surface it and glue it up. Then we can make Ellie happy with a community building bee and finish up with drinks at her house as soon as you get the carving done."

"We should get it up soon. I think Cook, the electric company guy from Perris, is bringing his supervisor out here in about a month," I said, switching from boatbuilding mode to California land developer. "Might impress him; make him see a future with more potential customers."

"Cook been out here again?" Bob asked. "Have any news?"

"News? Not him," Larry stated. "I think he is paid to work as a professional road block. We're just an excuse for him to get out of the office every Friday afternoon. Likes to waste my time with his newest dozen reasons the power lines can't come out here."

"It'll happen," Bob stated, walking over to the kitchen for the usual cool drinks. "Just got to keep the pressure up. Lin, the builders' supply place on the highway has a special price on screen doors this week. You really need one to keep this silly mutt outside. Got tired of your complaining about flies and bees last summer."

So I stopped in and ordered a screen door when I drove to buy extra wine and supplies for the people I'd invited for the weekend. I wasn't worried about the three-week delivery delay. I'd lived without a screen door for a year and a half, but the thought of a fly-free kitchen occupied my thoughts as I tried to keep pace with the roadrunner that led me across the washouts and rippling creek on my way home into Bull Canyon. But this now familiar bird easily outpaced me as he cut right across the tightest bends.

From the moment the alarm went off at dawn on Saturday, I was glad help was on its way. "Forget the coffee," Larry commanded, "we've got to get those fires going, take an hour or two just to warm the tubs." So I pitched in and shoved firewood and kindling under each of the old cast-iron bath tubs we'd bought for twenty dollars from "Bernie-down-by-the-Tracks." The tubs sat side-by-side mounted a foot above the ground on pedestals of bricks. Lee Newhouse had welded steel elbows with shut-off valves into the drains. A length of galvanized pipe led to the wooden mold which, over the past two weeks, had become Dog's favorite earth-cooled sleeping spot. Meanwhile, Larry arranged rows of metal road signs (we'd found another dozen buried beneath tumble weeds and sage when we cleared the firebreak) to protect the boat, the workbenches and the wooden walls of the shed. As he listed his preparations for the day, I agreed he'd planned for every contingency, agreed he and I could probably have handled it all ourselves, agreed it really was time for breakfast when the first load of friends turned up at ten and took over my job of moving firewood from stack to flames.

Three hours later, when Larry slowed down enough to grab a plateful of salads and turkey from the picnic Mom laid out, he put his arm around me and gave a squeeze. "Thanks, Lin, we couldn't have kept those fires burning if you hadn't invited everyone out here." We stood for a moment watching as fifteen eager friends stoked the fires, carried sixty-pound lumps of lead and eased them into the tubs, then laughed like children when solid metal floated lightly across the shimmering pool of silver that was slowly filling each tub. Larry called another ten directives my way as he handed his empty plate to me. "Better get more cold drinks, rustle up some Band-Aids for Grant. Got any old hot pads we can use later? Couple buckets of water might be good too." By late afternoon, as the last sheet of lead was slid carefully into the almost-full tub to slowly melt down like dabs of butter on hot rum punch, every person, Mom included, sported smudges of soot across frequently mopped foreheads, dirty shirts and weary smiles. Larry skimmed the dross from the top of the two bubbling pools of lead. Then Doug Schmuck made a ceremony of adding thirty pounds of lead wine bottle seals gathered by dozens of waterfront friends from who knows how many shared bottles of wine. "I hereby christen thee a keel to carry forward the tradition of parties with the Pardeys," he intoned.

Larry took his huge wrench and began to open the big outlet tap on the first tub. "Grab the damn cat," he shouted as Dog daintily began to step into the mold, intent on curling up for a nap.

"Grab the fire extinguishers," I yelled, realizing how quickly that 600-degree metal could start a fire if it happened to splash onto any nearby timber. Every one of us stood in awed silence as the first ton and a half of molten lead flowed in a steamy hissing stream of silver. As it hit the cold plywood cavity Larry had settled down into the floor, a huge cloud of green smoke mushroomed toward the open sides of the boatshed.

Larry walked confidently around to position his pipe wrench on the second valve. I didn't see it happen. I only heard the communal gasp. Then I turned to look. Larry had the broken heat-softened handle of the bronze valve at his feet. The handle had twisted right off. Now there was no way to open the valve. The second lot of lead was firmly sealed inside the tub, the fire beneath it beginning to cool as it consumed the very last of the scrap wood we had. Larry's face was a study of stunned panic."Got to get that lead into the mold fast or it will all stratify, ruin the whole thing — four weeks work down the drain. Lin, get metal buckets, shovels..." No one moved except Grant, who I saw running toward his car. Then, Jean, the lady from the marine chandlery who had come out for this "once in a lifetime event, at least in my lifetime," now calmly said, "Can't you make a trough out of those metal signs and just unscrew that pipe? I do that to get water to my horse-trough when I can't find a hose." I am amazed to this day at the cooperation and speedy action that followed. Within minutes Larry yelled, "Stand back. This is either going to work a treat or we'll have a 3200-pound mass of hot lead all over the shop, but here goes." A last twist of the pipe and hot molten metal gushed forth, found its guiding trough and rushed to join the pool just beginning to cool in the mold.

A scream of triumph roared into the sky to mingle with the second mushroom cloud of green-gray smoke that rose a hundred feet into the air.

Lee Newhouse's truck came screeching to a stop at the top of the driveway. I could see the look of concern slide off his face as soon as he saw the contented crowd surveying the still bubbling lead now safely contained in its mold.

"When I saw two huge clouds of smoke and heard screaming and shouting, thought your place had exploded into flames," he said. "Should have remembered you were pouring today. Ma told me there were lots of cars headed up your way. She saw Jimmie and Barb's truck, your folks, and some others she'd noticed head up here before. Kind of wish she had more company out here."

"Why didn't you bring her up here today?" I asked. "I dropped in last week and said come by."

"Na, you got lots of yer own friends. I've seen lots of hot metal before. She needs to have more of her own kin around. Almost be worth paying for electricity if it would get the kids out here more often."

I thought of his words while I worked alongside my mother to heat up hot chocolate and lay out an array of desserts as the cool of evening set in. Rommel trotted in for what I knew would be the last time this year and without even looking, I yelled, "Cindy, stay outside."

"You really should get a screen door," Mom scolded for the fifth time that fast-paced day. Now that I actually had time to slow down and relax I should have told her of the door I had on order. Instead, I found myself snapping back, "Don't need one."

"You really do need one. I'll pay for it as a gift to celebrate you owning this place. I'm so glad you've got a home you can call your own, even if it is only half yours. But you really need a screen to keep out the flies this summer."

"Mom, this is not our home. It's a good investment. You just helped us build one more part of our real home. I don't want a screen door, a picket fence, a rose garden! I want a boat, adventures, faraway places," I stated firmly.

In the silence that followed I wondered how I'd reverted to the rebellious fourteen-year-old who refused to like the blue dress my Mom pointed out as we shopped together, just because she had seen it first? Back then I had felt like she was always making decisions for me instead of letting me grow up. Now I was grown up. Or at least I thought I was. So my only excuse for my snippy reaction was the stream of demands Larry had made since early morning, the emotional stress of a near catastrophe, the exhaustion and excitement of the long but fulfilling day. But I didn't have the slightest inclination to smooth the situation over.

"Guess Dad and I will just have to enjoy knowing that you two are going to be around for another year. It's really been fun today. I like your friends, but glad Rommel's not staying. Not fair to Cindy."

I felt like a real crumb as she brushed off my rude words. "Hey, Mom, we'll be around a lot longer than a year. Probably two more to finish the boat now we don't have to worry about the three-year-lease we originally asked for. Then there will be sea trials. You'll be tired of us by the time we finally set sail again."

Any awkwardness was buried in a deluge of camaraderie as the whole lead-pouring crew came in to devour the succulent apricot pies, the rich creamy brownies and big tub of mocha almond fudge ice cream we'd set out.

"Hey, Grant," Barbara asked, "Why'd you rush out to your car when Larry broke that valve off?"

"Went for my emergency oxygen gear. Never seen a man look closer to a heart attack in my life. What a day," Grant answered. His words were echoed by each of our weary friends as they drove off. Then, as Mom climbed into the car to leave, she added, "Remember, I'll pay for a screen door. Just get one next time you go to town."

Later, as we crawled into bed, Larry spoke up. "Say I told you so. You deserve to. Would have been nearly impossible without our friends. What was your Mom talking about?"

"Nothing," was all I said. And I said nothing, either, about the insanity that led me to drive into town the next day, haunted and taunted by the image of my defiant fourteen-year-old self as I cancelled my order for the screen door I knew I really should have.

Chapter 15

Changing Times

"Ruby, don't take your love to town," Larry sang as he loaded three bags of dirty laundry into the truck. I laughed and joined in on the next line of lyrics as I added my box of letters to be mailed, papers to be copied.

"Pick up some of those burritos Mariano's friend makes," Larry called as I backed out. "Get some ice cream, too. Then you won't have to cook anything when you get home."

As soon as I drove clear of the narrows and bumped across the summer-dried streambed to burst free of the hills which blocked every station but "WHWB, country music from Riverside — home of Don Williams," I punched the buttons to pick up an all-news station from L.A. and re-connect with the outside world. "Heavy congestion on the 5, stalled truck in center lane north of Wilshire exit. 805 South, accident in lane two," the radio intoned, highlighting the hassles facing early morning commuters in the cities to the north as I drove onto the sleepy streets of Lake Elsinore.

Tuesday, my day in town, had by now settled into a soul-soothing routine. A quick chat with Elena, the laundromat manager, then a stop for Mexican sweet cakes at the fruit stand run by her family, a hello to Glen who had a tray with hot tea ready and waiting for me at the café next to my ersatz "in-town" office.

"How are things going in the outback," Jean would invariably ask as she opened the door of the music shop for me, then went to clear a space among the crystal punchbowls, silk floral arrangements and wedding cake decorations. We'd share the tea and hot fresh cookies along with our weekly stories. Then I'd settle in to begin whittling down my list of calls, ordering a never-ending array of nuts, bolts, sealants, arranging rendezvous with friends, talking with magazine editors who had grudgingly grown to accept the limitations of our phone-less state.

Halfway through the list I'd take a break and stroll "across town" five blocks to where I hoped our post office box would be crammed with letters from faraway friends plus a check or two from magazine editors. Then, a stop at the local bank for cash to begin a round of shopping interrupted with telephone breaks at my bridal-arch dominated home base.

When I looked back at my introduction to this small town, I realized two things helped me quickly overcome the normal reticence of the local shopkeepers: the good fortune of meeting Jean and her son Larry, and my decision to do as much business as possible right in Elsinore. After only a dozen or so "days in town," I had found my walk broken into short chunks, as I felt compelled to open a dozen different shop doors and call in, "Don't have anything on my list from your place today — how things going?"

"Wish more of the folks living out in the hills shopped here," Richard, owner of the local lumber-cum-hardware-cum-garden-supply yard had griped soon after we first met. "They bank in Corona on their way home from work, so they do their shopping in Corona. Only come in here for a few screws or some bug spray on a Saturday morning. They're hurting this town."

There were times when I was tempted to drive "out beyond the valley," too. I'd search the aisles of the old Alamo supermarket for such "up-market" items as cheddar cheese and find my choice limited to American cheese. I'd look in vain for French style mustard, dill weed, or green peppercorns amid eleven varieties of powdered chili peppers, or brussels sprouts among the limited choice in the dimly-lit fresh vegetable section. But, the sheer personality of the small town shops and offices captivated me. "Miss Pardey, you don't have to fill in all those account numbers," the teller at the locally-owned bank would say. "You've got too much to do in one day. I'll write them in for you. Usually do it all by name anyway." But a few weeks later she and then the manager refused to accept a check from a British bank, saying "Never seen nothing like this. Well, if you insist, you can leave it here until the owner comes in on Friday — I'll see if he thinks it's real money." Then I came to appreciate why so few newcomers banked there.

When the floods of our first winter washed away the highway bridge

north of town and cut off the only road leading between Corona and San Diego, politicians in the fast-growing towns of Temecula and Canyon Lake, south of Elsinore, forced the State highway department to forge ahead with plans for a proper freeway. Ahead of it came far-sighted developers who gave free land to a larger banking group and and also to a big-brand supermarket chain right next to where they planned to build an off-ramp, three miles beyond Main Street. Even after these things were built, loyalty kept me tied to the old town bank, loyalty secured by Dave, the local sheriff.

"Looks really good up here," he'd called as he and his partner drove in to our yard late one Friday. "Can't stay for coffee, but Janet down at the bank knew I patrolled this road. Said to stop in and tell ya, your account's overdrawn."

I rushed into town Monday morning. "Dave shouldn't have worried you. Was supposed to tell you to drop in on your regular day. We wouldn't bounce any of your checks, just wanted to warn you, so you wouldn't spend too much over the weekend."

The only thing that kept me tied to the old post office next to the fire department was that I had no other choice. "Rules say you can get general delivery for thirty days. You've used that up," the postmaster warned a month after we moved to the canyon.

"No problem, here's my application for a post-office box," I replied.

"Can't give you one, aren't any addresses up that canyon. Against the law to set up boxes unless you've got a physical address," he snapped.

"Then you'll have to let me use general delivery!" I stated.

"Nope. I'll give you five days extra, but after that we'll return all mail to sender."

Jean was sympathetic when I went back to use the phone again, but commented, "Lin, you know jobs are scarce out here. Post office folks have some of the best-paying secure ones. They can't risk giving out a box to someone who might be fencing stolen stuff or running illegal immigrants or growing pot. It's all been done out in those hills. You could get your mail sent here."

But I was tired of having my mail addressed "care of," tired of waiting for someone else to open their shop. I wanted to pick up my mail at my convenience. By the time I had the truck laden with groceries, my cooler filled with ice cream and other frozen treats, and the seat next to me covered with the clean, folded laundry topped with hot, scrumptious smelling burritos, I was furious. "I finally come home to my own country and I get treated like a crook!" I blasted at Larry the minute I drove in. "I'm an American and it's my right to receive my mail."

"Calm down and think about what Jean said," Larry commented, as he tried to counter my anger with logic. "The little guys can't bend the rules, so go back to town tomorrow and call someone higher up."

"'Phone calls cost money, trips to town take time."

"Mail returned to sender costs money and time, too," he stated, giving me a hug.

So the next day I retraced my steps, dug through the county-wide phone directory and five calls later reached the secretary for the head of the U.S. Post Office for all of California. "I will not be treated like a potential crook. If your boss doesn't solve this problem, I'm going to write every senator in California."

On my next visit to the Post Office, I was handed a formal letter: "To finalize your special exemption, please list three references. I have instructed my employees to issue you a post office box today," signed Postmaster General, California district.

"It's a hick town and no matter what anyone says, I know it's never going to change," Pete Shomler stated when I told him of my post office woes. "That's why I like it. Not much to tempt Sandy. Get's more done out here cause she isn't interested in going into town."

But within a few months of our arrival, I began to notice small but definite signs of change in Lake Elsinore. During the heat of our first canyon summer, we had driven down to the north end of the lake past the scruffy but busy No-Tel Motel, to the air conditioned Pantry Café, where home cooking really was a lot like the best Mom could do. "Did you see those signs on the highway?" our favorite waitress asked. "Can you believe anyone would build four hundred new homes, then say you can buy one for only five percent down out here? Who's going to buy them. Where they gonna work?"

"Maybe developers have run out of cheap land everywhere else in California," Larry said. "Lots of cheap land around here."

"Cheap," Patty snorted. "Stuff's been going for cost of back taxes for the past ten years. I think those signs are an attempt to con someone into buying that useless old walnut grove."

As Larry and I drove back past five miles of mostly empty land between her café and the dirt road leading to the canyon, I asked, "You think anyone wants to own their own home bad enough to drive for an hour or more to get to work? Prices on that sign are half what they're asking in Corona, but..."

I asked Jimmie Moore the same thing when he came out a few weeks later. "The freeway's coming," he answered. "I saw survey marks alongside the road outside Corona. Only be a twenty-five minute drive then. Probably should be looking at land in the valley before they survey the route out here. Wish I knew exactly where they're going to put that freeway."

The town folks began to worry as big machinery arrived to level the old walnut grove and half-a-dozen other developers staked out plots of land for "Your dream of country living, three beds, two baths, only $1,000 down." Then, as a second lot of machines began to scrape the flat land south of the lake, five miles from the first slowly growing development, workers flooded into the laconic local trailer camps to create a mini-boom in the shops along Main Street. Jean glowed as her music sales, bridal and party gear rentals soared. But when the first survey marks showed the freeway leading well away from the lake and a sign went up three miles past Main Street near the new bank proclaiming, "Site of New Sav-On Drugs, Shops Available," Jean, like most of the shop owners I spoke with, began to feel uneasy.

A week later a sign went up right where our road, El Toro, left the two-lane highway: "Thirty acres flat land, perfect for future homes." Jimmie and Barbara arrived to say, "We're staying for a few days. Probably put a deposit on some lots near the lake. You two should do it, too. Anyone with spare cash would be a fool to leave it sitting in the bank getting eaten up by inflation. Even if you take the conservative route, buy another piece of land up here before folks believe you'll get electricity and phones in, you'll double or triple your money, especially with the new freeway."

By the end of that second summer, there was no denying — change was coming ever closer to our stone cottage. A seven-foot-high wood and stone replica of Bob Steele's elegant drawings now graced a patch of weeds alongside the corrugated dirt road three miles south of us to announce, "Welcome to Bull Canyon, private property, no hunting." Then Margie moved into Uncle John's cabin, two miles north of us.

The tidy but tiny two-room wooden cabin sat on a narrow sliver of land right at the crossroads. According to Ellie, Old Man Payonessa had given his work-mate this land as a gift because he played a good hand of poker. "John only got up here a few weeks every year, but sure made a good foursome when he got stuck by the rains. Died two years back. Hear he left the place to some niece. Wonder if she'll even come out here to look at it."

I learned that the niece not only came to look at the cabin, but was planning to move in full time the same way I learned most of the canyon news. Bob Steele drove in. "Can you believe it, damn fool butterball of a girl thinks she's gonna be a truck driver. When I went in to get paid for 'dozer work at the county offices, they wanted to know if this silly broad lived up here. Must be hard up to consider hiring a girl to drive a dump truck."

"I knew they'd be pretty hard up for drivers with all those tract homes and the highway comin' in," Margie told me when I drove up the road, using some bread I had just finished baking as an excuse to welcome her to the canyon. "Figure all the experienced drivers would desert the county and go for higher paying jobs with outside contractors." She went on to tell me how she'd grown tired of her waitress jobs when she was less than two years out of high school. So she'd taken a night course on truck driving at a local college. "Always wanted to drive a big truck. Got my license the day I turned twenty-one, and tried getting a job all over Orange and Riverside County. They all laughed at me, no experience, no job; no job, no union membership; no union card, no job. But I know they really meant 'no jobs for girls.' Now I've got my foot in the door and I'm keeping it there. Don't need real high pay 'cause I can live up here for free." She proudly showed me the tiny row of geraniums she'd planted to liven up the eucalyptus-shaded patch of bare earth surrounding her new home. "Guy from work said he'd come up next week and help me put a fence in so I can get a puppy to keep me company."

"A puppy," Sandy Shomler snorted when I drove up to get another signature on another set of papers. "She should get a pack of hounds to protect her from the dirt-bag bikers that roar around up there. She's only a few feet from the crossroads. Nothing hides her place from everyone's view. In fact, I'll go down and take her one of my spare pistols. Show her how to use it. Then those bastards will be sure to leave her alone. Pete says she looks like a chubby-cheeked kid, but still good enough to excite some of those idiots. Wonder if she needs some curtains. I've got lots of lace and trim left over from mine." Sandy proudly led me around the newest roofed-in room inside the stone walls of her slowly growing home. Calico curtains covered each window, matching covers hid the ratty cushions of Pedlars Village overstuffed chairs.

"Soon's Pete gets Larry to cut some more of those beams he found at the village, we can roof in the back rooms. Then when you get the phones in, Pete's got a great idea to make money out here."

Pete elaborated on his scheme when he came down to our boatshed with his rough timbers. "Start a war games park. City types can come up here, I'll break them into two teams and give them air guns with paint pellets and set them loose at both ends of the property. Let them hunt each other down. I'll organize them, Sandy can feed them, kids can wait on them and clean up their rooms. Be good money, entry fees, ammunition, food, beds, beer."

"I'd worry about them getting a bit rough and rowdy," I remarked.

"Nope, be too tired. And if they get out of hand, Sandy'll just let Mike loose on them." I couldn't help but agree as I remembered the size, the threatening bark of their bull mastiff watchdog.

"Glad you got that big saw here, saved me lots of cash," Pete said as he loaded his newest roof beams onto his tiny truck

A few days later, when the summer sun dropped behind the far hills to bring the canyon temperatures down twenty degrees, I convinced Larry to set aside his tools a few minutes early. "Come on," I urged. "We owe Bob for the last diesel delivery, want to pay him."

"Could wait for him to drop in, but I know you," he teased as we began walking up the steep winding road, "You just want to see if he's got anything done up there."

It had been almost four months since our last foray up the hill and for once, the changes that met our eyes were as expansive as the gestures Bob used to point them out. "Still have to live in that damn trailer," Marlys complained. "No plumbing in the new house. It hasn't even got any walls inside."

"Don't want walls. Want a big expansive feeling," Bob stated as he spread his arms to emphasis the vastness of the one-roomed solid stone house that encompassed over three-thousand square feet of stone flooring. Huge wooden beams supported a shingle roof, long eaves shaded the square spaces where oversized windows would some day be installed to frame stunning vistas of rock-strewn, brush covered hills and shadow filled canyons.

"Not going to live in here and sweat all summer, freeze all winter. Need some walls, at least for the bedrooms," Marlys stated.

"Won't be a problem. Lin and I are going to get the electricity up here soon. Ever heard of air conditioning?" Bob retorted.

"Who's going to pay for it? You're too busy movin' hills up here to go out and make money. I'm maxed out on all my credit cards."

"Moving hills to make some real money," Bob stated. "You want to get rid of your credit card bills, give me a blow job and I'll pay them all off," he called over his shoulder as he led us off for a tour of his land development scheme.

A web of roads now wandered across his 260 acres of land. "Got ten really good house sites staked out already," Bob told us. "I figure those town folks have got about as much imagination as Marlys, but if I show them my house, show them a ready-to-go building pad, electric pole right there, telephone outlet, give them a dream. Then they can bring a house-trailer up here to use on weekends and I'll contract to build them a home to match mine." Looking back across the rocky hills, his enormous stone creation did look impressive, with its bold roof that soared across the wide dirt area that would some day be a three-car-wide shaded entry. And the views from each potential site would be great; that is, if you ignored the green slime-covered puddles that graced the bottoms of seven deep pits Bob grandly described as lakes in his sales pitch to us.

"Who's going to pay for all the electric lines, the phone lines," I asked.

"Bank," was Bob's quick answer. "Soon's electricity gets here, I get my house finished. It'll be collateral, it and all this land. Get a building loan and pay it off from the income I'll get when I sell these sites."

"He might just pull it all off," Larry commented as we walked back to our stone cottage nestled in its tree-protected canyon. "Too bad he can't go easier on Marlys, get her involved, too." Dog purred and strutted beside us. When I bent to unhook Cindy from the chain that kept her from following us, I said, "Everyone's sure depending on the electricity coming in. Not sure it's going to happen. I don't feel Bob and I are one inch closer than we were four months ago. I'm not even sure I want it up here. It definitely would change things."

"Change is a fact of life." Larry answered. "Better to grab hold and be a part of it, try to make it happen so it suits you. Resist and you could get run over."

That second summer, the brutal midday heat bore in with more force than ever. The humidity, even at night, dropped to the point that I put lotion on five or six times a day to keep my skin from feeling like over-stretched parchment. Even the outer leaves on all the trees around us lost their resilience and turned a dull, dead gray as the glaring sun and scorching wind sucked away their moisture. Larry watched as the planking he was fitting to the framework of the boat began to dry and shrink until his perfect fits showed lines of light at each seam. Finally he made up a new shopping list for me, and within a few days the shop again had walls — heavy clear plastic replacing the plywood he'd cut away only a year before to let the breeze blow in. A huge, secondhand industrial swamp-cooler graced one

end of the shed. A hose dripped slowly all day long to wet the dirt beneath the towering framework. The humidity inside the shed rose enough to stabilize the hard teak timbers that Larry worked into long thin boards, and then riveted onto black locust wood frames with copper nails.

I'd spend each afternoon sanding the newest pieces of fresh wood he'd finished, scouting out any of his leftover pencil markings, any cross-grain scratches he'd missed and smoothing them away with sandpaper before laying on the first coat of varnish. My concentration cut off the constant roar of the generator, the whir of the fans that brought the temperatures down to where I could enjoy my work if I did it clad only in a pair of bikini bottoms. My concentration also cut off the sound of an approaching truck. It was only when Larry pulled open the small side door of the shed that I realized the Newhouses had come to check their beehives and collect the sawdust and wood shavings from around the machinery. They did such a fine job of acting that I thought I'd gone unnoticed as I snuck out the back door of the shed, a pair of work gloves hiding my naked top.

"Ma Newhouse wants to know where she can buy a glove-shaped bikini for her daughter," Bob called when he drove in with another tank full of diesel late that week. "You seen Margy, our dump-truck driver lately?"

Larry laughed as he recalled Margie's recently acquired pack of dogs preceding her up our driveway at five that morning. They had become such a familiar sight they barely raised more than a welcoming bark from Cindy. "She came walking down here for the third time this month, flat battery. Had to drive up and jump start her car. I'd be ticked off, but she's really trying to make a go of it. Says she'll be able to afford a new battery when she gets her next pay check."

"You and the road-crew manager, giving her slack 'cause she's a girl. I think he's got the hots for Margie," Bob stated.

"Not going to do him much good," I added as I filled tall glasses with ice and lemonade. "Margie made it clear she's planning to stay single, less complicated for a truck driver. She says if we ever get phones up here she's going to start looking for work on an eighteen-wheeler, doesn't want romantic connections to get in the way."

Margie's early morning intrusions were only a small inconvenience because the 110-degree midday temperatures had forced us to change our working schedule. Now we set the alarm so we were up before dawn to revel in the last soothing night breezes. As soon as light filled the canyon, I shut every window in the house and lowered every shade except for the one behind my office chair. Then we both set to work until the glare of the midday sun hammered Larry into a slippery mass of sweat. Just before noon I'd hear the kitchen door open, the shower start up and Larry groan with relief as the cold water washed over him.

I'd switch on the window-mounted air conditioner Jimmie and Barbara had loaned us and listen carefully as the generator took on this latest load through the 300-foot long extension cord that snaked from the cottage to the boatshed. If it staggered and shut down, Larry would have to go back out into the blazing sun to restart the boatyard humidifiers that were far more important to our long-term project than a few hours of coolness.

Then the two of us would lie together in the relative coolness of the stone-surrounded room. If the air conditioner managed to override the heat of the pounding sun, we'd savor the intimacy of a shared siesta. Refreshed by the break in our day, we'd usually talk of the projects we were working on, the schemes we had planned, the problems we saw looming as we waited for the sun to drop behind the steep hills on the other side of the stream. Then, refreshed and focused, we'd return to work for a few hours more stopping only when the late twilight of summer called an end to our working day.

When I look back at afternoons like these, I realize our marriage has always had one distinct difference from the norm. Because we set our own daily rhythms, we'd usually had the time to discuss fears and concerns, to encourage whoever was feeling overworked, snowed under, frustrated. More often than not, one or the other of us came up with a new tack to pursue or turned these sessions into a morale-boosting pep talk.

"Larry, I'm wasting my time with the electricity. Now it's too hot for Cook to drive out here, Bob goes by the electric company offices every week and still gets the runaround. You know — 'We're working on it. You are on the list; need another paper for the right of ways.' Don't you think it would be better if I used the time to write a few extra articles so we can buy a bigger generator?" I said, as we lay on the sweat-dampened cover and listened to the inadequate whir of the air conditioner. "And the telephones — every time I call the Perris office, they say, 'No right of ways up past the cross roads and not enough users to justify the line cost.' They aren't even bound by the utilities commission. We'll never get phones up here but everyone in the canyon is talking like they are depending on me to get them."

"Don't quit now, pumpkin," Larry answered. "I think it's time you forgot about waiting for someone else to get something moving. I think Bob's gotten a bit bored with the whole idea. We always seem to get more done when we get on with it ourselves. I've been thinking about that hassle you had with the post office. Maybe the Perris office is a road block. Maybe you should switch into over drive, drive right over the local guys' heads and go to the top."

"Easy to say, Larry, but really hard without a phone. No one's ever in when I call them. Secretary says leave a number, they'll call you back."

"If it was easy, everyone would be doing it," Larry answered. "Why don't you fight for the phones first, then you can go after the electric company more easily," he suggested as he headed for the shower.

I tried to settle the responsibility for getting through to the right phone company person more comfortably on my shoulders as I dressed to join him and push for a few hours more progress out in the boatshed now the sun had fallen behind the sheltering hills.

His words echoed in the back of my mind each week when I drove into town. As the relentless heat gave way to the shorter days of autumn, the freeway crept ever closer to the valley, and more housing tract signs began to spring up, even before the foundations for the first were a reality.

"If you get a phone up there, be no reason for you to come in here," Jean commented as we shared our ritual Tuesday morning Mexican pastries and town gossip. "You're doing most of your shopping over at the new supermarket. You've finally switched to the new bank like most of us. No reason to come to Main Street. The town's already starting to fade; toy shop's closing down next month."

"That won't happen. I have to come for my mail, and my weekly guitar lesson," I said. But I knew she was probably right. Now the path of the freeway was clearly delineated, it would route me and everyone else clear of Main Street directly to the next off-ramp decorated with glaring, towering signs of the new cut-rate gas stations next to the fancy 24-hour laundromat, complete with electronic pinball machines. Soon I'd be able to shop and do my laundry in the evenings and save a whole day of my working week if I could only get those phones in.

I was so occupied with my thoughts I almost walked right into Dave, the sheriff. "Hey, Lin, seen your neighbor lately? Margie's caused a bit of an upset at the town maintenance department," Dave said. "How about you keep an eye on her. She's pretty isolated, you know."

"What are your worrying about?" I asked. "Margie's definitely independent."

"Yup, that's what her boyfriend says. It's made him really unhappy. Just check in on her when you can."

I had barely digested this when Glenn, one of the local firemen called, "Been wanting to talk to you. Chief and I were assessing the situation around here. Another high-risk fire season coming and your side of the canyon's got heavy growth. Besides, that boat of yours is becoming pretty valuable — hate to see it go up in flames. Got any plans?"

"Mariano and his brother are already up there clearing our firebreak. We won't leave the place unattended till it rains. We'll keep the water tanks topped up," I answered.

"Sure wish someone had phones up there. Could give us an early warning if a fire did get started."

It was late afternoon when I drove past Pedlars Village on my way back toward the canyon. Jerry's highly-polished, chrome-decorated pickup truck sat next to the entry booth in the center of the vast empty parking lot. On impulse I drove in. "Jerry, do you think any of the folks here have some extra long lengths of hose going cheap? Fire season's coming up."

"I'll ask around," he answered. "Might be a real problem this year. Soon's that highway's in, it'll bring lots of city types out looking for dirt roads to play cowboy and Indians. They'll go up your canyon shooting rabbits, throwing cigarette butts out their windows. You got phones up there yet? Be a good idea to figure out some way to call out if you need help."

He glanced past the shanty homes of his vendors toward the far edge

of his land, where bulldozers had begun scraping and leveling alongside the marching rows of highway survey marks. "Freeway's gonna change everything around here," Jerry stated. "Gonna make a few people real rich when it comes in, gonna make a lotta folks unhappy."

"That's all I'm hearing today. Can't be that drastic," I said.

"Look at this place, Lin. Soon's Riverside officials can drive past and really look at it, they'll see a hundred reasons to shut me down — bad sewage, no fire lanes, illegal occupants. I'll probably sell the land to some shopping mall developer and make a bundle. But going to be real hard on my people. They'll lose their businesses, their homes, their whole way a doin' things. But that's change, can't stop it. Have a nice day and howdy to your man."

The quiet, unchanging hills of the canyon closed around me as I drove past our cottage to check on Margie.

"Word got to you too," she stated matter-of-factly. "Want something cool to drink?"

"Thanks, but I've got groceries in the back. Just stopped for a minute. Dave, the sheriff down in Elsinore told me he was worried — something about your boyfriend."

"Just because he's good enough to sleep with, good enough to go dancing, doesn't mean he's good enough to raise my child," Margie stated. "No law can make me marry him. I want this kid but sure as hell don't want a man to take care of, too."

Now I finally understood Dave's cryptic comments. A pregnant single woman alone in an isolated canyon cabin could present a problem for him. I found the thought a bit worrisome, too.

"Have to admire her determination," Larry said as he helped me carry groceries into the kitchen. "She seems to have it all worked out, secure job, babysitters organized. She might be the key to the phones, too. Didn't the vice-president of the phone company say you had to prove phones were vital. There's Margie, the fire department, Jerry's concerns. Maybe that highway coming in can do us some good. Nice to have phones to organize a whiskey plank party."

I sensed he was right. I now had the tools to lever change into this quiet, forgotten canyon. But as I stored away the last of my shopping, I recalled my stop at Pedlars Village where Jerry had lamented, "Gonna change everything around here. Gonna make a few people rich and a lot unhappy." Then I wondered which description would fit Larry and me a year or two down the line.

Chapter 16

Celebration

"Lin, you just want an excuse to throw a party," Bob Steele protested when he and I stopped at the Lone Palm Ranch on our way home from Perris.

"I think Lin is right," Ellie rejoined. "We have to get those officials every signature they asked for. Only way to get to folks to sign papers is throw another party. Good music, good beer. We've got the money in our fighting fund, should use it. Sounds like that lady from the phone company is on our side."

"That lady was a stooge," Bob snapped. "She's not going to do a thing for us."

Larry shared my more optimistic view when I reached home and described the latest meeting with the telephone and electric company people.

"El Toro Road was built wherever it was easiest, not exactly along that line on your maps," we'd been told by the cabal of electric company officials as we sat, Bob on the opposite side of the long conference table, the officials at the far end. "Never been surveyed. Road could be half a mile away from where it's drawn. Be a real mess if we put our lines in, then someone came along and proved our poles weren't on the right property. You need to get us signed right-of-ways from everyone in that canyon."

A disheveled, grey haired woman slid quietly into the seat next to me. "Sorry," she said. "Got sent out from the main telephone office in Riverside. Drive was longer than I expected. Perris is a pretty isolated place."

"This place isn't isolated; it's almost downtown compared to our canyon," I blurted out. "That's why we're trying to get phones in!" Bob's glowering look made me feel I'd been too aggressive. But when he and the other men began busily thumbing through the stack of papers, the newcomer quietly said to me, "You sound a bit angry."

"I've got a pregnant 21-year-old living by herself a mile up the canyon, four prize-winning show horses at a property a mile past there. My life's fortune is tied up in tons of boat building timber right in the middle of a brushfire prone area. Fire department says risk is higher than they've ever seen before. To call the fire guys, I have to drive five miles down a twisting dirt road to a payphone that doesn't work half the time. Floods washed our road away last year. We had to hike three miles to get out to our truck for almost three months because we couldn't phone every day and remind the county we had no road. That's isolation!"

"Reason I'm here is our local rep said you guys really need phones," she countered. "If only we could bring a line from Santa Rosa Mine Road, we could use it to connect up some orange grove owners who've been pestering us for years. Has your group looked at right-of-ways across the hills toward Riverside?"

As we drove back toward Bull Canyon, Bob commented, "Mr. Cook says if we get the right-of-ways down the canyon, Electric Company is obligated to give us power even if they lose money. Law says so." Then he added, "Waste of time looking for a route toward Riverside. No law controls the Phone Company, so they can do what they want."

Another month and another Bull Canyon Association barbecue had passed with no progress even though Mr. Cook drove up our track every Friday afternoon to tell us, "We're processing the paperwork." And every time he left, Larry would repeat, "There he goes, stalling us again, wasting my time just because he wants an excuse to get out of his office and go for a drive in the country."

"Get the telephone first, then you can use it to push for electricity." Larry's words broke through my thoughts each time I added to my calls-to-make-when-I-go-to-town list. With his encouragement, I decided to forge ahead without Bob Steele's help. Armed with maps and signed documents from the barbecue, I headed up El Toro Road towards the ramshackle house at Hecks Horse Ranch.

"Come on in. Shove that horse outta your way," Virginia called from the back room of her cottage. "Throw the plastic off the couch and sit down. Only be a minute."

"No problem. It's better to use the kitchen table," I answered as I crossed the straw-strewn canvas that covered the pine floor of the front room. "I need to spread out these property maps."

"Move back, that's a good girl," Virginia crooned as she shoved past her dappled grey mare to join me. "Here, let me wipe those damn horse hairs off the table. I've spent almost two days grooming her for the weekend show. Got to keep her inside. Let her out in the field this time of year and she'd have her tail full of burrs in no time. Be glad when we get a new barn built. Now what you got?"

I showed her the papers I'd brought. Virginia couldn't contain her glee. "Eureka! I mean really, really Eureka!" she yelled even before we'd exhausted the pile of new permissions we'd gathered. "Look here — this section touches the north corner of my property and my land connects with the land owned by that guy who gave the phone company a huge deposit four years ago. Run a line from here, across to here, do a small jog and we've got their continuous right of way from Ellie's Lone Palm right to Santa Rosa Road. Now you can go into Riverside and get the phone company moving."

By the time Virginia led me and her mare out onto the bleached grey wood of the verandah, the late September sun had begun its descent to paint the hills below us in golden hues. I drove slowly down the canyon, mentally rearranging my week, listing the shopping I could get done in the grand metropolis of Riverside when I carried my treasure trove of paperwork to the lady at the phone company the next day. As I passed the chain-link fence that now defined Margie's bare, carefully swept patch of land, I laughed at the changes this canyon had wrought in me; my acceptance of my neighbors' housekeeping standards, my comfort with the rhythms of life in an isolated country cottage, my growing confidence in my writing skills and my growing ability to put up with the constant intrusions that thrust their way into my "tidy little plans."

I pulled to a stop at the open door of the boatshed. Larry, his back to me, was working on a long plank, which was firmly secured to his shop-length workbench. The growl of the generator and the whirr of the swamp cooler fan hid the noise of my arrival, so I could sit quietly for a few moments to admire his dance-like movements, the sweeping strokes of his wood plane as he sidestepped smoothly down the length of the shop, then a swaying bend to sight along the smooth curve of the newest plank he was shaping. Each curled shaving of teak that fell represented progress which had slowly begun to affect me and my attitudes toward this sometimes magical-feeling canyon. Now that I could actually climb inside the hull of the vessel that would some day carry us across another ocean, I began to have glimpses of a future when I, too, would, as Larry and Jimmie both did, see the twenty-five acres we lived on not as a lovely safe haven but as, "a damned good investment, especially if we can get the power and phones up here."

I didn't disturb Larry but carried on to the house to try to get in one more hour of work on the piles of paper that Larry constantly assured me were just as important to our goals as the carefully shaped pieces of timber he was creating.

"We're going to need extra screws for the transom planking. Probably pay to order the ones for the deck and interior, too. Might get a quantity discount," Larry said about a week later. Habit, honed by the long, hot summer, had brought us both awake before the autumn dawn. Now that we no longer needed to rush to catch the coolest part of the day and then divide our working hours by taking a midday siesta, we could linger in bed and watch the September sunlight creep slowly over the hills. I had been waiting for a time like this, when we were both fresh and alert but unrushed, and Larry's latest materials requisition list gave me the opening I needed.

"Larry, we've got to hold off on buying too much this month. Not sure I'll have this book done for a while. So we can't count on the advance money to live on."

"Come on, Lin, you've never missed a deadline yet. And if we run low on money I'll stop work on the boat for a few weeks and take some outside jobs. My friend Sloan hinted he could use my help fixing some spar damage on his schooner. Relax. Things are going great! What's the worry?"

What is the worry? I asked myself later as I poured another cup of tea and gathered the notes I'd scribbled at our morning conference. But my feet seemed reluctant to walk thirty feet from the kitchen counter to my oversized desk, piled with "important" papers. My mind seemed to flit from responsibility to responsibility — get the telephone sign-up papers organized and ready to deliver, write another chapter, make a list of screws and bolts for Larry, edit the last chapter, add three more calls to my phone list, six items to the general shopping list, re-type the chapter I edited last week, write another letter to the public utilities commission complaining about the hold-ups at the Southern California Edison Company.

I knew Larry was right. Boat repair jobs were readily available for him outside the canyon. But each day he took to drive down to the coast just to earn money meant one more delay on his part of our boatbuilding project. To build something this big, this intricate, requires continuing enthusiasm, an enthusiasm that is difficult enough to keep up for three or four years, let alone five or six. I'd seen unfinished boats and the broken dreams they represented lying abandoned in storage yards up and down the coast, boats that didn't get built because their owners optimistically underestimated the time involved. They slowly lost interest, or ended up deserted by their partner as seven or eight years slid past and the possibility of setting off sailing grew ever more distant. It had been my idea to ensure our project kept moving by financing our daily expenditures with my writing. I was the one who was pressuring me, and I carried this pressure along with all my other thoughts across to the desk, sat down, carefully arranged my cup of tea, my pens, my footstool and stared at the blank writing pad I positioned front and center before bed every evening, to await each new writing day.

A bird flitted from garden pot to garden pot just outside my window. My glance flitted from paper stack to paper stack along the edges of my desk. Each stack seemed more urgent, more interesting, more accessible than the blank pad I studiously avoided. "Anything and everything is an excuse to avoid writing. Only reason I get anything done is I need the money," a magazine editor once told me.

Though the money my stories earned was affirming and very useful, seeing the ideas that had formed in my mind laid out in black and white had always been the reward that spurred me on. Up until this time, whenever I picked up my pen, eight hundred or a thousand words seemed to almost magically appear on paper, be it while I was standing a night watch at sea, waiting for my clothes to dry in a laundromat in some Latin port, or over the past months in the canyon, sitting in this same quiet corner. I had a list of dozens of good story ideas. Larry was so absolutely confident in my ability to transfer these ideas onto paper. I didn't want to disappoint him, almost as much as I didn't want to disappoint myself. Yet on this morning, my mind refused to block out the intrusions that could easily be dealt with later in the day. I finally wrote "Outline" at the top of the page. Then I got up and tried a new tack. I removed every stack of "things that should be attended to" papers from my desk and set each stack in a row on the floor against the wall where I could no longer see it. Now my almost blank pad looked even lonelier.

I got up and strolled to the kitchen to pour a fresh cup of tea. Through the kitchen window I could see Larry at work cutting into another chunk of timber to shape it into one more perfectly finished piece of the giant jigsaw that would become our boat. I envied him at that moment. He had a definite blueprint to work from. No one had drawn up a plan for me. I had to scour my imagination and come up with something to put down on my outline before I could begin to gather the bits I needed to construct the story that would follow.

I finally shoved the pad aside and picked up the work I'd done the day before and began to smooth out sentences written in a mad dashing script, to chase out repetitive words and inactive verbs and consider how to add the ideas Larry had contributed when I had read my chapter to him at breakfast. By the time I had turned the previously tidy black and white pages into a scrawl of red and blue corrections, I found myself caught up in the world I wrote about. Soon a generous scribble of notes made their way onto my "outline for chapter 19" pad. And with the pad no longer glaring pristinely white, my hand seemed to take off on its own until I was lost in a torrent of words.

◇◇

In the very earliest days of our relationship, I'd admired Larry's ability to be singlemindedly and completely involved in whatever project was at hand, so determined to see rapid progress that he'd work from dawn to dusk, seven days a week, completely unaware and uninterested in the world outside, never once feeling he was missing any "pleasures." When I suggested he needed a day off, a lazy afternoon at the beach, a change of pace, he'd retort, "I'm the luckiest guy alive. I'm not spending the best part of my life working for 'the man.' I've got a grand partner to share my ideas. We're getting lots done. Why do I need time off?"

I'd slowly proven to him that I needed "time off" and the stimulus other people offered, and that he needed time out to step back and think about what we were doing, where we were going. Eventually, he came to value the rhythm that came with looking forward to a set pattern of days off. "I actually do a lot of good planning and thinking when I back off," he'd say, as if to justify his lack of productivity to himself. Our trips down to sail on *Seraffyn* had provided a definite reason for this break in our country life. Now that she was no longer part of our life, I really missed the excuse she had provided to take time off. To compensate, we began inviting friends from outside the canyon to join us for old-fashioned country weekends.

"Okay Lin, what do you think constitutes the good life?" Lillian Jarman asked one late autumn evening as the fire blazed and oil lamps lit the remains of a leisurely meal of succulent lamb and couscous spiced with mint from my garden pots. Lillian and I had met and almost instantly become fast friends seven years before when Larry and I sailed into Rhodes, one of the outermost islands of the Greek Archipelago. Lillian was a charter boat cook, and had just come in to port for the week to stock up on provisions then wait for the next guests to arrive. From the minute we met, her madcap sense of humor had captivated Larry and turned me into a willing accomplice as we spent as much time together as we could. We'd kept in contact through the years, and now Lillian had rejoined "real life," returning to the academic world she'd known before she ran off with a sailor. Though the first hours of her visit had been filled with laughter, an extra glass of wine, the crackling of the fire, a coyote's call echoing through the hills to the north and occasional hoots from our resident owl had seemed to bring out her far more philosophical side.

I thought for only a few minutes. "That's easy. Good health. Time to contemplate and appreciate what we have. Someone to share it with. One's own individual accomplishments. Celebration and community." I counted each item off on my fingers.

Lillian jumped up from the beanbag she'd been sharing with her boyfriend to grab a piece of paper. "That's good, Lin. I'll write it down. Be fun to read this list in ten years time."

When I sat down to start the new working week, I pinned my copy of the list she'd written to the bulletin board on the wall next to me. And that day in September, my mind refreshed from a fulsome weekend with Lillian, words flowed on to my writing pad almost as if by magic. I put a mental check mark next to the first four requisites for a good life. The final chapter of my book took form that morning. By the time Larry came in for lunch, I was anxious to tell him he was right, I would meet my deadline. "That's great," he commented between mouthfuls. "I'm sure I'll have the last plank ready to go on the boat in three weeks. I think we can safely invite everyone up here for a Whiskey Plank party." I got out a blank pad of paper and began making up an invitation list, a things-to-do-to-be-ready list and a party shopping list, then checked off in my mind the last item on Lillian's handwritten sheet.

The way the day was flowing, I wasn't particularly surprised when Bob Steele's battered Ford pickup skidded to a stop at the top of the driveway late that afternoon, followed closely by Ellie's dust covered Cadillac convertible. "Big delivery truck just dropped off ten coils of cable at my place," Ellie shouted. "Driver said the phone company ordered them. They wouldn't spend money on cables if they weren't going to put the lines in. Let's celebrate!"

"I wouldn't rush out and celebrate yet," Bob said. "Cable's cheap. Still a long way from getting us any connections — got to put up poles, string the cables, put in exchange boxes. Probably just sent the cable to keep you guys from bugging them."

"Larry and I are planning a celebration anyway — everyone's invited. We're having a Whiskey Plank party up here on the 30th," I interjected as a way of defusing Bob's pessimistic comment.

"What the hell's a Whiskey Plank party?" Bob countered.

"Last plank you put on a boat's called a whiskey plank," Larry explained. "In the old days, boat builders got a big progress payment from the owners when the hull was finally closed in. So they promised the building crew a case of whiskey to encourage them to plank the boat up quickly. This marks a real important turning point in our boatbuilding project. Means we're past the halfway mark. Good reason to celebrate!" Then he led Bob into the boatshed.

Jealousy can be a strange thing. From where I stood in the driveway I could hear Bob praising Larry for the latest progress he'd made just as every visitor seemed to. I felt the pangs of resentment momentarily cloud my excitement over the phone cables. Even after Ellie drove away, I waited and listened, wishing I could hear some word of praise. But I knew there was nothing Larry could point to and say, "Look at Lin's beautiful varnish work," for I had done almost nothing on the boat over the past few months. With Larry's never faltering encouragement, I'd devoted all my spare time to the telephone quest. Though everything he'd accomplished was clearly visible, I still had nothing to show.

Strangely these thoughts came back to haunt me less than a month later. By then we really did have reasons to celebrate. A thin strip of disturbed dirt stretched the total length of El Toro Road and up beyond the Hecks' horse farm to show where the telephone company had trenched in the cable that meant phones would soon connect me and my neighbors to the whole world. My book advance had arrived in the mail, and Larry had the last plank for the boat perfectly fitted. He'd laid out all the tools he and our party guests would need to fit and fasten it in place.

I'd sent out invitations to a long list of friends, family, our Bull Canyon neighbors and each of the folks who had come up to see the progress on our boat over the past two years. Dozens had decided to bring along their campers, their tents or just their sleeping bags and stay for the weekend. Mom arrived two days early to make up long tables using planks and sawhorses from the boatyard. "I know your friends," she'd said as we carried another piece of scaffolding timber across the yard. "They'll bring tons of food for the pot luck. I'll drive into town in the morning and get something nice to cover these boards." Larry's folks had driven down from Canada, and his mom had kept both the oven in the propane stove and the one in the wood burner busy as she baked a generous supply of her specialty apple pies. The crowd kept growing and as Mom had predicted, by Saturday afternoon food filled the tables to overflowing.

"You did it, Lin," yelled Ellie as she teetered up the long driveway in her

patent leather high heels carefully keeping the chiller she'd filled with her favorite cocktails away from the knee length mink coat she wore. "Guy came up yesterday to ask me what color phone I wanted."

"No, we all did it. Bob, you, Virginia — Virginia got a hold of all the folks up her way," I reminded Ellie.

"Hell, Steele had nothing to do with the phones," Pete commented. "He's obsessed with getting the electricity. Now they trenched in the phone line instead of putting it on poles, he says we'll never get power. No way to share the cost of stringing the lines. Doesn't much matter to me, generator's working fine. Phones are what I really wanted and from what I hear, you did it." Then he actually patted me on the back.

"Pete may want the phones, but not me. I'll take the electricity any time," Sandy said. "I could do a lot more sewing then. Pete hates the sound of the generator running just so I can make clothes for the kids. You get the electricity in and I could make you some really nice curtains for your back room if you want. I looked around in there, needs some fancying up, and you've got all that silky material lying around on that shelf."

As the sun began its descent behind the hills, Larry invited each of a dozen friends to drive in a fastening to secure the Whiskey Plank in place. A great cheer went up with the last ringing blow of the rivet hammer. Three large ceramic jugs of whiskey I'd secured especially for this party began to make their rounds. "Food's ready," Mom called, and at least two hundred people began sampling the huge array of dishes while several friends began tuning their guitars and banjos.

I should have felt nothing but elation at that moment. Every one of our projects was on track. Everyone seemed to be having a good time at a celebration I had brought to fruition. Yet I had a slight sense of unease as one small corner of my mind kept fitting together isolated snippets of conversation until a disturbing picture began to form.

As I had spent the afternoon flitting from greeting new arrivals, to finding yet another plate or serving spoon, to getting a Band-Aid for a child's scraped knee then back to admire the latest dish someone had brought to add to the feast, I had tried to find a time to include my canyon neighbors. I went out of my way to talk to them and introduce them to outsiders I thought they'd find interesting. "Got any beer?" Pete had asked. "Don't see your city friends bringing nothin' but wine. Sure a lot of talk about boats. Any of them do any shooting?"

"Ma's right pleased you got the phones in for us," Lee Newhouse had commented. "Here's some really good sage honey for your city folks to try. But don't think we'll stay very long. These are your real friends — Ma doesn't really feel she fits here."

I'd had far more success with Marlys. Each time I noticed her she was in animated conversation with yet another of our waterfront friends, face glowing, hands flying as she described canyon floods, house-building disasters, country life. Bob Steele, on the other hand, seemed to be standing back, away from almost everyone including his neighbors and for the first time ever, appeared to avoid me. Even Jimmie Moore commented on this. "I think Steele's got his nose bent cause he bet me the electricity would get in first. Not sure he likes all the attention his wife is getting either."

As the light began to fade I finally cornered Bob. "You were right about building that sign and getting together a canyon association, " I said to him. "No other way we'd have gotten the phones in. As soon as I clear up from this party let's meet and talk about pressuring the electric company." He not only ignored my suggestion but mumbled, "Got some important things to do.

I'll be leaving as soon as I can round up Marlys. You'd better keep an eye on Sandy and her thieving little brats. Been hiding all sorts of food over behind that big Diadora Pine near the road," he added. Then he spotted Marlys and charged over to take her elbow and guide her away from the latest group of admirers. Though I couldn't hear what was said between them, it was obvious Bob was far more eager to leave than his wife.

Pete Shomler watched them start down the driveway and seemed reluctant to be the only canyon dweller left. "Food's mostly gone, no real reason to stay. Come on, Sandy, round the kids up and let's get going," he called.

"You take the car and drive up. Me and the kids will walk," Sandy had answered. "Lin better be careful, Steele's got his nose out of joint cause you're getting all the credit for the phones coming in. He can get kinda nasty when he doesn't feel like he's the kingpin," she said just before she went to find her handbag and the inevitable flashlight all of us in the canyon carried each time we left our doorstep.

But these snippets of canyon politics were quickly swamped by the reality of the Whiskey Plank celebration that continued through that night and most of the next day. As the desert evening cold crept in, people began

splitting into three distinct groups. Some filled the fire-warmed living room, others lingered in the boatyard where the generators quiet mumble kept Larry's work lights shinning. I joined several of our more contemplative friends as they gathered around the open fire in our outdoor pit. There, for a while, I let my mind drift as they discussed the outside world's concerns about ever-increasing interest rates, Israel threatening to take over the Golan Heights, the appointment of the first woman to the U.S. Supreme Court. I was more interested in the lovely sounds of bluegrass music coming from the boatshed, sounds which drifted across the darkness to blend quite easily with the laughter and guitar music from the cottage. Cheers and clapping inside the cottage began swelling until I couldn't make out what tune was being played on the two guitars. Then my brother Allen came hurriedly out to where I sat and hissed into my ear, "Lin go in there and talk to your mother!"

"What's wrong?" I asked as I jumped up to wend my way past the crowd that was nibbling at the slowly dwindling supply of food on the kitchen counters. When we reached the doorway of the big fire-warmed front room Allen didn't say a word. He just pointed. Now I could make out the tune the guitars played. In the center of the oil lamp lit room, surrounded by a crowd who clapped and cheered, my mother danced to the strains of "The Stripper," slowly, coquettishly removing yet another piece of clothing.

"Go on, stop her!" Allen stated firmly. Then he noticed that I too was clapping and cheering, proud to be the daughter of a woman who for that magical moment was beautiful, full of rhythm and grace. "You're just as bad as she is," my brother said turning to leave.

I had a great desire to rush right in and join my mother. But as the last strains of the music faded, leaving Mom glowing with satisfaction, covered only by a sheen of perspiration plus bra and panties, I realized I didn't have that right for this was her moment and hers alone.

Chapter 17

Telephone

"Hi ya, kiddo, boat looks good. Where's the telephone? Couple of calls I've got to make," Allen said as soon as he stepped out of his car.

"It's Thanksgiving, and I don't want to think about that damned phone. It's stored away for the weekend." I called over my shoulder as I helped my two nieces carry the first load of extra food into the kitchen.

My brother rushed past us to scour each room of the house. "Lin, people don't just put phones away. Where is it?"

But I did put the phone away. Whenever I wasn't using it I pulled the plug and stored it in a drawer. It stayed there from seven every evening until noon the next day. I had little choice because, once connected directly to the outside world, I found I lacked self-control. In fact, I became an absolute telephone trollop the minute that useful but invasive instrument became a reality. During the first week, I called every family member, every friend, every editor I worked with, using as my excuse the need to give them my phone number. Instead of making a list of things I wanted to research at the library during my day in town, I called the librarian three times a week and she willingly looked things up then called me back with the answer plus some town gossip. I called the electric company and was soon on a first-name basis with the secretaries of every supervisor in the Perris office.

In the beginning it seemed efficient. Then the calls started coming the other way, editors asking for a short article or a photograph, friends wanting to chat, neighbors needing to talk about our push for electricity or to relate the most recent bit of news. My writing production disappeared, and I actually found myself lying to Larry about what I'd been doing during my morning office sessions. The telephone invasion made its presence felt in the afternoon when I went out to work with Larry. Its shrill ring would echo across the yard. I'd scramble out of the boat and rush the hundred yards toward the house to arrive just as the ringing stopped. Since I was at the house, I'd go in and pour cool drinks to take back with me. I'd linger in the kitchen for a few minutes hoping whoever had just hung up would try again. Within three weeks, Larry was threatening to tear the phone connection out of the kitchen wall. "I hate the goddamn thing," he snapped when I came back to the dinner table after spending fifteen minutes telling my mother it was fine if she invited a few extra friends to join us for lunch that weekend. "If you can't just let it ring and ignore it, why don't you at least turn it off when we are eating?"

Within four weeks, I'd been offered some very tidy sums for assignments editors could easily direct my way now I was in phone contact. But I didn't seem to have any time to write them. Then the first phone bill arrived and with it, a reality check. It wasn't only the dollar amount that shocked me but the duration times listed for my long-distance phone calls. For almost two years, I'd solved all my communication issues by using Jean's telephone in town for two hours, one day a week. Now I'd spent more than seventy-five hours with my ear pressed against the outside world and, if I was candid with myself, the majority of that time was spent in pleasurable but idle chatter.

I soon came to relish the freedom and logic provided by a small black box with blinking red lights. The battery-powered answer machine, tucked away in the far corner of the kitchen, let me forget about rushing to pick up a ringing phone, let me go back to a life where I decided when to let the outside world intrude into my day. And now I wanted to hold onto the magic of our yearly "Country Thanksgiving." For the next few days, I wanted to be completely absorbed by the warmth of family and friends, all of us isolated and insulated from the cares and concerns of the outside world. I explained this to Allen when he threatened to drive back down Bull Canyon to use the payphone at Pedlars Village.

Then another car rumbled up the long driveway. I waved and hurried back to the kitchen to clear a space for the newest batch of food. "Lin, be a bit reasonable," my mother quietly suggested. "Plug in the phone for your brother and let him make his calls. You can unplug it again as soon as he finishes. You don't want to ruin our weekend by insisting on having everything your way. Besides, Allen probably has some patient he's worried about."

As all my kitchen helpers set to work mixing, chopping, spreading,

I couldn't completely ignore the intrusion of the "few calls" Allen made. Even though he carried the phone receiver to the far extent of its long cable, for the next half hour we all had to keep our voices down and stifle the laughter that usually filled the kitchen. Then just as Allen hung up, Dean yelled from the front yard, "Can I borrow the phone? Want to tell my brother we'll be coming out to his place day after tomorrow."

The changes wrought by the telephone, both good and bad, reached into every corner of my life. Almost immediately, the comfortable pattern of my week changed. Since I didn't need to be in town during the day to make phone calls, Larry suggested we drive in together late in the afternoon to get groceries. "We can take along our laundry, drop it at the full service place near the big new supermarket, pick up our mail and read it while we have a

meal at the Mexican cafe, then we can come back with all the laundry done," he said. When we returned to the stone cottage later that evening he added, "Worked well didn't it? You got someone else to do the washing and folding, saved you a whole day. No dishes to wash up tonight and I enjoyed taking you out for dinner." It wasn't until a few weeks later when I drove down the canyon to pay for my last phone calls at Jean's shop that I realized, by saving a day I'd given up something almost as valuable.

"Missed having you come in the past few weeks," Jean said as she opened the gift I'd brought along to thank her for providing me an in-town telephone space. I, too, missed our ritual of morning tea, pastries and town news, my glimpses of local life as I ate lunch in the rustic cafe, the uncomplicated sharing of concerns and pleasures with folks I saw for a few minutes each week. Even as I promised to stop in occasionally just to say hello, I sensed this might be the last time I found myself surrounded by the eclectic mixture of drum sets, guitars, bridal decorations and fancy porcelain dolls in Jean's Music and Bridal shop, the last time this anachronistic strip of small privately owned shops on Main Street was of any true importance in my world.

I picked up burritos and headed right back to the canyon, eager to get in a few extra hours work on the boat. Ellie was raking up windblown eucalyptus leaves by the small pond under her single palm tree as I drove by. She waved and I slowed just a bit to yell, "I'll call when it gets dark, got to talk about the last visit from Cook!"

"I saw Ellie on the way in," I said to Larry as I sanded another section of the boats planking. "Said I'd call her tonight. Would have stopped for a chat but I really do want to get some more of the interior sanded today. One thing I can say for getting the phone in, I definitely have more time to spend out here. But I kind of miss stopping to have a cold drink with her. She's always upbeat."

"You entertain her and she wastes an hour or two of your time," Larry retorted just a bit sharply.

"It's not wasting time," I snapped back. "It's being neighborly. Since we got the phone in I never stop at the Lone Palm, we haven't seen how the Newhouses' gardens are doing, haven't seen how the new porch on Sandy's place looks. No one's stopped here except Steele when he came to deliver diesel last week. Only time we actually see any of them is when we pass on the road. We rarely stop and talk then, just wave and yell hello."

I thought Larry was concentrating on the deck beam he was shaping, but when he spoke, I realized he'd been calculating his answer as carefully as his cut. "I kind of like it better this way," he said. "I'm in working mode.

Time matters, especially daylight time. It's quicker and easier to talk about canyon stuff on the phone after dark. Besides, this way our neighbors don't keep track of each move we make, each thing that happens around here. Have you noticed how Sandy prowls around examining everything you own? Makes me a bit uncomfortable.

If you really want to see the canyon folks we can go up at the end of the day, or on the weekend. Or you can invite them here. Make it a true social visit."

By the end of the week, I had tangible proof of the time the telephone saved me. After almost a month of afternoons spent in preparation work, I was ready to apply the final coat of varnish throughout the whole interior of the boat. To me this was a monumental moment, one which showed how much my personality had changed during the years I'd spent with Larry.

Not only my mother, but my favorite teachers had often warned me about my tendency to start different projects because they seemed interesting, then get bored or distracted by something else that caught my attention.

"Lin, when are you going to finish the dress you started a month ago?" my mother would ask.

"I decided I didn't like the way it fit me," I'd say as an excuse, than tuck the unfinished product away in the back of my closet with the unfinished basket I'd decided to make six months before that.

Mom, prompted by my high school counselor, would yell in exasperation, "You have got to stop being a butterfly, flitting from one interest to another. You have got to learn to finish things or you'll waste your whole life," as I dropped out of the debate society just as I'd dropped out of the civics club, the canoe team, the play production group and eventually college, too. When I began dating I got fully caught up in each of my latest boyfriend's obsessions. I learned to drive a hot rod on the local drag strip while I went steady with Dave; I took skiing lessons and spent every spare hour reading about skiing technique when I dated Mike. Then it was dog breeding, chess, bridge. I threw myself into these forays with a sense of pure pleasure, but at some point my interest seemed to wane just as my interest in the man of the moment faded. I realize now that I had been acting like a mental butterfly, searching for the perfect obsession but without the imagination to find it on my own.

I count myself lucky that it was Larry who introduced me to the first obsession that could truly hold my interest. A few days after we met, he borrowed a small dinghy and rowed me halfway across Newport Bay to show me a boat just like the one he was starting to build. I asked, "How can one person expect to finish something as big as this? It's a really daunting task." Larry's answer sustained me through all the projects and years of our relationship.

"You don't build a boat, Lin," he'd stated. "You build a keel timber. When that's finished, you build a stem. Think of each piece as a separate goal in itself

and watch the pieces fit together until you have a complete boat. That way you can enjoy each step and celebrate each triumph without getting overwhelmed."

Looking back at the months of work I had put in — sanding, coating, then re-sanding each piece of timber until there were three coats of varnish on every plank, every frame and now finishing a final careful sanding — reminded me again that I had learned to stick to a task until it was finished if the long-term goal, be it a productive garden, a new book, a new boat or a new voyage, was one I truly desired.

The next morning, I got up at dawn and rushed out to the boatyard to hose down every inch of the earthen floor. Then, even before I ate breakfast, I climbed into the boat with the vacuum cleaner and sucked up every bit of dust, every wood shaving. That done, I removed the key from the generator so Larry couldn't accidentally start up the bandsaw or any of his dust-throwing power tools. I rushed to change out of my work clothes into fresh ones I hoped would be dust free. Finally, I left my shoes on the ladder as I climbed inside the hull, and after carefully wiping every surface with a tack rag to gather up any specks of dust, I began applying a thick even coat of golden colored varnish. I worked as fast as I could in hopes the varnish would have time to dry before the afternoon breezes could stir up any dust. "Get out of the boatshed, you could get dust in my varnish," I yelled when I heard Larry begin chiseling away at the outside of the hull. "Go edit my manuscript until I'm finished."

"Aren't you taking this all a bit too seriously? It is, after all, just a boat," Larry replied. "Most of the planking and frames will be covered up with bunks and cabinets." But as I glanced back at the rich sheen along the sections of hull I'd already coated I realized I *was* taking it seriously. The timber literally sparkled with its mirror-like finish, I felt wonderful about my work and enjoyed the serenity that came with feeling I'd completed one more goal I'd set myself.

Before I had a chance to start coffee the next morning, Larry said, "Let's go take a look, see how it came out. Varnish should be good and hard. Won't matter if we get dust in the boat now."

"No comments about any sags or runs. I tried for a real good job but the light wasn't always perfect. Remember most of it's going to get covered up anyway," I cautioned him as we approached the shed.

"Oh, shit," Larry exclaimed as soon as he had climbed onto the scaffolding surrounding the boat and could see inside the hull. I thought he was trying to tease me until he turned and said, "You'd better come up and take a look. Remember, anything can be fixed."

Tears began welling as soon as I climbed up next to him. From bow to stern and back again, across frames and planks, along the keel and up the sides of the boat, embedded paw prints scarred all my careful work. Shadow Cat, alias Dog, lay asleep in the lowest spot in the hull, curled around the gnawed and battered remains of a packrat. I stood in stunned silence slowly absorbing this disaster, tears tracking down my face. "I'll help you fix it," Larry said as he put his arm around me. "If we both work together bet we get it sanded in less than a week. I'll even help you lay on the varnish. Five coats of varnish will make it look even better than it does right now with only four. Just consider this a good intermediate coat."

It was almost three weeks before I could look back and admit Shadow Cat had just been doing his job. By then I'd found the hours I spent working within inches of Larry, sharing the almost mechanical task of sanding, gave us the time to sort out a new challenge the telephone brought into our lives.

Chapter 18

Telephone II

"You won't believe what I just heard at the chandlery," Lee yelled down the phone line. "They've got a ham radio hook up with the cruising boats in Mexico. Real bad storm just hit Cabo San Lucas, dozens of yachts stranded on the beach. You know that famous sailor Bernard Moitessier? His boat was one of the first to drag its anchor. It's being pounded in the surf right now. This is a big story, you guys should get moving on it!" We had just started to walk out of the house, headed for a weekend of sailing with Jimmie and Barbara, when the phone rang. Lee Washburn, a yacht skipper who worked out of San Diego, was bombastically enthusiastic about everything, including our boatbuilding project, but now as I listened to his report I couldn't imagine how it fit into our lives. I hung up and repeated his story to Larry then watched another of my "tidy little plans" disintegrate.

"Call and tell Jimmie we won't be coming down to the beach." Larry began ticking off each thought. "Call the chandlery in San Diego and get some hard facts, call your editor and ask her for some expense money. If what Lee's told you is true, they'll want this story."

"It's a story for a reporter, not for me," I said as I dialed the chandlery. But with each new fact I learned, more questions began forming in my mind. Even though it was the weekend, three phone calls had me in contact with the editor at *Sail Magazine*. Larry had been right. Keith Taylor didn't hesitate. "Forget about the money, get the story," he insisted. Within an hour I had grown from freelance journalist to reporter, "on assignment." Christmas was only two weeks away. Cabo San Lucas is a favorite holiday destination. There wasn't one airplane seat available at any price. Yet the story loomed so important in Keith's mind he told us, "Charter a plane." Five hours after getting Lee's call, the two of us, an overnight bag and two bags full of cameras were winging our way south in a single engine Cessna for the long haul to the tip of Baja California.

Eight hours and two fueling stops later, as we circled above the now sparkling tranquil roadstead fronting Cabo San Lucas, I turned to Larry and said, "I'm not sure I'll be able to handle this." Beneath us, scattered along almost two miles of golden sand, lay shattered yachts strewn like discarded toys. Broken spars, torn sails, shredded upholstery and flotsam driven ashore by the fierce winds and pounding seas, cast long shadows in the last rays of sunshine. "One of those wrecks laying down there could have been the boat we're building," I added. "What am I going to say to these people?"

We landed at the dirt airstrip and flagged down a taxi to take us to the beach, then walked into the living nightmare of twenty-nine families who'd watched their boats and dreams dashed to bits by an unseasonable storm. For two days, I interviewed cruisers who'd lost almost everything they owned. Some were people I'd met during the seminars we'd presented, others we'd met in ports we'd visited through the years. Even the folks we'd never met seemed drawn to tell me the most intimate details of their battle with wind, breaking seas, dark and fear. I sought out harbor officials who were trying to coordinate clean up efforts, prevent vandalism and help homeless sailors find ways to carry on with their lives, while at the same time sticking to immigration and customs regulations. Meanwhile, Larry shot roll after roll of photos and, when he ran out film, set to work helping salvage boats and gear.

Two days later, our pilot, who had also stayed on to be helpful, said he had to get back to his "real" job as an attorney. I climbed into the cabin of his plane feeling emotionally exhausted and almost immediately began to question my actions. Maybe I should have been getting my hands dirty, pitching in and working instead of adding to the victims' emotional anguish with my insistent questions.

These thoughts stayed with me as my mornings were spent with the telephone glued to my ear. Hour after hour, I questioned international weather agencies and Mexican officials trying to piece together a story line.

I checked quotes, had conferences with Patience Wales, the editor who was handling my story and helping me choose ways to pare down and organize the over-abundance of information I'd gathered. Each afternoon, Larry would stop his woodworking and join me inside the hull of the boat to sand away cat and packrat paw prints. "Do you think reporters make things worse for everyone by being so intrusive?" I asked Larry. "I couldn't believe the way some of those people poured out their souls to me. They told me how careless they'd been, the mistakes they made, how hopeless and confused they felt. I'm not sure they need me to share their pain with the whole world."

Larry replied, "There are lots of lessons other folks could learn from what we saw. Remember what the crew on that big schooner said — someone needs to tell the story and they are glad it's going to be you. You've been out there so people will believe what you say. Figure a way to get it all on paper and you might keep someone else from making the same mistakes. That's your job now."

"Every one of them should have gotten out of that anchorage the minute the wind shifted to the south. That was their big mistake — they waited around for someone else to move first." I answered, "But if I say that I make them look foolish. Besides I wasn't in their shoes. I'm not sure how I would have acted in the same situation. I can't criticize them in print. They'll hate me and these folks are part of our real world, we could meet up with any one of them when we finish this boat and head off cruising."

"How about starting from a completely different perspective," Larry suggested. "How about figuring out what people did right instead of what they did wrong. Some of them did leave the anchorage early in the day. Some of them did get their boats out to sea even when the winds were blowing 50 knots and the breakers were 15-feet high. Isn't it about time sailing reporters started telling the stories of winners instead of losers? I know the losers' stories are far more dramatic, but I don't think they are nearly as important."

"Problem is, folks who made the right decisions just sailed away and kept on cruising so we never heard from them," I replied. "The folks who got in trouble were all right there on the beach so I could get their stories."

"So track the winners down," Larry stated as he climbed out of the boat to get some fresh sandpaper and tune the radio so we could hear Glenn Campbell singing "Wichita Lineman," our current favorite from our translation station.

I came to appreciate the width of the world the telephone brought into the calm of my isolated canyon home as I set off on this new tack. My morning phone call expense sheet increased to match the airline charter fees and our afternoon sanding sessions helped me mold the information into two long stories. Larry had set me on the right path. Readers and editors did like his "learn from the winners" approach. What I hadn't expected was that this path would have such a profound effect on my writing life.

◇◇

Gentle winter rains had fed the streams of the canyon that winter. Green shoots of grass and desert sage brought out flocks of quail to scratch for food in the front yard where the swelling buds of the chinaberry trees showed spring was not far away. A very pregnant looking bobcat got herself chased into the tree just down from the boatyard when she tried to sneak food from Cindy's bowl. Larry and I both heard wild snarling intertwined with angry barking and rushed down to marvel at the wide spotted head and black-tufted ears of the 30-pound wildcat. It hissed at us as we stood holding firmly onto Cindy's collar. Its short, black-tipped tail curled and uncurled slowly, tensely. Then we backed away, dragging the dog with us as the wild cat leapt clear of its perch and disappeared into the growth of the stream bed. While we walked past the boatshed Larry offered, "I'll give you a hand cleaning the house so you can relax before Eric shows up."

"No, you keep on working. I've got everything under control," I answered. I paused to look at the boat, which now sported its first coat of white paint. "I'll get in a few more hours writing."

But I didn't write one more word that day; instead I massaged my ego by thumbing through the magazines that contained my Cabo stories. There it was, not only in *Sail Magazine* but in three foreign ones as well, with Larry's photos punctuating each important point. That flying excursion to Cabo San Lucas had earned us enough extra money to let me ease off on my writing schedule. Then Keith called to tell me his magazine had increased its circulation and won awards because of my work. "How about letting us put your name on the magazine's masthead," he'd suggested. "You could become editorial advisor and give us the same number of stories you already do. Only catch, you'd have to give us exclusive North American rights for your articles." His offer, which included a regular paycheck, meant I could relax and have fewer concerns about keeping our canyon boat building project financially viable and on track. It also solidified my feeling that I was finally a "real" writer.

Then in early spring, another unexpected telephone call topped up my already overflowing ego. The vice chairman of W.W. Norton and Company, Inc. Publishing was on his way to visit. Eric Swenson, who had commissioned three of our books already, said it would be good to talk about my

writing plans in person. Oh, how I loved that telephone. Forgotten were the hours of frustrating meetings it had taken to get the lines up the canyon, forgotten was the slowly dwindling contact with canyon folks since it arrived — my life was far too full to remember that!

"Where can I change? I don't want to slow up your work," Eric Swenson asked as he stepped from his rental car. "I brought along some work clothes — I am sure I can help you sand something and we can talk while we work." Eric looked far more approachable when he left his carefully tailored suit and black leather shoes in the back room. The afternoon sped by as he admired the work Larry had done. Eric regaled us with stories of the sailing personalities who had joined him for ocean races on his elegant yacht, the famous authors, many of them household names, who wrote books commissioned by him, the ins and outs of his publishing world and the biographies and university text books that earned the "real money." As the sun sank lower and the first chill of evening crept in, I left the boatyard and went to light the front room fire. Then I put a carefully prepared chicken and rotund loaf of bread dough in the oven. I was feeling quite proud of the atmosphere I'd created for the moment when I would present Eric with my newest book proposal. The oil lamps in each room burned brightly through clean shiny chimneys. The table, set in front of the crackling fireplace, was laid with a crisp cloth that blended beautifully with porcelain plates discovered in the back alleys of Pedlars Village. My notes, partially hidden by the napkin next to my plate, weren't too obtrusive. "Hey, Lin, you can really relax about money now," Larry stated as soon as he walked in. "Eric has offered me $7500 as an advance for a book on boat building. That's the biggest advance we've ever had. Sure glad I've been taking all those photos."

I slipped my notes under my dinner plate and tried to forget them as Larry reveled in the plans for his book. Then, with the second bottle of wine, Eric asked who played the guitar. As the fire dwindled and became a bed of gently glowing embers, I let my writer's ego slip aside and savored conversation that ebbed and flowed between occasional bursts of shared fireside songs. I climbed into bed that night feeling quite smug about the way I'd entertained a publisher who had come all the way across the country to my home for a literary meeting.

When we finished lunch the next day, I finally got to pull out my notes. Eric listened for only a few minutes before saying, "How about sending me the usual quick synopsis and outline. You know what your readers want better than I do. Soon as you send me something on paper I'll arrange an advance."

I felt just a bit chagrined at being denied my chance to talk about me. But as Eric appeared from the back room, once again formally outfitted in tailored silver suit, crisp shirt and tie then climbed into his rental car, I regained my composure. "Can't thank you enough for coming all the way out, it's really been encouraging," I said.

"Detouring out here to visit with you two has been a real treat for me." Eric said as he prepared to drive off. "Now I have to go to work. I'm scheduled to meet with Curt Gentry this afternoon. He's the man who actually did the writing on *Helter Skelter.* We gave him a half-million dollar advance for a biography of J. Edgar Hoover. That was three years ago. My job is to extract a manuscript from him."

I stood rooted in place, smile fixed, as my ego slowly dissolved. The ring of the telephone shattered the quiet. "Better grab that before they hang up," Larry said. "I'm going to get started planking up the transom. Let's talk about my book at lunch time."

I watched Larry stride away, buoyed by thoughts of gaining both a new boat and his own book from our time here in the canyon. I could already see it. I'd do the typing, editing, organizing but only his name would appear on the cover of the book that gained the biggest advance we'd ever been offered. I walked slowly into the house, unplugged the phone without answering it, poured a cup of tea then sat down on the hearth.

"Bit of a comeuppance. You were letting your head get too big," my inner voice taunted me. "You can't expect to be center stage all the time. Better not dampen Larry's enthusiasm. He'll need your support on his book project."

By the time Larry came in for lunch, I'd begun to find my sense of humor again, humor I'd need in spades when, only a few days later, a seemingly small mishap made me the center of far more attention than I wanted.

Two black-jacket wasps decided to make their home in one of my dishwashing gloves. And a large bee happened to be underfoot when I put the glove on. Two stings on my wrist, plus a sting in the arch of my foot and my body spun into an allergic reaction. For the next month, Larry rushed me from doctor to hospital, from allergy clinic to homeopathic practitioner, in an attempt to control the resulting reaction that made my eyes swell shut some mornings, my lips swell to cracking point on others. An unusual reaction to strong antihistamines meant the skin covering most of my joints turned brittle and cracked open to leave me itching and bleeding. Sleepless nights led to unproductive days. Tears were rarely far from my eyes as I tried to keep up with writing, boatyard time, and homemaking, never sure what my mood would be as Larry urged me to try every remedy friends suggested. Grant Gould finally found ways I could control the reaction or calm it down when it happened. But this meant stopping to take cool baking soda baths sometimes twice or three times a day.

Then we took off to go sailing for three days with Jimmie and Barbara. Almost as soon as we drove over the hills separating the warm dry desert from the moisture of the coastline, I began to feel different. When I awoke on board their boat the next morning, I found, for the first time in weeks, my skin had stopped itching, my eyes and lips were normal sized and I felt well rested.

"How's your skin today," Jimmie called to ask the day after we returned to the canyon. "Woke up with swollen eyes again. Must be allergic to something up here," I answered.

"Guess you better push harder for the electricity," Jimmie urged. "Get the power out there and I'll send out the big air conditioner I pulled out of a house I'm rebuilding. Then you could close up the house to keep away from all the plant pollen and dust this summer."

I had put the quest for electricity on the back burner soon after the phones arrived, partially because I had become absorbed with my "professional life," and more recently with my health problems. But also, in the back of my mind, was a bit of selfishness. The telephone had wrought such dramatic changes in Bull Canyon, I worried that electricity could destroy even more of what made life out here seem unique. But now, as Jimmie urged me onward and I fought my daily battle to keep clear of the pollen, weeds and stinging insects that surrounded me, I began to sense I could never expect to live in this canyon, never make the cottage my home even after we returned from the voyages that lay ahead. I hung up the phone and went out into the front yard. The rocky hills, tree-shaded boatyard, wildflower-laced ravines and ivy-trimmed stone cottage looked just the same as they had the day before. But for the first time, I began seeing them for what they really were: a stopping place and a good long-term investment. And electricity definitely would improve our investment.

Now on afternoons when my itching skin would not tolerate the dust and wood shavings of the boatyard, I set to work picking up the threads of the electricity quest. Bob Steele had stopped in to deliver diesel for the generator that morning. "Soon as you guys finish transferring that fuel, come on over for some coffee," I called across the yard. "Let's talk about the electricity. We need to figure out how to get past the Perris office — it's nothing but a roadblock. We have to go above Cook's head or we'll never get power up here."

Mr. Cook had stopped driving out to the canyon since the phones came in; instead, he called every week or two to say his office had found another problem with the paperwork. "You go above Cook's head and you'll ruin all the work I've put in. He's on the case. He's the key to the power," Bob said as he grabbed a handful of cookies but refused to settle onto the heavy-duty chair we kept just for him. "Just because you happened to luck out by kissing up to that telephone lady, you think you can magically find one person who will hand us electricity. No, it's a matter of working through the system and Cook is the system." Bob left abruptly, no quest for canyon gossip, no stories about bulldozer mishaps. Then I listened with resentment as my morning writing time dissolved and progress in the boatyard ground to a halt while Larry listed the reasons he was convinced Mr. Cook was a foil, a yes man sent out to keep us from bugging the higher-ups at the SoCal Edison Corporation. "Shadow Cat kills rats, that's his job. Cook stalls customers, that's his job," Larry stated firmly. "He makes sure SoCal Edison doesn't have to lay out money on capital investments that don't pay off. If we want power, we have to bypass Cook."

Soon after lunch, the phone rang and my day continued its downward spiral.

"Lin, I was just talking to Allen," Mom's voice poured cheerfully down 120 miles of telephone line. "He says you've got a dentist appointment with him early Tuesday morning. That means you'll be up here Monday night. Tuesday is Passover. Come stay with Dad and I both nights. That way you can help me prepare dinner."

"Mom, I'd really like to join everyone but I can't take extra time off right now. I'm way behind. Two days off is bad enough — Passover dinner with the family would mean three days away," I answered. But Mom bulldozed ahead, reminding me of the decade of family celebrations I had missed. "You need time away from the sage, the sawdust, Larry, boat building, the stress of canyon politics," she insisted. "That's what's triggering your allergies."

By the time Larry came in from the boatyard I had reluctantly marked my calendar with this unwanted intrusion. "You look stressed out," Larry remarked. "Why don't you forget cooking. We can run down to Elsinore for

some Mexican food."

"It's not the cooking. It's my mother. I don't want to hurt her feelings but I just don't feel like taking three days off next week. I need to go pick up some timber, do some shopping, get my teeth fixed but..."

Before I could finish, Larry grabbed the phone and dialed Mom's number. Tears began pouring down my face as I heard the barely contained explosion waiting under his forceful tone, "Marion, you are out of line. You know Lin's not well. You've got her so upset that her skin is acting up again. She was okay this morning but now the insides of her arms look like raw hamburger. Remember she's her own person first, my wife second and your daughter third and I won't put up with you pressuring *my wife*." He slammed the receiver down, grabbed a glass from the sink and poured a shot of whiskey in it.

I sat in stunned silence. I knew Larry had been trying to help as he charged in to defend me. But I was already picturing the emotional fallout his forceful cancellation of my mother's plans would cause. As I continued preparing dinner, my mind rejected every idea that flitted onto the mental list I'd already labeled, "How-to-mend-the-rift-with-my-mother." Larry, confused by my silence, went to shower off the day's accumulation of sweat, wood shavings and sawdust.

The phone's harsh ringing finally broke the silence. "Lin, what a wonderful man you have. You are lucky to have found someone who cares so much," Mom said in a voice that carried a tinge of envy. Then, to cement her credentials as a proper Jewish mother, she went on. "There's no problem now. You can come for Passover dinner, get your teeth fixed and only be away for one night. I called your brother and made him change your appointment to Wednesday morning."

Chapter 19

Country Roads

"What took you so long?" Larry called. "Did you blow a tire? Is the truck okay? Expected you back a long time ago."

"Decided to get groceries while I was out of the canyon," I answered. "Then El Toro Road went missing and I had to find it."

I didn't hear his reply as I rushed to transfer melting ice cream into our propane fueled freezer. But when I walked out to the boatshed carrying a tray laden with icy lemonade, fresh pastries and dog biscuits, Larry stated, "Roads don't go missing. What really happened?"

The freeway had now grown from a rumor to an approaching reality. Most of my Lake Elsinore friends, and many of the folks in the canyon, viewed its arrival with trepidation. I shared some of their concerns but still was entranced by the engineering finesse, the marvel of organization I could see whenever we drove past the various sections that lay within sight of the old highway. Overpass bridges seemed to appear magically in the center of open fields. A month or two later, wide scars of flattened earth arrived to connect each bridge as the eventual roadway marched relentless toward us. Four days before when we had driven out of the canyon, I had noticed the clouds of dust sent up by heavy machinery working on the hills to the north. Today I had a pile of manuscripts to send off to various magazines, so I'd headed into town just after lunch. When I drew up at the intersection where the dirt track of El Toro Road met the two-lane highway, my path was blocked by a pickup truck. Its driver rolled down his window and called, "Many folks live up that way?"

I made a quick mental count. "Eight of us, maybe a few more if you include the folks up above Lindell. Not sure how many are at home right now. Why you asking?"

"Supervisor told me to ask if I saw someone come down this track," he replied.

As I waited in line at the post office, the only thing I heard people talking about was "the freeway." The same thing held true as I worked my way through my shopping list.

"Two more folks called it quits and have moved on," the manager of the local hardware store stated. "My business is holding up because I get wholesale orders from the builders who are finishing the shops near the new market."

"Not sure why everyone is running away from Main Street," Jean said when I overcame my guilt and decided to take time for a cool drink and a chat with her. "There is going to be a freeway off-ramp here at Main Street too. Still be traffic but guess the new shops look fresher, more modern. Main Street is definitely dying. Time for me to think of moving on."

Jean's words rang in my mind as I drove toward home. I crossed the railway tracks then turned onto the dirt lane leading to the highway. A high barricade of earth stood between me and El Toro Road. I climbed out of the truck and stood on the running board hoping to figure a way to get around the obstruction. Huge graders grumbled along a freeway-wide field of churned up dirt. I could see no signs of "my road." I got back in the truck and drove along the rough track bordering the snaking mound of earth until I found a workman. "What has happened to El Toro Road?" I yelled above the noise of the earthmovers.

"Never heard of it," he called back.

It took me most of an hour to get past construction hold-ups then find the temporary construction site offices; it took more time for the foreman to locate his road drawings. "Guess this dirt track here must be what you're talking about," he said pointing to a thin line that snaked up into my hills. "Crew that's been doing the surveying said almost no one uses it so I didn't worry about posting any signs. Guess he was wrong. Here's what you do. Just drive south two miles to Highway 74, then turn left onto Dexter Road. Head north and follow that for a mile. It ends right at your track. You'll get home that way from now on. Must be pretty nice living way up in a quiet place like that."

"It is if you aren't allergic to dust," I commented. "Freeway sure is changing things down here, but doubt it will have that much effect up in the canyon."

I had to laugh as Larry insisted on driving down to verify my "missing road" story. We continued around the diversion another two miles to where a handmade sign now stood, describing the route to El Toro Road. "Guess that shows how moveable a dirt road is," Larry commented.

Jimmie Moore echoed his words a week later when he and Barbara arrived for a weekend stay. After the usual tour to inspect progress on the boat, then the springs and water system, the slightly more productive garden I now limited to a dozen old washtubs, and the newly painted back room, we settled down at the table I'd set under the chinaberry trees in front of the stone cottage. As I began pouring a second round of iced lemonade, the rumble of a large truck slowly grew to overpower the buzz of the season's first cicadas. A cloud of dust marked the truck's slow progress up El Toro Road. "Must be bringing Bob Steele's Cat back," Larry commented. "Last time he brought me diesel, Steele said he was almost finished with the job he was doing over in Riverside. He didn't seem too happy about it. Don't think he has any other work lined up."

I covered the nibbles and pitcher with a towel as the cloud of dust came closer. Jimmie and Larry walked over to the edge of the yard to watch the heavily laden truck rumble slowly along the road beneath them. "Sure does shake the ground up here. Can't be doing the old cottage any good," Jimmie said. ""Be awfully nice if Old Man Payonessa had cut his track on the other side of the stream instead of on this side."

I went into the house for more ice cubes. "While you're in there, can you call Bob Steele and ask him to come down for a drink so we can talk about moving the road," Larry called.

"We can't just move a county road," I protested as I sensed yet another mass of paperwork and phone calls intruding into my writing life.

"Why not? Freeway crew showed you how moveable a dirt road is," Jimmie countered. "You've got the paperwork to prove the El Toro Road has never been surveyed. County can't prove where it belongs. We own the land on both sides of the stream. If we build a better road, the county won't care."

Then Larry took over, bombarding me with reasons to get involved with this latest scheme. "It will be far less prone to washouts, keep the house quieter and cleaner and give us a nice flat area where the old road is right now. That way Jimmie can build a corral for the horse Barbara wants to buy. She's talking of moving up here and playing with horses when we get the boat finished. Bet Steele would love to see the road moved; make it easier to get to his place since he wouldn't have to cross the stream." And it will add to the eventual resale value of the Stone Cottage — that's what it's really about, I thought, as I dialed Bob Steele's number.

As the evening wore on, I, too, became infected with the road moving bug, especially when Bob offered the use of his bulldozer for free and Barbara said, "If I can have my corral, then I'll pay for hiring the dump truck. You just organize getting the folks in the canyon to help move the small rocks. I'm sure they'll all be glad to see the last of this blind corner."

◇◇

For the first time since telephones arrived, Sandy Shomlers' little Toyota screeched to a stop next to the back door on Monday morning. "Great idea. Moving the road to our side of the creek means we can always get out, even if Steele does go ahead and cut off our access across his land," Sandy stated as she marched into the kitchen. "Haven't been here in a while, what's new? Ya think Steele's got another lady in Riverside. He's been a real grump since he brought his digger back from there."

"The only thing I've done to the house this year is fix up the closet and paint the back room where Jimmie and Barb always stay," I said as I shredded lettuce leaves I'd carefully gathered from my garden pots. "Go take a look if you want."

"You really should get a proper cover for this coat," Sandy called from the back room. I wiped my hands and went in to see her gently stroking the thick fox collar on the luxurious kidskin winter coat she'd taken out of the closet.

"My sister-in-law up in Canada gave that to me on a long-term loan." I explained, trying not to appear annoyed at what felt more like prying than neighborly interest. "She gained some weight. It made her feel guilty hanging in her closet. I feel like a princess when I wear it. Promised to send it back as soon as we get the boat finished." Then I steered our conversation back to the road moving plans while I waited impatiently for Sandy to finish the coffee and cookies I'd felt obliged to offer her.

"Brought you a list of things we'll need for the job," Bob Steele said the next day as he reached for another cookie to dip in his coffee. "You could probably find some cheap buckets at Bernie's, down by the tracks. Newhouses said they'd come up on Saturday. Said it won't help them but might encourage the county to keep the whole road in better condition. I heard their kids are thinking of moving out here if the electricity comes in. Freeloaders wouldn't want to live without TV. I told them we've pretty much given up on getting power. Ma Newhouse didn't seem too put off. Likes the phone a lot, says it makes her feel safer but she worries about having more bills to pay. Not too eager to have electric bills either — not the way Marlys expects to keep the place air conditioned all summer, heated all winter."

"Marlys going to be here on Saturday?" I asked. "I want to figure out how much food I'll need to feed the road moving team."

"Don't really care," Bob answered as he laced up his shoes to leave. "She wouldn't be any help. Too worried about her damned fingernails to pick up any rocks."

Maryls was there. So was a full-sized dump truck, Bob's D-8 Cat, Pete Shomler's rusty ancient tractor, plus each of our neighbors, some city friends who thought roadmoving sounded like fun, plus the cat named Dog. By the time I carried the second pot of coffee down the driveway and wended my way past mounds of earth to fill waiting cups, the outlines of a third of a mile of new road had been gouged out among the huge boulders, sagebrush and tumbleweeds on the far side of the trees that marked the course of the almost dry streambed. By mid-afternoon, a clean wide swath of roadway was clearly taking shape, twice the width of the old road, and with far gentler curves. It was high above the line scoured by the heaviest rush of the previous winter's rainwater and banked so, with luck, it would stay intact even if the stream went on a rampage.

Between trips along the length of the project, then up and down our long driveway to get fresh jugs of iced lemonade, more cookies, more Band-Aids for the troup of volunteers, I joined in to walk along the plowed earth with the foot soldiers, filling a bucket with any small rocks that were left standing, tossing them along the mounds that edged the new road. Above the din of machinery, occasional laugher and snatches of song, I could hear Cindy barking madly from the lead we'd rigged up between two trees in the front yard to keep up the pretense she was a guard dog and to keep her from running off as she sometimes did once she left her own yard.

"I'm sick of dust, sick of rocks," Marlys groaned as the afternoon shadows began to lengthen. "Not sure it's worth trying to impress Bob anymore. He's never going to want a kid, that's always been my idea. I never wanted to live in the country, that's always been his idea. Now he's found a deal on a big generator. Says he can install it to take care of our house and maybe even a few that he claims folks are going to let him build over by one of his dry lakes. But it's all probably talk. He'll buy that machine and leave it sitting till it's dead, just like the five hundred trees he killed last year. Bob snips at me whenever I ask if he's talked to the electric company people. I can't bear the thought of another summer up here with out air conditioning."

I was thinking about her words as Larry and I were laying in the big brass bed, listening to Jimmie and Barbara whispering and laughing in the back room. "Tomorrow I'll be driving that dump truck," Larry said, sounding as eager as a kid waiting to try out a new toy. "Owner showed me how it works. He said it didn't pay for him to drive up here for a few hours work. We'll probably get it all done by noon. Then Bob says he can dig up the two culverts from the old road and transfer them over later in the week. He'll choose a time when we know no one will be coming up the road. Until then, we'll leave both roads open and folks can choose which way they want to go. They'll all take the new road. It looks so much better. Everyone in the canyon is going to love it."

"Yes, but will the county guys love it? Will the electric folks use it as another excuse to put us off?" I asked.

"Won't even notice we moved it," he answered quietly humming the latest John Denver song as we watched the moonlight dance among the leaves outside our window.

Three days later, Larry was fully engrossed out in the boatyard where he was smoothing wide luxuriously grained planks of teak to form cabin sides for the boat. Now that the hull was completely finished, he'd begun the far less demanding work of closing in the deck. I was at my desk, my mind far away, sailing through the islands of Malaysia. My fingers were flying over the keys of my typewriter. The sound of a covey of cars and trucks moving slowly along the clean new ribbon of road outside my front room office window broke through my concentration. "Larry, I think the county noticed we moved their road," I stated when I reached the boatshed.

"Ignore them, they'll just go away," he answered brusquely when I described the convoy of officially marked vehicles that were driving up and down the length of our newest project. But when two hardhat wearing officials began walking up the long driveway, he grabbed one of the cabin side planks and climbed onto the deck of the boat, then stated, "You go talk to them. I haven't got the patience to deal with their bullshit. Besides, someone has to get something done around here."

"You have any idea who did this," the county road supervisor growled as soon as he saw me.

"All of us up here pitched in. Sure looks good, doesn't it? Twice as wide as the old road, cut out that horrid blind corner under the stone cottage,"

I chirped, hoping sheer bravado would soften the frowns of a glowering team of men who now surrounded me. "Wish you guys hadn't seen it until we moved the two culverts and smoothed out the last bits where the new road meets the old one. You'd be really impressed then!"

"I don't care how good it looks. I'm not impressed at all. You don't just go and move a county road!" yelled the man whose badge carried the grand title of Senior Road Engineer.

"You're not the one who had to call the ambulance after a head-on collision at that damned blind corner. You're not the one who has to worry about losing the road the minute the rain comes down. It's not your land this road's on," I was now getting almost as loud as he'd been.

"Everyone calm down," the man behind the "Supervisor, Riverside Roads" badge said. "Miss, folks don't normally just move a road like this. Got a phone call from some lady. Didn't give her name. No one believed her, sounded like a crank. But since we were checking out the road plans for the new subdivision and school they're thinking of building at the bottom of El Toro Road, thought we'd come up and take a look. Pretty big surprise. Let's take a walk uphill, just the two of us and you can tell me what happened here."

Later that afternoon, Bob Steele stopped by. "Heard there's a real big subdivision going in a few miles down the hill. Stopped to talk to one of the road surveyors on my way in," he said as he climbed out of his truck. "Things are finally going to happen out here. Real estate prices will sky rocket when city folks see this open land. Same guy told me the county road guys were grumbling about our road up here. Hope you didn't tell them it was my idea to move the road. Might want some work from them some day."

"Not sure who told them we'd built our own road," Larry replied. "But don't worry, Lin snowed them. She had them eating out her hand by the time she was finished."

"Not so sure I snowed them," I called from my desk where I was trying to finish the work I'd started that morning. "I just showed them their road was a wreck. Final outcome was, we agreed to leave both roads open for two weeks. Let the folks who live up here choose which one they like best. If they use ours the most, we can dig up the county culverts and use them. We can't lose. Our road is obviously better so I doubt we'll ever see anyone from county roads up here again, especially after I told them our Association lawyers would demand a proper survey for the whole length of Bull Canyon if they hassled us too much."

"Who's this lawyer?" Bob demanded.

"You know we don't have one. Just made that up after listening to all the power company guys spouting on about legal right-of-ways. Seemed to do the trick," I replied. "Larry, why don't you get Bob to help you move those mast timbers. Then you two can talk about road moving somewhere else. Someone around here has to get something done today."

But I didn't settle down at my desk. Instead I snuck out the back door of the cottage, then climbed down the bank behind the house. With Cindy at my side, Dog prancing ahead, I had my own quiet walk along the new, elegant sweep of country road that definitely helped improve the property values of a place that, as each day passed, was beginning to feel less like my home.

Chapter 20

Electricity

"Page ten, nine, eight," I counted as I sorted carbon copied pages into separate piles. One more chapter of *Seraffyn's Oriental Adventure* finished, only five more to write and I'd have this book finished. Then we'd get a big juicy check. I already had plans for this latest advance. Larry was installing the last of the framework for bunks, a chart table, a galley. I was eager to order the stainless steel galley stove so he could fit that in, too. At the far end of my bedroom/office/front room a window-mounted air conditioner rumbled quietly, sending in just enough cool, dust-free, pollen-free breeze to keep the shuttered room from feeling stuffy or overheated. Will it do the job when summer really settles in? I wondered. As if it read my thoughts, the air conditioner's fan seemed to stagger. Moments later it stopped. In the sudden silence I realized the boatyard generator was no longer adding its low rumble to the canyon's natural background noises.

I wasn't surprised to hear the kitchen screen door — which I'd broken down and ordered a few months back — fly open, nor were Larry's first words unexpected: "Sorry, Pumpkin, have to unplug your air con, generator can't handle that extra load and still start up my planner. Be using the planner most of the day. You having any luck with the electric company?"

My reluctance to bring electricity into the canyon had been replaced by sheer frustration as I spent a large part of each afternoon on the telephone exploring potential routes around the roadblocks thrown up by the Perris office of the electric company. Just the previous day I'd discovered the reason our constant complaints to the Public Utilities Commission seemed to be falling on deaf ears. The commission's job was to make sure the electric company did not take unfair advantage of its position as a huge monopoly. "Your letter has been sent out for action," the PUC customer service lady parroted, as she had a dozen times before. But this time, some instinct urged me to ask, "Who exactly did you send it to for action?" Armed with that name, I called the Los Angeles office of the electric company. My reaction was mild compared to Larry's when, later that evening, I relayed the story to him. "PUC did what? They just forwarded your letter to SoCal Edison Office in LA? Then the LA office just sends it to the Perris office for action? I can't believe it," Larry stormed. "Those letters all end up on Cook's desk. He covers his ass by writing back, 'We're looking into it.' Then nothing gets done. What good is the PUC if they take the word of the exact person who is trying to cover up the whole affair? What a worthless, stupid system."

Ellie's reaction was far more subdued. "You and I are the only ones who seem interested in fighting for electricity anymore. Maybe I should look into that generator Bob talked about. My wrinkles are going to get even worse this summer if I can't shut this place up and keep the dust down."

Shearlane and Robert Duke arrived soon after I spoke to Ellie. I'd invited them out so I could share Shearlane's excitement over her promotion from reporter to editor for the Life section of the *Los Angeles Times*. After exhausting the subject of her new position, dinner drifted by, filled with talk about the boat Robert planned to buy, their shared dream of some day sailing away to a place where they could try writing without deadlines, editorial guidelines, political restrictions. As the late spring light faded away, I lit oil lamps. The soft glow of the golden flames prompted me to share the story of Ellie's wrinkle woes. As their laughter died away, I launched into a litany of electricity quest roadblocks.

I am convinced I have a mental radar detector working somewhere inside me. Time after time it has snapped into action countless times when I have been in need of inspiration. When I have been trying to solve problems with my writing, scout out materials for Larry's building projects or to resolve some financial quandary, I seem to turn around a few times and suddenly just the right person, be it a friend or a stranger who happens to be in a line beside me, is there to give me the information I need.

Shearlane's reporter antennae seemed to snap to full attention as I related the two-year-long saga. She began firing questions, then stated, "I may be part of your answer. You have to use real pressure. Make the electric company feel exposed."

On Monday morning I called the secretary to the Vice President for Development and Infrastructure, Southern California Edison Corp,

Los Angeles Office: "Please give me your exact address. I need the room and floor number, not just the street address." Following Shearlane's plan, I left my name and number then I called again. After three attempts to get past the secretary, I instigated step two of our action plan. "Forecast is for temperatures of 103 degrees in the shade later this week," I told the secretary. "Because your Perris office has been stalling for two years, I have no power out here to run air conditioning. I need to work, deadlines to meet. So I'll have to move into your air conditioned offices to keep going. I'll be there at 10 a.m. Wednesday, sleeping bag, food, typewriter. Reporter and photographer for the *L.A. Times* will be there at 3 p.m. to interview me. They'll probably want to ask your boss why he's done nothing about all the letters from the PUC."

I gave her Shearlane's phone number then hung up and tried to settle in and write an outline for the next chapter. But I couldn't concentrate. Instead I began making a new list — "Things to take with me to Edison Offices" — as I eagerly anticipated my stint as an anti-big-business activist.

Time groaned slowly along when I headed out to the boatyard after lunch. I tried to keep focused on sanding the teak Larry had cut and shaped into narrow, bevel-edged strakes. He'd begun fitting each piece carefully to create bunk and cabinet fronts. I kept finding excuses to stop sanding and climb out of the boat. First it was to get extra sandpaper, then to get a dusting brush. Each time I made a quick run to the house to check for phone messages. Each time I was disappointed when the warning light on the answering machine sat dark and unblinking. Each time I returned to the boatyard, Larry would say, "Don't expect anyone to do anything until you actually show up with your sleeping bag. Are you really ready to push your way in and make a fuss?"

"I'm ready to try almost anything if it gets me talking to a person who has some real authority. I need a definite yes or a definite no so we can get on with life." I answered as, for the fifth time that afternoon, I climbed back up the ladder, onto the deck of the boat then down another ladder to where I was supposed to be working.

"You might be getting some action," Shearlane's voice rang with barely contained laughter that evening. "Got a call from the public relations folks at the electric company late this afternoon. I think they were checking to see if you really had a reporter on tap. You've got their attention now."

Shearlane was right about attention. By mid-morning the next day, two different electric company engineers had called asking to set up a meeting with the representative of the Bull Canyon Association Committee for Electrification (that was me!). My response: "I am tired of talk and besides I have to meet reporters at the L.A. offices tomorrow."

The man in charge of new power line installation called. "We've located power poles and cable. I think we can start construction in two weeks." My response: "We've had all sorts of promises before. We won't stop our pressure until we actually see something physical to prove it's going to happen."

Just after lunch, Mr. Cook roared up our driveway, then jumped from his car looking disheveled and worried. "You sure have stirred up a hornet's nest," he grumbled. "L.A. office has grabbed all the equipment we'd put aside for repairs, all the poles we've been saving to take an extra line to the industrial complex they're building at the new freeway off-ramp. They say your job is top priority, but don't know what good all the gear will be when we haven't got any spare linemen out here. All our crew are in the middle of other jobs. Whatever you are up to, call it off. You'll get your power as soon as I can arrange a crew. If you make any more fuss, I'll lose my job!"

I waited impatiently until Larry came in from the boatyard, showered and settled on a kitchen stool, a large pitcher of lemonade plus a bottle of rum in front of him. Then I dialed Shearlane's number and made sure Larry could hear what I was saying. "I've heard of the power of the press, today I've seen it in action," I exclaimed. "Larry told me he couldn't believe how tough I acted, but I finally got really ticked off. Told Cook I didn't give a damn about his job, we needed power to the canyon right now. Then I showed him my sleeping bag and camping gear all rolled up and ready in the back of the truck. He went really pale. He used my phone, then sat out in his car for two hours until a big truck arrived. Cook even forgot about his clean white shirt and polished shoes as he helped them unload three huge coils of cable right on our old road. Assured us poles will be trucked in and work started on Monday."

I made absolutely no excuses for abandoning my desk when Monday arrived. Ellie's Cadillac cruised into the yard before I finished my morning tea. "No one can stop it now," she called. "Linemen came by my house before I had climbed out of bed. Told them to make their headquarters here in your yard. Lots more shade than anywhere else and besides, wouldn't want everyone seeing me before I got brushed and painted in the morning. You'd better warn them about snakes. Found a rattler curled up in the woodshed a few days back."

Larry, too, abandoned his attempts to work on the boat as the different work teams arrived, each needing directions to the secluded households of our neighbors, each obviously awed by the isolation and ruggedness of the canyon. It soon became obvious that these men had been pulled away from their usual work in the sprawling city to the north.

"You really got cougars up this way? They as dangerous as we hear?" the leader of the pole digging team asked. "Think we should talk to the sheriff before we do the work up above Lindell Road? Those drug dealers your neighbor told us about could still be hiding stuff in the hills up there." I realized the men must have met up with Bob Steele when they were stringing poles and wires along the bulldozed roads and ponds he'd dug on his 260-acre plateau. I could imagine Bob's glee as he'd filled their ears with stories that were old even before Larry and I moved into the canyon.

I found tweezers to pull thorns from unprotected fingers, and then reassured the team. "Cougars will be scared off by all your racket. Same with rattlers. Just make lots of noise and don't step over any big rocks without checking first. Biggest danger out here is getting buried under a mound of bullshit or butted by that crazy goat of Sandy's. It's on the loose again."

Three weeks after Shearlane and Robert's visit, with the crews finally finished, I found myself unwilling to climb out of bed in the morning. "Your allergy bothering you?" Larry asked with barely suppressed frustration. "Your eyes aren't swollen, skin looks good. Be great to get in a whole day's work without constantly having to answer questions for those power company guys. Jimmie says his electrician will come up this weekend to get the house wired and run the power over from the pole. You did a good job. Bet you're ready to settle in and finish the book."

I lay ready to do absolutely nothing as Larry made himself a pot of coffee, slathered peanut butter and jam on two slices of bread then almost ran toward the next piece of timber that lay waiting for his attention in the boatshed. The first cicadas started up their sun-warmed rhythm. I heard the generator roar to life then settle in for what would be its last week of rumbling. The realization slowly dawned. I was experiencing withdrawal symptoms, withdrawal from the adrenal surge brought on by fighting a well-defined battle, withdrawal from the sense of power that came with having the Edison Company officials and their minions rushing to satisfy me. Then there had been the attention from canyon dwellers. They had each come by to sign final papers that would let them take power from the main lines into their homes. People who owned empty parcels of canyon land arrived to indicate where they might eventually bulldoze a living pad on the property electricity made far more interesting, more valuable. Each had been eager to hear details of the ruse that had finally broken the maze of red tape. Everyone showered me with words of appreciation, even when I reminded them of the groundwork various canyon folks had laid.

Everyone except Bob Steele. But Pete Shomler had warned me, "Bob's nose is really bent. He's raving on about pushy women. I told him I didn't care who got the power in just as long as we got it! Not sure what's really bugging him, he's been really shitty lately. Been so bad Marlys says she's never coming back, says he wants her to leave. He's even gotten nasty to me and the kids."

I realized I missed Bob Steele's big bold presence, just as I missed the bustle of the linemen who had gratefully settled in the shaded front yard during lunch breaks, joking, relaxed and full of stories. Invariably each newcomer had walked over to the boatyard to question Larry about the ocean going boat he was creating almost on top of a mountain in a desert canyon fifty miles from the sea. If I wandered over after lunch, I'd often find a line of unlaced, dust-covered, metal-cleated boots piled at the bottom of the ladder. I'd listen as Larry talked of the sheer pleasure of turning random pieces of rough-sawn timber into a strictly controlled structure that had to be water tight from all directions, strong, and at the same time, graceful and beautiful. "How did I learn to do this?" Larry answered. "Woodworking seemed to come naturally to me. I just pick up a chisel and it fits my hand. I love building boats; it's the ultimate wood-working challenge. In fact, if I knew I was going to live forever I'd build a new boat every five years. Only problem is I love to sail, too. Be good to get this baby free from the canyon and head her off across an ocean, see how she feels."

"Why would you want to leave a beautiful place like this?" one of the linemen asked. His sentiment seemed to be shared by all of these city men. I overheard fragments of their conversations as they took breaks between adding poles, lines, and connections. "Great hunting, neighbors far enough away to give you some privacy, fine place to raise a few horses. My kids would love living out here."

"What a wonderful, safe place for me and my family, no city gangs, no drive-by shootings or crazy drivers. I could feel really secure out here. Can't imagine why that guy's talking about giving up a place like this. I sure wouldn't want to be out in a storm in that boat."

Now all the linemen had packed up. I knew it was time to settle down and work toward getting our boat finished so someday in the not too distant future, we could sail away from allergy-inducing canyon dust, autumn fires, winter floods, telephone and electrical bills and toward the unfettered life I remembered from the days before we'd found Bull Canyon.

I climbed out of bed, my lethargy still stronger than my work ethic.

Cup of tea in hand, I wandered down to the old stretch of road, Cindy trotting unleashed beside me. "Get back here," I called as she rushed to investigate an enticing smell. A roadrunner shot out from under the dog's searching nose, its neck outstretched, its legs a blur. I watched as the bird streaked downhill drawing my eyes toward the rugged beauty of the canyon. For that moment I glimpsed the same vision those city-bred and city-frustrated linemen had seen. To them this land looked untamed, open, a refuge and a playground. Then I began to think about the work I'd been ignoring, work that I could now give my undivided attention. I turned to head back to the stone cottage and lost sight of the roadrunner as it sped westward just as we would do some day, when the time had come to sail away.

◇◇

"You seen the cat around?" Larry asked a few days later.

"Can't really say I have," I answered as I raked up wood shavings from under the boat. "In fact, can't remember seeing Dog for the past day or two. I remember it following the linemen up towards Steele's plateau last week but since then been too busy to really notice. He been eating his food?"

"That's why I asked," Larry said. "The bowl I keep on the workbench doesn't look like it's been touched for a few days."

"Your damned cat has been prowling around up here for a week," Bob growled when I phoned him. "One of the females must be in heat. If you don't keep control of that animal, coyotes will get him."

"Been a lot of howling last few nights," Sandy said. "But I haven't seen your cat. No trees up this way so if it's been wandering away from the buildings, wouldn't stand much chance against a pack of coyotes."

Three days later, Pete Shomler drove in, honked and waited in his car. Cindy stood her ground in the doorway of the boatshed, barking and growling as if she really was a watchdog. I snapped a lead on her, and then walked over. "You can stop looking for that dumb cat," Pete stated. "Here's what's left of her. Stevie found it near the shed where our cats bed down. Better go by the pound next time you're in town and get three or four kittens. One or two of them might be smart enough to survive. Going to be lots of mice and rats invading your house when the weather turns colder." He handed me the chewed remains of a fuzzy white and grey tail that had, only a few days before, waved and undulated in the air over the inquisitive and useful animal that had been a hard working part of our country cottage team.

After a sluggish morning, I spent the afternoon going through the almost mechanical motions required to cut woodplugs out of offcuts of timber. My mind was free to meander since Larry was engrossed in building fancy raised-panel doors for the cabinets he'd finished. But instead of thinking of the boat or about the chapter I was writing during my now interruption-free mornings, I kept looking over to where Dog's empty food bowl still sat on Larry's workbench. That cat had spent his life unrestrained, free to wander wherever he pleased, bound to the buildings we currently called home only by the tenuous need for occasional warmth, a bit of extra food when rat hunting was slow and possibly the pleasure of human hands stroking hard-to-itch spots. The cat's roaming ways, its very freedom, had gotten it killed.

I glanced across the yard to where Cindy had settled calmly at the end of her long lead, bone between her paws. She looked content, safe. Her tranquility brought to mind the linemen's comment, "I could feel really secure out here." But did the stone cottage really offer security? Or was it just an illusion? For I knew the very restraints that kept Cindy from wandering off made her totally dependant on us. If we weren't there to feed her, to provide her water and take her for a long run each day, she too would perish.

As I walked over toward the house to shower off the woodchips that dusted me from head to toe, I stopped for a moment and glanced first at the boatshed then at the stone cottage. For that moment, I questioned my desire to sail away instead of savoring this place we'd worked hard to change into a comfortable home. I wondered if Larry and I were tempting fate with our desire to launch this boat and spend the next years of our life wandering freely wherever we wanted to go. Then I noticed a flight of Canadian geese winging northward above me and as I watched the ragged V they formed I realized, for me there really was no choice. I knew the cottage offered an appearance of security but the boat would soon give me the ongoing adventure I craved.

Chapter 21

The Far Side of Success

Now that we had an unlimited supply of electricity available at the flick of a switch, our third summer in the canyon seemed to slide almost unnoticed into autumn. The huge air conditioner shoved refrigerated air in from one end of the boatshed. The swamp cooler threw its moisturized coolness in from the other, so the scorching heat no longer forced Larry to stop for a midday siesta. As the September days grew shorter, we scoured the back lanes of Pedlars Village for secondhand work lamps and extension cords. They soon festooned the boatshed and let Larry keep working late into the evening. His productivity soared. The deck of the boat quickly closed in as he bolted thick teak cabinsides in place.

Inside the cottage, overhead fans whirled cool air into each room. The electric-light-extended work hours, a second-hand electric typewriter, plus freedom from "canyon business," meant my book manuscript and the articles I'd promised to write rushed toward completion. I now had afternoons free to work in comfortable companionship with Larry, fitting woodplugs into the deck strakes he'd screwed in place. The sun porch of the cottage became a dust-free working space. Late in the day, I'd retreat there to put the final coats of varnish on raised panel cabinet doors Larry had lovingly formed using black walnut and birds-eye maple. We'd often delay dinner until eight or nine o'clock. Then we'd fall into bed and count coups, ticking off each small obstacle we'd overcome, each project we'd finished.

As much as we enjoyed the immediate physical improvements electricity added to our lives, I couldn't keep from feeling slightly uneasy as I noticed the underlying changes it brought to the canyon.

Less than a week after the power officially arrived, a slightly weathered mobile home appeared alongside Ma Newhouse's garden. A few days later I took a broken drill bit down to Casa Nueva for welding. As I walked up to his workshop, Lee Newhouse glanced toward the trailer, his expression betraying a rare sense of annoyance, then said, "Ma's pretty happy to have her daughter and grandkid up here for a good long visit. Keeps her from being lonely all day, so I shouldn't complain. But food bill is going up. I'll have to plow up a bit more land to add to Ma's garden. Sure would have liked a bit of time to dig a pad farther away from the house before they arrived. Been a lot more private for all of us. But minute they heard we had electricity, they drove on up and settled on the only flat spot there was. Glad her man's got work, even if it is only a delivery job. Power company deposit took most of my savings."

A few days later, Lee drove in to fill his pickup truck with the wood shavings I had raked into a pile just outside the boatshed. "Better go up and check my hives while I'm here," he said. Then he turned to the quiet seven-year-old he'd brought along with him. "Little Rufus here is going to have to learn a bit about handling bees. Seems he'll be living with us permanent like. Might as well show him the best producing hives I've got."

Another surprise was waiting for me when I stopped by the Lone Palm Ranch for the first time in almost a month. "Come and take a look at the plans for my house," Ellie called even before I got out of the truck. "Bob's going to bring his bulldozer up and start building a road to a pad right up at the top of my property. I'll have a better view than anyone. Bob says his banker will loan me money to build it against the three pieces of land I plan to divide off. If I sell just two of them I can pay off the loan. Bob says electricity, phones, now we've got it, land's going to sell for really good prices."

"You really want to divide up this land just to build a house?" I asked Ellie. "Are you sure you want to have neighbors so close? Thought you liked having space around you."

"You know the kind of folks who buy land out here. They're all dreamers," Ellie answered. "Takes them years and years to get around to building. I get the kind of house I've always wanted, air conditioning, a humidifier so my skin doesn't keep adding wrinkles and wall-to-wall carpet while I can enjoy it. I'll be dead before anything really changes. Sure glad potential buyers won't have to drive past Newhouse's place; it's looking downright trashy since both his kids have moved their families in."

I had tried to ignore the unsightly extra trailer, the latest collection of rusting cars that had been added to those already scattered along the edges of the stream at Casa Nuevo. During the previous week, the Newhouses' son and his partner had also arrived with their dented mobile home to "save money so we can buy ourselves some land up here someday, too." Then I watched as Lee erected a television aerial on top of the hill behind their house and ran cables to three different abodes. "Ma can't say no to the kids, can she?" he commented. I could appreciate Ma and Pa's dilemma and finally understood why they had been less than enthusiastic about getting power into the canyon.

I had very mixed emotions as I listened to Barbara, Jimmie and Larry talking about the sewage that must be seeping down into the stream now that three households were sharing a septic system that was, from Ma Newhouse's description, little better than a barrel-sized hole in the

The complete tribe — Larry's family and mine. That's my mom, fifth from the right.

ground. "Planning to get my crew out here. I want to start building a house on the lot up the road from here in the next few weeks," Jimmie said. "I need something to keep them busy 'cause not much going on in Laguna right now. Besides, it's time I start making some money out of all this land. Soon as I submit my drawings, there's going to be county inspectors driving up here. Hope Newhouse fixes his sewage system and cleans up the place before one of the inspectors notices it. Codes allow for only one household on any single property. Reason I bought this land up here is it's already divided into seventeen titles. But Newhouse only owns that single lot. Now that could be a real problem for him."

I have always wondered if there was any connection between the phone call I made the next day and the traumatic event that took place about six weeks later. But I felt compelled to share Jimmie's concerns with Lee Newhouse. He listened quietly then replied, "Can't close my doors to my own family. With all the bills coming in, don't have money to fix up much of anything. Just have to deal with the county if something happens. Heard they don't look if no one complains."

With the approach of fire season, Mariano and his brothers had been up to clear the firebreak around all our buildings. We joined in to do a thorough pre-winter clean up in the boatyard and cottage in preparation for a party we'd scheduled to celebrate another milestone. The boat now had a name carved deeply into the highly varnished transom. I'd painstakingly added gold leaf to highlight each letter, then Larry secured a sheet in place to hide the name. I'd sent out invitations to friends and family, and then hand delivered one to each of our canyon neighbors. Margie, her pregnancy far advanced, had a trucking job that would keep her away that weekend. Sandy Shomler, alerted by the rattle of my truck as it bumped up her rutted approach road, was standing in her doorway. When I pulled to a stop in front of the ever-growing structure that now sported a covered-in porch, even though the back rooms had empty spaces where windows would someday be, I was a bit surprised that she didn't invite me to stop for a cool drink. Instead she called, "Best you stay in the truck, Mike's on the loose. Can't come down that weekend. Pete'll be working and he insists I stay where I can hear the phone. I hate that damned phone, like a ball and chain keeping me at his beck and call all the time."

"I might drop in but don't expect Marlys," Bob Steele said offhandedly. "She's gone to live near her goddamned job, right next to that smart-dressing snob she calls her boss. Thinks without her paycheck I'll never get the bank to give me a loan. Never get the money to divide off my land and start building a spec house. Says even with power and phones the land up here's useless. Dumb bitch is in for a real surprise!"

Two weeks later, a crowd of partygoers worked together, rolling our half-ton generator out of the old concrete shed. A sailing friend had bought it to provide electricity on his schooner. And as I watched it being loaded onto the bed of his truck my thoughts turned to Bob Steele. I realized I wouldn't miss the roar of the generator but I already missed the connection to canyon folks that Bob's gossip-filled fuel deliveries had kept intact. The next morning, another event put one more chink in my connection to Bull Canyon.

After Larry unveiled the name we'd chosen to keep the connection to his families Welsh background, I sprayed champagne on *Taleisin*'s transom in imitation of the dousing she'd get when she was actually being launched into seawater. Then the party began in earnest. Sunrise the next morning revealed almost forty leftover party-goers camped in disarray around the property.

"Come on, let's get this boat moved before we lose any more of our workers," Jimmie Moore ordered after Mom had finished dishing out mounds of pancakes along with the leftovers from the previous night's potluck dinner. The same truck that had carried the generator away had also brought a very

solid steel boat cradle that the owner had loaned to us. This arrangement saved him storage fees and us the cost of building or renting a cradle when the time came to truck our boat down to the sea. Now all of the wooden struts that attached the nearly finished 8-ton hull to the sturdy uprights of the boatshed had to be removed. Then the boat had to be lifted just enough to slide the steel cradle under her, all the time making sure that, as each support was shifted out of the way others were in place to keep her steady. I'd worried about this whole procedure ever since we'd been offered the cradle.

"Why don't we hire a crane — Bob told me we could get one up here for three hundred bucks. Sloan is paying us more than $1500 for the generator, so we've got the money. Be absolutely safe that way," I'd suggested.

"You're the one who taught me folks like working together to move big things. Besides, I'd have to remove some of the boatshed roof to crane the boat into a cradle. Far less complicated this way. We can save the money and buy an anchor with it," Larry answered. Then he added, "Pick up two more hydraulic jacks next time you run in to town."

I found myself torn between wanting to protect the boat and wanting to spend time with the women who were giving my house and kitchen a post-party clean up. I ran out to the boatyard every few minutes to watch twenty men debating tactics and joking as they jacked, wedged, added pipe rollers then slowly moved the cradle closer to the boat. I could sense that, as usual, Larry had thought this whole process through — each call for another wedge, another block was answered with, "There's a stack waiting right in the corner of the shed. Take it slowly; if we don't do anything quickly we can't get into any trouble."

As I turned to head back to the kitchen I heard Larry say, "Okay, Dean, now start jacking the boat up real slow, just enough to roll the cradle under the forefoot of the boat, then we move this block."

"STOP!" That single shouted word echoed against the hills surrounding the boatshed. I froze.

If ever the phrase "deafening silence" held true, it was at that moment. Everyone had jumped clear of the possible trajectory of a falling boat and now stood, as if rooted in place, looking for the potential danger. Then they turned toward the source of the warning. Mike, my brother-in-law, stood still as a stone, his hand pointing beneath the boat, a shocked look on his face. The look turned slowly from shocked to mischievous as he stated, "Larry, do you realize you are trusting your life savings and three years of hard work to a $14.95 K-Mart jack?" My heart slowly returned to a normal rhythm as laughter rang out from everyone. Everyone, that is, except Larry, whose face was only gradually regaining its natural rosy color. Then he, too, joined the camaraderie that flowed as *Taleisin* slid slowly from her well-grounded building supports into the highly moveable transport cradle.

◇◇

"What do you think of Newhouse taking his hives away? Didn't he say they were some of his very best producers?" Larry asked me about a week after the name unveiling party. I had been a bit surprised when Lee arrived that morning, accompanied by his taciturn middle-aged son, and said he was moving his hives so I wouldn't have to worry about being stung ever again. "Besides, might be a better idea to have these bees up near the Shomler's place," Lee added when I tried to reassure him by saying I never saw any bees near the house. In actuality, I'd thought he'd driven up to show off the new truck he'd bought and was using his bees as an excuse. But he soon made it clear the truck was no reason for celebration. "County showed up about three weeks back. Said they'd slap all kinds of fines on me if I didn't move my kids off or fix up the place," Lee said. "Took a lot of talking but they agreed to hold off on the fines if I filled out the right

papers and paid to divide up my land. Then they made me agree to put in a fence to hide the metal I keep for my work, the cars my son plans to fix up and sell. Cheapest sewage system they'll accept is going to set me back half a year's wages. Almost had my house all paid off. Was planning to retire in six months. Now I've been forced to take out a bigger bank loan. Means I can't retire for five more years. So I'll be doing that 120-mile round trip a lot more times. Old truck used so much fuel I figured I might as well up my loan and get one that will save me some money."

"I think he bought that truck to bolster his ego," I said to Larry as we settled down for dinner. "It's sort of a consolation prize for having to keep working. Sandy told Ma Newhouse, we're the ones who dobbed them in. Figured all the city folks who come up to visit us and watch our boat project don't understand country life and complained about the place looking messy. But Newhouse says it could just as easily have been Steele or any of the other land owners up the road. They've all got "for sale" signs out, they all want to improve their property values. Might even been one of the real-estate salespeople who are nosing around out here. He thinks Sandy's got a bee in her bonnet about us. She's probably worried because their plumbing and electrics aren't up to county standards either."

"Newhouse should have fixed things up before the county stepped in. He did have warning," Larry answered. "He broke all the rules. Too bad he's ended up saddled with a big debt but I'm not unhappy to see him cleaning up his property. Doesn't look like such a garbage dump now. Remember, Lin, we'll want to sell this place some day, too." Then, as if to shut off talk of canyon business, Larry picked up the drawing pad that always sat next to him at dinner time. We were lost in a discussion of the materials we'd need to build the spars that would some day grace the hull that was beginning to gleam under its first coats of white paint.

I wasn't particularly surprised at the frenzied welcome Cindy gave us when we returned late in the evening after a foray away from the canyon. She usually gave us a warm welcome even when we'd only left her latched onto her running lead for an evening away. Now we'd been gone for two nights so I assumed she was really hungry. We'd driven to San Diego to present a slideshow, and then done the usual round of metal dealers, fastening companies and timber yards. "Let's leave everything in the truck for tonight and climb right into bed, I'm exhausted," Larry stated as he searched for the key to unlock the house. I calmed the dog down enough to unclip her long lead, picked up her empty food bowl, turned off the dripping faucet that kept her water bowl full then headed for the kitchen. Larry had just switched on the kitchen light and I ran right into his stock-still back. "Don't move, you could get hurt," he yelped. He moved carefully aside. It took more than a few moments to absorb what I was seeing. Slowly the mess that covered the kitchen floor began to separate itself into individual components. Smashed canisters of flour, sugar, coffee and tea spread their glass and contents to mingle with the remains of the dozen kerosene lamps we'd used to light the cottage. "Don't touch it," Larry said when I bent down to pick up the one unbroken glass lamp that lay amidst the mess. "Call the police while I check the other rooms."

"Who knew you'd be away?" the police officer asked as he began to fill out his report. We'd shown him the shattered panes of the French style sunroom door where the vandal had entered. He noted the broken remains of the typewriter that had been attacked with the hammer that lay beside it on my office/bedroom/living room floor. The list of stolen items was shorter than the list of broken ones; my sister-in-law's fox-trimmed leather coat, a length of heavy golden colored silk from our time in Singapore, an embroidered piece of fabric from an isolated group of native people near Panama. Even in the boatyard we could find nothing missing though the vandal had ripped up every page of the drawings for the boat we were building. "You guys are pretty lucky," the officer stated. "Those tools out in that shop, the gear you got in your sun porch could have been worth a fortune to someone who knew how to pawn it. This definitely wasn't done by some dope-head or regular thief looking for money. Looks more like someone who's jealous or has a grudge against you. From the stuff that's missing, stuff that's been thrown around, I'd guess it was a woman. Made a mess for you to clean up but not like a real vandal. You should see some of the rotten stuff they do... slashed curtains, shit on the walls."

Real vandal or not, I couldn't sleep that night as I tried to rearrange the shackles this break-in had tightened around my mind. "Did you tell anyone we were leaving?" I whispered to Larry who tossed and turned beside me.

"Haven't talked to anyone in the canyon for at least two weeks," he answered. "I did see Sandy's car down at Newhouse's when we drove out, saw Ellie working around her place. Probably no need to actually tell anyone anything; you know how word spreads around here."

"I'm going to call Ellie in the morning. Maybe she'll go talk to the canyon folks with me 'cause I think I know who did it and I plan to get Elaine's coat back," I stated, my anger shoving sleep even farther away.

"Forget talking to anyone about it," Larry replied as he got out of bed then poured himself another glass of whiskey. "Remember, this time we've got insurance to pay Elaine for her coat, fix the door, buy you a typewriter. I think the less you say to any of the neighbors about this, the better. But we have to turn lights on and leave the radio playing when we go out from now on."

I thought of the carefully chosen bronze boat gear, the gleaming compass and heavy anchors that were now starting to fill the sunroom to the point we called it the Gold Room. I pictured the damage someone could so easily inflict on *Taleisin* that, now that it had a real name, seemed to have an actual personality. I realized lights on or lights off, I could no longer feel comfortable leaving it all unprotected for more than a few hours at a time until we found out who broke into the house.

Lee Newhouse stopped me as I drove past his property two days later. "Cops been around asking questions. Insisted on quizzing my kids, too," Lee said. "Sorry to hear what happened but don't blame us, don't hold no grudges against you guys. Only one around here that does is Sandy and she's too smart to do something like that."

"Guess everyone in the canyon knows about the break-in," I said to Larry that evening. "I talked with the cops and they said they can't really do anything more about the case. But I know who I think did it and I want to confront her so I can feel completely safe again."

"Let it lie, Lin," Larry said giving me a hug. "You won't feel comfortable even if you could prove exactly who did it. That's what happens when someone violates your space. Makes you aware of how vulnerable you are. You might be right in your suspicions but you might also open up a hornet's nest if you step in without real proof. Let's just get on with our own life."

For the first few weeks after the break-in, I was able to lose myself in the work of editing the book manuscript that had come back from my publisher. Jimmie and Barbara began spending almost every weekend up at the cottage, Jimmie to clear and mark out the land for his latest construction project and Barbara to indulge her latest pleasure; each time they drove up from the beach, they stopped to pick up the horse she had bought. "Can't call this place the Black Star Ranch without some kind of ranch things happening," Barbara had joked the first time they drove up with the horse trailer bumping along behind their truck. Their weekend stays gave Larry and me a chance to get away from the canyon for more than a few hours at a time. But the need to leave the canyon mid-week to do slideshows and book signings led to a moment of inspiration. "Looks good," Larry said as I showed him the cards I'd handwritten using my best imitation of calligraphy. "Not sure it will work, but worth a try."

Less than a week later I knew I'd solved my most immediate problem. "What a fine idea. Put me down for Tuesday through Friday the 5th," my Mom said. "Ida and Sid are coming out from the east coast for a visit, they'd love a country holiday." Several other friends responded with equal enthusiasm after reading the cards I'd sent out which read; "You have just won a free, all-expense paid holiday in the country. Accommodations, food and wine provided. Bring nothing but a change of clothes. Please inform me of any dietary preferences." Each recipient felt they truly had won something worthwhile. But as I put their names down alongside the speaking engagements on my calendar, I couldn't ignore my sense of loss. With the advent of electricity, it seemed spontaneity, security and comfortable interaction with my canyon neighbors had been relegated to the past along with the oil lamps I'd found smashed by the vandal I could suspect but never name.

"Call the minute you get home," read the note propped on the kitchen counter. During a very successful three-day journey to Santa Barbara, we'd earned enough to pay for two dozen bronze castings the foundry had made from Larry's carefully shaped wooden patterns and found time to go sailing on Jimmie's bright red sloop. My skin had felt wonderfully clear of allergic tendencies. My mind had been fully at rest since I knew my folks would reach the cottage only a few hours after we left. Now we'd returned home to find Cindy happily gnawing a huge soup bone on the front doorstep, lights shining in a spotlessly clean kitchen, the last of the wine-spiced beef stew I'd made for Mom and her guests simmering at the back of the carefully banked wood burning stove. "Everything looks great here. I'll call Mom after we eat some dinner, give her time to reach home," I said to Larry when he walked in holding six long beautifully tapered and detailed lengths of bronze that would soon be attached to the hull of the boat to support the mast that, at the moment, was just a pile of rough looking timber lying alongside the boatshed.

"Thank you, thank you, thank you," Mom blurted. "Gave Ida a holiday she'll never forget. She and Sid thought they were in the wild west when we drove up to your place. Hawks flying, coyotes calling out. The owl that lives next to the back window really spooked them. They'd never used a big wood-burning fireplace before. The weekend would have really impressed them even if Margie hadn't tried to have her baby at your place."

"Margie what?" I stammered in disbelief.

"Haven't you been in your back room? Sheets and blankets are piled in the corner. I rinsed out the worst, but you'll want to give them a good wash. Day before yesterday just before midnight, a real racket woke me up, dogs barking and howling, cat snarling. I went into the kitchen and saw a tiny beam of light flashing through the trees, pack of dogs bounding up your driveway, Cindy charging about barking, someone calling your name. I turned on some lights, got a hold of Cindy and in staggers Margie. She was trying to drive herself to the hospital. Didn't stop to close her gate, dogs followed her down the road. Then her car broke down halfway between her place and yours. She walked downhill expecting to find you. Contractions were happening every few minutes. Dad and I had no idea where the nearest hospital was so I called Ellie. She said stay put. Said she'd come right up and guide us out the back way, quicker than going down canyon. I got Margie to lay down in the back room and by the time Ellie finally drove in, Margie's water broke. I got her cleaned up; Ida made a bed for her in back of our car. Dad drove, I sat in back holding Margie's hand, Ida and Sid went with Ellie. We all got over to Riverside hospital just in time for Margie to have her baby."

"Glad you were here to help her. I wouldn't have had the slightest idea of what to do. Not sure I could have coped," I said when I could finally edge a word in between her excited recitation.

"I could have killed Ellie," Mom went on as if my interruption had never made it down the phone line. "She took almost an hour to get from her place to yours. Didn't even say sorry when I asked what took so long. Just said she had to put her makeup on, didn't want to scare any cop that might stop us on the way."

The image of Ellie, primped and dressed like a lady, leading the cops on a merry chase as she rushed through the night on her rescue mission stayed with me as I climbed into bed. I chided myself for feeling jealous at missing all the excitement. Then, just before I drifted off to sleep, my mind unraveled some gems I would keep and savor from among the words Mom had uttered. "You would have coped," she'd told me. "That's one thing you learned from me. When things seem to get out of hand, you know how to dig in and do what's necessary." I smiled to myself as I recognized the compliment she'd implied. And in Mom's final words, coming at the tail of that compliment, lay the secret to her apparently boundless energy: "When everything's back in control, you might feel like having a nervous breakdown but by then you realize it would just be a waste of time!"

Chapter 22

Rodeo

"That there one's the meanest of the bunch, Miss Lin," Jerry said as he pointed to a brown-and-white bull placidly meandering around the wooden holding pen below us. "Called *Turn the Crank Frank*. Devil twists to the right in the middle of his high kick just to get you off balance."

Earlier in the week, Virginia Heck had ridden up our driveway on her handsome grey mare. "Just a little thank-you gift," she'd said. "Phone and electric's made my daughter a lot happier out here. She's busy getting ready to compete in the barrel race at the rodeo. It's down by the lake this weekend. Got you some reserve-seating tickets. Can't stop for a drink right now, I've got to get started grooming this lady if I'm going to show her properly."

We had just located the roped-off special seating area in the temporary rodeo arena when the diminutive owner of Pedlars Village came over to greet us. "Nice to see you, Miss Lin," he'd said sweeping his large white hat off to reveal a network of scars running across his forehead and up into his less than abundant hair. "Never noticed you at last year's rodeo."

"We've never been to a rodeo before," I told him.

"I've been at rodeos since before I could walk. Rode in more than I can count. If I didn't think I'd make a fool of myself, I'd be out there on one of them bulls today," Jerry said as he graciously led us to the front bench. He then excused himself, saying, "I'll come back when the action starts up, answer some questions for you. Lot more to riding a bucking bull than just having a strong grip."

Hands reached up to touch the brims of cowboy hats as Jerry worked his way through the crowd. Several competitors, clearly distinguishable by large numbered squares pinned to the back of their shirts, climbed down from their perches along the slatted barricades and fences surrounding the arena and reached out to shake Jerry's hand or engage him in conversation.

As we watched the first hour's events, I began to notice distinct differences among the cowboys waiting to enter the arena. The riders who roped calves, wrestled steers or rode cutting horses stood out, dressed in bright embroidered shirts like the ones I'd seen in the windows of the expensive western clothing shops of Riverside. Agile and quick-moving, they tended to be long, lean and loose-limbed. The group that surrounded Jerry not only looked quieter, tougher, but with their shorter limbs and more tightly knit bodies, they moved slower, more deliberately. Amidst these bucking bull riders, Jerry didn't appear to be nearly as short, bowlegged nor anachronistic as he did when we saw him surrounded by the folks at Pedlars Village.

"Good money for the winner today, couple of the best riders on the circuit are in town to show the locals what it takes," Jerry said when he settled into the seat between Larry and me.

"Do the organizers pay professionals to come and attract the crowds?" I asked as the first rider began to lower himself carefully onto the relatively quiet looking bull wedged tightly in the starting chute.

"Sort of the other way around. Pros look for small-town rodeos that offer decent prize money without the heavy competition. But it's really the points they're after. As long as it's a sanctioned rodeo, even a third-place finish will give them points toward a chance at championship competitions. Don't have the points, don't get an invite to state level rodeos. State level, then national level, that's where the real money is. Win there and you get enough to give you a decent stake in life. Just like I did."

A loudspeaker blared out, "Dennis Lane riding *Bucking Crazy*." The gate in front of us flew open. Jerry tensed. The crowd began screaming. And for a split second nothing happened. Suddenly the bull appeared to explode into the ring, twisting as it leapt clear then sending its hind legs wildly skyward. The rider leaned back, feet flying, one heavily gloved hand gripped under the braided rope that was his only connection to the bull, the other hand waving high above his head. For eight amazingly long seconds, twelve hundred pounds of raging animal reared, twisted and threw its head back as if trying to destroy the unwanted burden clinging to its back. Then suddenly a loud buzzer blared out and the rider leapt for freedom, flying off to land awkwardly on all fours in the churned-up manure and dust, yet ready to spring clear of the flailing hooves of the bull. "Good ride," Jerry shouted into my ear, "but he'll lose some points cause he didn't stay in rhythm with that bull. Bull's a pretty high scorer, too, never made the same move twice, kept the rider guessing; I'd have liked riding him."

"You actually liked getting thrown around like that? Most dangerous looking thing I have ever seen," I commented as Jerry intently watched the next rider adjusting his grip on the bull that snorted and kicked at the slats of the starting chute.

"When I settle myself onto that bull, nod my head, and they throw that chute open, I'm truly living," Jerry answered. "Those eight seconds, flying on that animal's back, hearing the crowds roar, getting the bull to twist and turn and be as wild looking as he can, absolutely nothing in the world matters except showing my style, impressing the judges."

"Dale Jones riding *Flirting with Disaster*," the loudspeaker blared. Our conversation paused as the next rider flew free of the bull almost as soon as it twisted out of the chute, the bull's front legs hitting the ground hard as its rear legs seemed to fly out at a ninety-degree angle to its body. In the relative quiet that followed, Jerry continued, "Besides, who are you to talk about danger. You plan to head out onto the ocean in a little boat,

no prize money waiting for you — just pirates, sharks, storms, no one to help you. Worse that happens on a bull is you get thrown off, kicked, break a few bones."

No one but us seemed to laugh when the speaker blared out the next bull's name, "Joey Street riding *Preparation H.*" Jerry watched silently, seeming to study every move made by rider and bull as everyone waited for the chute to open. Now that we began to understand some of the finer points of the competition, we also joined the roar of the crowd and felt the excitement that surged into the ring along with bull and rider. We felt the disappointment mixed with relief when the rider was thrown clear and just missed being crushed against the arena side. In my excitement I almost missed Jerry's words as he said, "Smashed up my forehead then broke my shoulder on a bull that kicked like that. Not the worst break I had but took the longest to heal. Next ride, got the points, took the prize money but tore my groin muscles up too much to compete any more. That's when I bought my land. Now I have to leave here today and tell folks at the village I've sold them out to the highest bidder. Bulldozers come in next month to turn the only real home I've ever had into a business park. Not sure I did the right thing, not sure where all my folks are going to go, not sure where I'll go, either."

When the last bucking bull rider lost his chance at prize money and clambered up the wooden siding of the arena just in time to clear the menacing horns of a bull aptly named *Fear Me*, Jerry touched his hat brim lightly, turned and walked off toward the entrance of the rodeo. High-heeled cowboy boots scuffing up the dust, tight-fitting jeans emphasizing the rolling gait that defied any thought of fitting into a business suit, I could sense his confusion as he struggled to find the right words to tell his tenants he'd played his hand and the money he'd won had changed their world. Larry, too, seemed to catch Jerry's mood, for as we walked back to our truck I could hear him quietly singing Kenny Roger's song, "The Gambler."

Pedlars Village wasn't the only land to face the relentless power of encroaching development that month. The relatively hill-free acres at the entrance to El Toro Road had now been flattened into submission. The half-mile-long stretch of roadbed that crossed these acres had been widened and smoothed to perfection in preparation for paving. Strings and flags marked off individual house blocks, and already more than a dozen concrete foundations were beginning to take form under signs announcing, "Live your Dream, only 10% down, 150 New Homes starting at $69,500."

"Won't change the canyon much," I commented to Larry as we drove home.

"You're probably right," he answered. "Developers don't want to deal with hills. They'll stick down here in the flat lands. Too bad 'cause I am darned tired of this dirt road. Seems the corrugations get rougher every year."

As soon as we reached the top of the driveway, Larry rushed toward the boatshed saying, "Still got a few hours more light. I want to get two pieces of the mast glued up so I can shape them tomorrow morning."

After the excitement of the rodeo I wasn't feeling as ambitious as he was. The first excuse that leapt to my mind was, it's too late in the day to varnish anything, light's beginning to fade. I went into the cottage and sat down at my desk. My mind wouldn't settle into the scattering of notes for the novel that Larry had encouraged me to take on as my next writing project. Instead I found myself doing nothing but staring out the window.

Across the canyon from my window there was a tumble of huge rocks just above the spring that fed the waterfall. On one upright boulder, a finger-painted maze of ochre and black lines served as a reminder of the people who wandered through these hills long before the Spaniards arrived with their horses, guns and gods. When we first moved to the canyon, I'd eagerly taken visitors up to share the sense of peace that seemed to surround this hilltop aerie. I'd pointed out the black lines of soot scorched into the crevices of the

rock where cook fires had once burned, the broken slabs of rocks which might have, at one time, formed a roof to protect the natural dyes of the painting and help them withstand centuries of sun, wind and rain. Larry, in his practical way, talked of the perfection of this spot for hunter gatherers, "It's just within easy bow shot of the spring, and you could crouch behind that rock and no game would see you. Spring has never dried up since we've been here so there'd always be growth to attract the animals." Some of our visitors would say, "You should report these paintings to the archaeology department at the university. They'd want to explore around here to see if there is a midden." But both Bob Steele and Pete Shomler, the only other canyon folks who knew of this site, had made it clear they wanted no part of university types, "stomping all around, no thought to who owns the land, poking their noses into stuff they shouldn't." And though this native painting was technically just inside the boundary of the land Larry and I now half-owned, I resisted the temptation to learn more about the truly original inhabitants of Bull Canyon because I worried the magic, the special spirit of this place, might disappear in an over-abundance of scientific explanations.

Through my restlessness that late afternoon, I recalled the simple geometric lines scribbled by some earlier canyon-dweller, possibly when he was in a pensive mood similar to mine. I called to Cindy, and then for the first time in almost a year walked across the creek and along Bob Steele's newly graded access road to clamber up to the rocks that sheltered the maze. As I sat down, almost all signs of man-made change were hidden from my view by the swell of the hill below me. Now that I could not see the power lines, the winding dirt road, our boatshed or the scattered homesteads of our neighbors, the vista before me looked almost the same as it must have two hundred years ago, beginning with the gurgling green-edged waterfall, then leading down through the rock jumble of pink and gold canyon hills to the shining silver glimmer of the lake and ending with the sheer black wall of the coastal mountains ten miles to the west. My mind seemed to settle, and as it did I began to fathom just how much the advent of electricity and telephones had changed my thinking about this canyon.

When we'd first come to live here, Bull Canyon had felt wonderfully wild, primitive yet peaceful, quiet and far away from normality. Where others might have seen inconveniences, I'd seen nothing but adventure and interesting challenges. Every day had seemed to bring new wonders and new triumphs, from finding ways to guarantee we had water when and where we wanted it, to conquering the rodents that had as much right to live in these hills as we did. As we settled in to canyon life the adventures and discoveries became smaller but were still magical. I began noticing that the hummingbirds arrived just as the first red and yellow flowers bloomed on the acacia bushes lining the edge of the driveway, and the quail flocked to our yard only when the wild grains that grew there began to yellow and drop their seeds. With this familiarity came a special intimacy. I welcomed each returning bird, each new wild flower, almost like an old friend.

But once the utilities were turned on, this intimacy, along with the camaraderie of the canyon folks, had seemed to disappear. With air conditioning easy to switch on, as soon as the heat of the day beat down on us, we closed ourselves up into the boatshed or cottage instead of throwing open every possible window or finding a shady spot out in the yard to catch the breezes and notice the sounds, sights and aromas that spoke of changing seasons. With two small electric heaters easily warming the whole cottage at the flick of a switch, we rarely lit up the big fireplace. This definitely saved me time. I didn't have to worry about clearing out ashes or sweeping hearths. But we also didn't set out to explore along the stream beds and crevices of the canyon like we had when we foraged for dead trees to cut into firewood. No longer did I feel the pleasure of aiming an ax just so to get cleanly split kindling nor hear the ring my well-placed blows echoed back to me along with the calls of canyon creatures. Even our radio-listening habits had been changed now that we could plug into the power. With a bigger, more powerful radio, we got better reception and began listening to classic music, rock and roll stations and current affairs programs from the big cities to the west.

Just as the advent of the telephone had opened our canyon life to outside contact and loosened the connection to our neighbours, now the electricity seemed to be closing us off from the high desert land. As I sat on the hilltop watching the black shadows of evening slowly creep up the hills beyond our cottage, I realized many of the original charms of canyon life were now just a nuisance. Its isolation meant potential exposure to thieves and vandals, plus I had to spend at least two or three days a week feeling like a roadrunner as I drove up and down El Toro Road then onto the freeways and highways to the north in search of the ever growing list of specialty nautical items we needed as the boat grew closer to a reality. Since it was convenient to stop at one of the shopping malls along my route, I no longer took the extra time to drive into Lake Elsinore and the warm familiarity of shops run by people I'd come to know. Today's visit to the rodeo was the first time I'd seen any of my casual town friends in two or three months. And now, just like Larry, each time I had to drive up the long dirt road that had once been the reason to slow down and shrug off the outside world, to greet neighbors and notice the wildflowers and circling hawks, I resented the noise, dust, truck-juddering corrugations and narrow turns that kept me from rushing home to get one or two extra hours on "the project."

A golden brown eagle soared below me; its wings steady in the updraft generated by the last rays of the setting sun. I watched as it swooped downward to disappear from my sight among the brush near the creek, and then soared upward with a tiny mouse firmly gripped in its talons. I thought again about Jerry. He'd laughed off our concerns at the dangers of bull riding, saying the life we led was far more frightening. Maybe to him we did seem *Bucking Crazy* to willingly head out into the potentially rough weather that lay in wait at sea. But as I slowly began my descent, I realized that to me, the storms we faced at sea had been less emotionally stressful than those we faced right here as we lived on land and built a boat in Bull Canyon.

Chapter 23

Defining Fair

"You guys got a match? Can't find my damned cigarette lighter," Jo Caphart called as she flung open the door of the boatshed. "How about that cool drink you've been promising me?"

I was brushing the first coat of varnish onto the newly finished cabinsides of the boat. The hum of the air conditioner and the blare of the radio had masked any sounds of Jo's arrival. This was the first time she had come for a casual visit. Her only other visits had been when she signed the paperwork necessary to run first telephone, then electric cables, to her trailer at the crossroads north of us. So Jo's midafternoon drop-in was completely unexpected.

"Why don't you show Jo the boat, I'll get some cold drinks," Larry called from the back corner of the shed where he was assembling framework for a hatch. This was not his usual reaction to unexpected daytime interruptions. So I knew he, too, had been caught off guard.

"How about adding something to spice up that drink?" Jo called as he left. She climbed the ladder and took a perfunctory look at the boat, and then climbed back down to march determinedly toward the cottage.

Larry had a pitcher of iced lemonade and a bottle of rum waiting. At Jo's direction he poured an almost equal amount of both into a tall glass, then he lit yet another of her endless chain of cigarettes. When he added a generous splash of rum to his own lemonade I began to suspect Jo's visit was only part of the reason Larry had so willingly put aside his work. I pushed my concerns to the back of my mind, determined to enjoy the break in routine, the chance to review the canyon utilities fight with another satisfied participant now that distance let the humorous moments shine through. More than an hour slid by greased with laughter and rum when suddenly Jo looked at her watch. "Mind if I use your telephone. I'd better call for a tow truck before closing time."

"Engine problems? I can drive up and take a look," Larry offered.

"Engine's fine. No need to drive anywhere. Car's a couple hundred yards up the road. I was headed to town. Missed the corner. Car's upside down in the stream. Lighter's somewhere in there, but I couldn't find it. Perfect excuse to finally stop in and have a drink with you two."

By the time Jo's abused car was pulled out of the stream, turned upright and hauled off down hill, I had lost my usual sense of determination. "Let's clean up then go in to town and find something for dinner. Haven't been to the Pantry Café in months," I suggested.

"Good idea," Larry agreed. "I've been wanting to make an appointment with you. I think we've got to do some serious talking."

From the day we decided to live together, Larry and I found we rarely quarreled. The few disagreements we had tended to be quickly settled through a small act of diplomacy by one or the other of us. Then about a year after we met, a seemingly major argument did sneak into our lives. It was sparked by a disagreement that had lain smoldering and unspoken until it threatened to tear asunder the relationship we both hoped could work long-term for us. We weathered that storm but in its wake realized we needed to create some guidelines for discussing future differences. We'd spent several evenings refining these rules. Then in an act we both saw as the first true commitment we'd made to each other, we wrote them down:

> **Rule 1** — If you have something bothering you, don't hold it in and don't explode. Instead, make a definite appointment to discuss it. That way the other person knows whatever you want to discuss is really important to you.
>
> **Rule 2** — Arrange for the meeting to take place in a neutral spot, not right at home. If possible have the spot be free of outside distractions.
>
> **Rule 3** — Only the person who calls the meeting has the right to bring up their grievances. No rebutting, no bringing up complaints, this is the instigator's chance to point out problems and ask for solutions.
>
> **Rule 4** — If one or the other feels like walking out and slamming the door, you can only stay away for five minutes then you have to come back, listen and ask questions until you truly understand what is bothering your partner.
>
> **Rule 5** — Never say, "You always..."
>
> **Rule 6** — Never say, "You never..."

Through the years these rules had led to occasional hours-long, sometimes tear-laden discussions in back corners of cafés, on secluded stretches of beach. One time when we were sailing offshore with the nearest land at least a thousand miles away, I remember living up to the spirit of the rules by inviting Larry to meet me on the foredeck of the boat at cocktail time. Even though the foredeck was only a dozen feet away from where we spent the majority of our time at sea, it did represent a neutral place. The somewhat formal invitation to meet gave both of us time to think about our life together before we sat down to talk. Through the years, we have learned the frustrations that led to problems between us almost always came about because of outside pressures — being tied up in some foreign port while we waited for weather to change, getting caught up in family problems, writing deadlines, too many visitors or most often, having to wait for someone else to make a decision before we could get on with our own plans. Now as I changed into non-boatyard clothes and fed Cindy, I mentally added the afternoon-long interruption of Jo's unexpected appearance to the list of things that had not gone to plan over the past weeks.

I thought back to those moments when I'd tried to ignore the explosive cursing that came from the boatshed far more often than normal. Normal was, an occasional curse when a nut slipped free and skittered into the bilges of the boat, or a string of swear words over a skinned knuckle, a bruised shin or any of the small mishaps that are part and parcel of working around timber, scaffolding and machinery. But recently Larry's work had not been going smoothly. Small mishaps like finding a flaw in a piece of timber he'd saved for a special purpose, or breaking off a screw as he twisted it into place, seemed to provoke angry reactions that stalled his production for an hour at a time. Larger mishaps, ones he'd normally have taken an hour or two to get over, now sent him into an all-day spin. I'd heard the sound of a large piece of timber snapping apart one morning, followed by his angry shouts. Minutes later Larry came stomping into the house and poured himself a shot of whiskey. I knew he'd spent three days shaping a long strake of very expensive, difficult to replace teak timber to fit along the outside of the hull as a protective rubbing rail. He'd gone out just after breakfast that morning to finally fasten it in place. It had broken and no amount of sympathy from me seemed to help. He spent the rest of that day laying in the back room reading a book. By the next day he'd decided to take a different tack, using oak, which is far more flexible than teak and progress resumed. Then a few days later, as he worked methodically to bend one of the very expensive bronze chainplates so it would lay neatly in place, a casting flaw appeared, one that rendered the chainplate useless. His reaction was to throw the offending metal through the plastic window of the boatshed before once again stomping into the kitchen and grabbing the whiskey bottle.

Though I had been feeling quite good about my time in the boatyard, my mornings at my desk had not been flowing smoothly. Like many — maybe even most — writers who manage to get a book published, I wanted to write a novel. "That will prove I am a 'real' writer," I'd said during one of our leisurely weekends with Shearlane and Robert Duke the previous winter. Shearlane had agreed wholeheartedly since she too was infected with "novelitis." We'd spent the rest of the evening and much of the next morning in a roundtable discussion of the story I might someday write, based like most of my favorite novels, on a true event.

Five years previously, when we had been voyaging across the Indian Ocean, we made our landfall in Galle, on the southern tip of Sri Lanka. There we had a strange, in fact, disturbing, encounter with the owner of a Canadian-flagged, 50-foot yacht called *Crusader*. Don Sorte definitely was the most audacious, rude, often unscrupulous, sometimes exceptionally brave person we had ever met. Hard-hat, deep-sea diver, small-time con artist, adventurer, underwater rescue expert and co-inventor of the very first successful miniature submarine. Unfortunately, he was not a good seaman. Our lives became intertwined when his yacht went down during a massive cyclone, taking not only Don's life but those of five young backpackers who paid to sail with him across the Bay of Bengal. We weathered the same extreme conditions and came through relatively unscathed, but we were on a more seaworthy vessel. When we sailed in to Malaysia, we'd been caught up in the search efforts launched after Sorte's last radio call. The aftermath of his story continued to intrude in our lives long after official searches were called off. Over the next five years, we received letters and visits from families of the missing youngsters, from vendors in Canada who received deposits to help outfit Sorte's boat but never had their final bills fully paid. We even were contacted by the CIA, as it appears Don was suspected of selling highly classified submarine design information to the Soviet Union. We were questioned about reported — but never confirmed — sightings of the yacht in the highly restricted waters of the Soviet-influenced Andaman Islands two years after the event.

"I think Larry is right," Shearlane said when she climbed into the car to leave. "You could make a great novel out of that story. It's time you tried something new, something really challenging."

The morning after Shearlane and Robert's visit, Larry woke with yet another list of motives, character interactions and intrigues that could be added to the potential novel. Over the next weeks, instead of playing the guitar to while away the last moments of each day, Larry and I played with ideas to add to the notepad labeled, "Crusader Novel."

"Why don't you make a bet on yourself?" Larry had suggested when the first half of his boatbuilding book advance arrived. "Now we've got enough cash to pay for the materials to finish the boat, why not take ten or fifteen percent of the money we got from selling *Seraffyn* and use it to live on for the next six months. That way you can forget about sailing articles and spend your mornings writing that novel." At first his faith in my skills, his sheer pleasure as each evening I read my day's work aloud, had been heartwarming and inspiring. At first I was truly excited to explore this completely new mental territory, especially when I sent the first three chapters and my rough outline to Eric at W.W. Norton and got an encouraging letter back saying, "Could be a real ripper, get on with it. Let me see another four or five chapters and I might be able to send you an advance." But as the weeks passed, my imagination began to yield fewer and fewer words, and my outline became ever more like a pair of shackles than a guiding light. I blamed Larry's recent bouts of boiling frustration for my slowly dwindling writing production.

I also blamed Jimmie Moore for distracting me further from my work by what I saw as a continued assault on the cash that remained from selling *Seraffyn.* "Land — if I had any spare cash I'd be buying all the land I could around here. It'll never be cheaper," he'd kept telling us. "People are desperate to sell. You can name your price. Banks don't have any money to loan, you've got cash to put deposits down. Inflation is just eating up everything you get from CDs. Land is inflation-proof."

Jimmie's advice echoed the headlines that filled the newspapers and radio talk shows. It was 1982 and President Reagan was fighting to pull the U.S. out of its deepest recession since the 1930s. Inflation in the U.S. was running at 11 percent a year. "For Sale" signs were popping up everywhere, proclaiming, "owner financing available." At the same time there were reports of banks and savings and loan companies failing in alarming numbers as interests rates topped 20 percent even for the most secure of loans. So each time Larry suggested we take a look at some of the land for sale around the lake I felt my stomach knot up. I'd try to deter his interest by reminding him about the increasing number of people who were late on mortgage payments for homes Jimmie and Barbara had built and financed.

That evening as we drove down toward the valley, both of us were lost in contemplation. We chose the quietest corner of the café and ordered our meal. Then the silence settled so darkly around us I began to fear I'd somehow missed a fissure that had now grown into a potentially unbridgeable chasm in our relationship.

"Larry, I know you're not feeling good about something. Let's get it out in the open," I finally said.

“That’s an understatement. I feel really terrible. I don’t know how to ask this but…I guess what I’m trying to say is…Lin, I don’t think I’ve ever before broken a promise to you but…” Larry lapsed back into stony silence.

“Nothing can be that bad. We’re having some setbacks, but we’ve got our finances under control. You’re making progress on the boat. I’m getting some writing done. Things look okay to me. So come on, what’s bugging you? Blurt it out!” I demanded.

“Okay, here is the bottom line,” Larry said. “This whole damned boatbuilding project is taking too long. I don’t want to be stuck in the canyon worrying my way through another fire season, I am tired of waiting for something to set off another of your allergic reactions. I’m worried Jimmie and Barbara are going to move into the cottage when they really get started on the house up E Road; the stone house is half theirs you know. So I want to finish the boat and get away from Bull Canyon and go sailing again! That’s why we came out here in the first place. I know I promised you a chance to be a novelist, but I need your help out in the boatyard full time. I know that’s not fair to you but it’s what I want!”

I picked at the bits of salad left on my plate and thought for a moment. Across the table, Larry finished his glass of wine and signaled to the waitress. I waited until she’d brought him a second glass, using the time to compose my next words.

“I know it’s you who has the right to do the complaining tonight,” I countered. “But if finishing the boat is what matters most we have got to stop getting involved with Jimmie’s talk of buying land. Investing in land is a full-time business; it takes a lot of research. Jimmie’s got you convinced it’s a sure way of making money but it smacks of gambling to me. Besides, everyone seems to be doing it right now and you’re the one that says, if everyone does it, it must be wrong!”

“That’s what my grandfather always said. I say, view it with suspicion,” Larry rejoined, a slight hint of humor lifting the edges of his frown. “If it will make you more comfortable I’ll stop talking about land. I’ll tell Jimmie to lay off, too. It’s a very small compensation for asking you to give up your novel.”

Larry listed the ways I could help him by working right alongside him, then tried to assure me we’d make time for novel writing once the boat was launched. But as his concerns poured out, my thoughts were complicated by a slowly growing realization; each day at my desk had made me ever more aware that fiction was not my forte. I didn’t like making up situations, inventing people who didn’t really exist. Larry had unwittingly given me a graceful way to exit from a project that was beyond my abilities. If I set aside my novel because he needed me, I would never have to say, "I failed."

Larry put his arm around my shoulders as we walked out to the truck, "You're truly generous," he said. "I can't imagine anyone else giving up their dream to make mine run more smoothly."

"We've got 50 years to get even," I replied, ignoring the tiniest twinge of guilt as I accepted praise for what was really no sacrifice at all.

The change in my daily routine definitely lifted Larry's spirits. In spite of adding hours of extra physical work to my day, the same change seemed to give me an almost boundless sense of energy. I still visited my desk for a few hours each week to keep up with my required editorial quota of one sailing article a month. But I reveled in spending most of my time doing "real" things, not trying to chase imaginary thoughts into words. In the boatyard I was no longer confined to sanding and varnishing wood that had already been worked into shape. Instead, I was truly working alongside Larry, learning new, albeit simple, wood- and metal-working skills, thinking through the mental processes that lay behind each decision he made. The boat seemed to rush toward completion.

"Right there, about three feet from where you are standing. That's where I think I see a high spot," I said as I scrunched down and squinted along the length of satiny smooth spruce that would soon tower above *Taleisin*. We'd gotten out of bed just after dawn that late summer morning, eager to get the first coat of varnish on the mast we had finished shaping over the past few weeks. Then we'd spent half of the morning looking carefully along the spar, turning it slowly and inspecting it time and again in search of any imperfections that would be magnified once several coats of varnish added a glossy sheen. As Larry stroked his wood plane lightly across the slightly raised spot I'd noted, I stepped back and contemplated the amazingly light and limber pole he'd built. At its base it was only as big around as a dessert plate, the upper portion tapered until at the mast head it was as narrow as my arm, yet it would tower almost five stories into the air and support sails to shove eight tons of boat through light winds and storms. I thought of how Larry had carefully selected the spruce timbers he'd glued together so the wood grain all ran long, strong and true, how he had hollowed out the center of the spar not only to make it lighter but so it could flex more easily without fracturing. "Remember, this mast doesn't have to support itself, it's just the strut that supports the sails. The wire rigging supports the mast. It's sort of like a good marriage, each partner adding completely different types of strength, working together, supporting each other but still staying flexible," Larry had explained when we discussed its delicate looking proportions.

Now he straightened up and took one last look along the length of the mast then said, "That's it, Lin, it's fair. Let's slap some varnish on it."

"Fair, unfair, amazing how I've learned to spot even the slightest hint of unfairness on a length of timber," I commented as I got two cans of varnish and brushes ready for us to use. "I never thought I'd be able to do that, be able to feel a piece of wood and decide if it was fair or not."

"It's not something you feel, it's not something you do, it's something you see. There isn't any question of maybe — either a line is fair or it isn't," Larry said as he laid the first stroke of golden liquid onto the timber. He hummed as we worked just feet away from each other then paused to say, "Too bad 'fair' isn't as clear cut when it comes to relationships."

There was an amusing symmetry in an incident that happened later that day. It definitely brought back memories of Jo Caphart's visit earlier in the month, a visit I credited with forcing us to confront the changing nature of our life together. The encounters brought on by this newest event added to my contemplation of fairness.

"You guys got a match, can't find my lighter," called Jerry Washburn, the farmer from Lindell Road, as he threw open the boatshed door. Once again, the hum of the air conditioner and the swamp cooler, along with the talk that ebbed and flowed between Larry and me, had masked any sound of an approaching pickup truck. "Been meaning to come over and see what you guys are up to ever since I pulled you out of that bog in front of my place," Jerry said. "Never came by 'cause I didn't want to waste my time. Thought you guys were just another pair of crazies talking big about what you were going to do and getting bogged down, then bugging off like all the other hippies who came to live out here. But Bob Steele came by a few weeks ago and said, 'Noah is ready to float off as soon as the next flood comes by.' Show me this boat he's been talking about."

We'd exchanged a few words with Jerry over the past three years, but only when heavy rains filled the river crossings and made it wiser to use the long steep route along Lindell Road and past his strawberry farm. So his visit, just like Jo's, was quite unexpected. But unlike Jo, he was truly intrigued by the boat and especially the big woodworking machinery that surrounded it. When I offered to get some cool drinks, Jerry turned to me and said, "Mind giving Steele a call? Ask him to bring his tractor down 'cause I just dropped my house on your road. Be a good idea to clear it off before someone wants to drive up the canyon."

As soon as I finished calling Bob, I walked over to the edge of the yard, absolutely unprepared for the sight waiting there. Jerry really had dropped a whole house, albeit a small one, but large enough to block the width of the road. In actuality, it had not fallen off the low trailer he used to move machinery around his small farm. Instead, the beams supporting the two-room wooden structure had broken, letting the house flop down around the trailer bed until its walls touched the ground. With its slightly crooked attitude, the fallen house brought to mind a lady with her skirt touching the floor as she does a proper curtsy.

Jerry didn't seem the least bit fazed by this mishap. "Thing was a freebie, was going to need some work anyway," he said as Larry threw a bunch of wedges, some jacks and lengths of timber into the bed of our pickup truck. Bob Steele came to a stop just a minute after we reached the wreckage. Beside him in the cab of his pickup truck was a woman plus two young children. "Couldn't figure out why you wanted my dozer down here," he stated. "But guess we do need it for this job. I'll bring it down with the small bucket. No reason for Darlene and the kids to be stuck here in this dust and heat, take them up to the house and be back down with the machine and some chains."

I wasn't at all surprised when Pete Shomler drove up the road while Larry and Jerry began unloading timbers. "Bob's just been down to look this mess over," I said. "Now he's gone to get his bulldozer so he can lift each end and let them slide these new timbers into place."

"Good thing. I need to get past this mess and up to my place pretty soon. For some strange reason, Bob's dug a ditch across the track leading from his place to mine so only way in is up my own track. Sure glad there's no rain forecast for a while. Crowd of shooters coming up for our first war games this weekend. Want to make sure Sandy and the kids keep working, only way we'll be ready," Pete stated. "Guess you met Bob's new family," he added putting a strong emphasis on the word new. "Funny isn't it. Always said he hated kids. Now he's talking about having some more. Put up a kiddies' swing set, been building a corral and looking at ponies. Says it makes the place look more family oriented, good for property sales. But I think he's found someone who makes him feel real big. With those kids, no job from what I heard, I figure this one's so grateful to have a guarenteed meal ticket she'll wait on him hand and foot and jump into bed anytime he wants."

Bob and his bulldozer soon came clanking and groaning down the hill-side track. As I watched the relaxed, efficient moves of the four men working together, as I listened to the joking camaraderie that echoed above the chugging of the bulldozer, I had a growing sense of nostalgia. I'd missed the friendly rivalry, the problem-solving assistance that had been shared so gen-

Lyle Hess, Taleisin's *designer.*

erously by our canyon neighbors in the past. First the telephones, then the advent of the electricity, Marlys' departure, the discomfort engendered by the unresolved vandalism of our house — each had changed the dynamics between all of us. But probably the greatest change of all was my attitude as both Larry and I began to focus our view outward beyond the canyon and toward the ocean.

The slightly skewed and splintered house rose slowly, first at one end then the other. The men thrust blocks and wedges under Bob's directions until it once again sat properly above the bed of Jerry's trailer.

"Come on up and I'll find some cold beers," I offered as everyone began tossing tools and chunks of splintered timber into truck beds. "Bob, how about bringing your new lady down for some coffee?"

Bob looked at me, then at Larry and said clearly and evenly, "Not worth the bother. You two will be moving on soon. No need to subject Darlene to any of Lin's silly stories about that bitch Marlys."

In the awkward silence that ensued, I wasn't surprised when Pete quietly turned and left without acknowledging my offer. As Jerry drove slowly up the road, the wooden house rocking gently above the trailer, Larry walked over and put his arm around me. "Sure doesn't seem like Marlys got a fair deal, does it?" he said. "She spent all those years working and financing Bob's shenanigans up there. All she wanted was to have some kids, some appreciation and a chance to live in a finished house."

The two of us separated when we reached the top of our driveway. Larry headed back into the boatshed, intent on finishing one more piece of woodwork before dinner. I headed over toward the stone cottage but instead of going inside to check for phone messages then start preparing our meal, I settled under the limbs of the diadora pine and swept my eyes around the homestead we'd repaired and built up together. As I sat there, I began to marvel at the flexible and strong partnership we'd formed, one that had been built piece by piece, then shaped slowly and carefully just like the mast we'd varnished that morning. Now, as I watched the evening shadows creep across the yard and up the sides of the boatshed, I realized, you might not be able to see it, you might not be able to define it, but you definitely could feel when a relationship was truly fair.

Chapter 24

The Long Road to Our World

"Set your launch date yet?" Jimmie asked the minute he walked through the door. "Everyone down at the beach is looking forward to the party."

"That's all we've been talking about for the past week," I answered. Then I set out the the rich spicy lasagna I'd prepared. Jimmie and Barbara's Friday evening arrival had become almost a ritual. As our canyon project was drawing toward completion, theirs was just beginning. Each weekend visit saw another section of foundation dug out for the spec house they were building half a mile up the canyon. As we sat down to eat, I added, "I still have a lot of work to do on the boat's interior. All of the cabinets need two more coats of varnish. Larry's just started on the mast fittings. I want to put more varnish on the spars while they are so easy to sand. Not much sense moving the boat away from here before we get it truly finished — got the tools, the bits and pieces to do the work. Crazy to commute a hundred miles to use a bandsaw!"

I knew Larry was anxious to see the boat afloat. Over the past few weeks, as we'd gone over the list of jobs-to-do, he'd added a tick mark next to project after project that could "just as easily be done once we launch the boat." In distinct contrast to Larry, I was in no hurry to see the boat rushed to completion. I was enjoying the tranquility, the sense of control that had settled into my life now I could focus almost completely on boat work and simple homemaking chores. So I'd hidden any signs of pollen-induced allergic skin reactions by wearing a long-sleeved worksuit, then used all my wiles to dampen Larry's impatience and diffuse his concerns about the upcoming fire season. And until this evening I'd been successful. But now, with Jimmie and Barbara at the table, each tendril of conversation seemed to lead back to, "when the boat heads down to the water." As the evening wore on, I realized this was the first time Jimmie or Barbara had urged us to think beyond the canyon.

I found myself alone with Jimmie later that evening and mentioned a news report I'd heard on the radio. "Can't believe another savings and loan company collapsed. What's that going to mean for builders like you?" I said.

"Means Barbara might just get to play with horses a lot more," Jimmie answered. "Money for all my builders' loans has dried up. I could lose everything except this land in Bull Canyon and my half share of this old house. Might have to move up here soon. Should work out okay since you are almost ready to launch your boat."

I tossed and turned as I listened to Larry's snoring, and caught muted snatches of tense-sounding conversation from the back room. Finally I got up and took the work list into the kitchen along with the calendar from my desk. Some time after midnight, I climbed back into bed and gently woke Larry. "Six weeks, that should give you time to finish rigging the mast," I said. "The upholstery guy is due up on Tuesday. Said he needs three weeks to do his work. We can have bunk cushions in time to move right on board so we won't have to drive all the way back up here every night. I think we should launch the last weekend of October."

"Sounds good to me," Larry said as he pulled me closer to his body. "But what made you change your mind so suddenly?"

"Halloween! Great time to have a big party. Just think, we'll have something else to celebrate on the same day each year; your birthday, our wedding, two boat launchings — you'll never forget our anniversary that way," I whispered. "If we get the boat moved down to the beach six weeks from now, we'll be out of the canyon before the fire season. I wouldn't have to worry about the winter rains making a mess of the road. Best of all, now that Jimmie needs to live in the cottage, we've solved the only really difficult problem we had. He says Cindy is such a part of the place he wants her to stay right here."

◇◇

I climbed the hill behind the cottage six weeks later, ostensibly to take photographs as *Taleisin* slowly emerged from her shed, but in actuality to have a quiet moment just to myself. Cindy laid her head on my knee as soon as I sat down on the rock pile next to the big water tank. The huge, low-slung trailer and heavy-duty truck that would carry the boat down to the sea had been maneuvered in to place the day before. A dozen friends had been up over the weekend to help remove two trees and widen the road at the bottom of the drive so the truck could negotiate its turn. Now the truckers were working with quiet assurance, deftly placing rollers under the boats' steel cradle. They'd set Larry and some friends to work, securing carpet around the long spars to pad them against the gravel and road debris that could mar their heavy coats of varnish as the boat we'd so carefully built was carried down the rough dirt road, across three streams and onto the freeway leading to the sea.

I let my mind drift as I watched from my lofty perch. The first puff of the afternoon breeze carried the scent of sage and rosemary. It shook the limbs of the chinaberry and sycamore trees to send brightly colored, brittle leaves skittering across the yard below me. The lonely cry of a hawk echoed across the canyon. I realized this was the last time I might sit here admiring the cottage Old Man Payonessa had built, the trees he'd planted, the tranquility and comfort he'd worked so hard to create in the middle of a rugged wilderness. I wondered what he would have thought of the changes

we'd wrought in his special canyon. Would he have welcomed the electricity, the phones? Would the slowly spreading fruit trees and nodding black locust trees I'd added have met his approval? Mentally I ticked off the changes we'd made and wondered if some future owner would call the barnlike building we'd be leaving behind "Old Man Pardey's boatshed."

Just as I realized I was saying a silent farewell to the home we'd created in Bull Canyon, my reverie was broken by the sound of the truck's winch as it sprang to life. A cheer went up as the bow of the boat we'd built glided slowly out into the sunshine. I almost forgot the camera in my hand as inch-by-inch *Taleisin* emerged from her shed, and for the first time I could see the full length of the sweeping lines Larry had so lovingly and meticulously created, the glowing colors of the varnish and paint I'd carefully brushed into place. I snapped off a dozen pictures then rushed down to watch for any overhanging branches, any unexpected snag that could scratch the boat as she was rolled carefully into place.

It was late afternoon when the trucking crew finished strapping *Taleisin* firmly onto the trailer, ready for her rough ride down our driveway and out through Bull Canyon. The driver informed us it was too late to head onto the crowded freeways leading to the sea. I wasn't disappointed at this overnight delay, it gave me a chance to slow down for one evening, to sleep in the stone cottage one last time. Over the past few weeks I'd cleaned out the cottage, and literally moved our life onto the boat. Every thing that couldn't fit on board had been given away. That morning, Dad had helped me disassemble the big brass bed and load it in his pickup truck, bound for my niece's bedroom, where she promised it would be ready any time we came to visit. Tonight we had planned to be in the shipyard and sleep on board.

Now Larry, exhausted, headed for the back room of the house the minute we returned from what would be our last visit with our favorite waitress, Patsy at the Pantry Café down in Lake Elsinore. He climbed into the double bed Jimmie and Barbara planned to use and within seconds was sound asleep.

I found myself unwilling to join him. Instead I wandered into the front room, which loomed large and unfamiliar with the bed gone, the shelves and desk bare of books. I sat on the hearth. Its stones felt cold and unfamiliar; I'd swept the fireplace completely clean of ashes in anticipation of Jimmie and Barbara's arrival some time in the next few weeks. As I sat there I recalled the first time I'd laid a fire then watched it spring alight to dispel the cold of this generous sized room and herald the first of many companionable evenings we'd spend in the stone cottage.

Everywhere I looked I could see memories, from the new strakes of wood at the bottom of each door which hid the ragged holes chewed by the rats we'd finally learned to keep at bay, to the hanging electrical lamps we'd added to supplement but never fully replace the oil lamps that lined the mantel piece above me. I made my way out through the kitchen, my hand gliding across the counter I'd scrubbed and polished that week to remove any signs of the hundreds of meals that had been prepared on its wide, sweeping surface. Then I walked outside to listen once more to the night sounds, as the last of a crescent moon descended into the V on the far side of the canyon.

I automatically put my hand out in expectation of Cindy placing her head in reach for a pat. Then I remembered the way she'd bounded eagerly out of the truck a few days earlier; she'd happily joined a brace of dogs at the friend's farm, where she would stay until the time came for her to return to the Stone Cottage with her new caretakers. At the time, I'd been slightly disappointed that Cindy seemed unfazed by my departure. And I hadn't been surprised when Larry told me, "I already miss my dog," as soon as I returned to the canyon with the empty truck.

When I finally climbed into the bed in the back room to snuggle up against Larry, my mind was at ease. I knew in my heart that my "tidy little plans" had worked. Not only had we built the boat as we'd set out to do, we'd saved this lovely stone cottage, too.

◇◇

"Get up, lots of work to do before everyone gets here." My mother's tone left no room for argument. "Tables to set up, food to get ready. Your dad's gone

off to get coffee and donuts so you don't have to cook any breakfast." It had been a week since the truckers gingerly transferred *Taleisin* and her cradle onto the shipyard's railcar. I really wanted to lay right where I was, in the luscious-feeling double bunk, admiring the swirling grain on the deckbeam above our pillows. I wanted to feast my eyes on the woodwork that glowed richly against the plush, green-velvet upholstery and enjoy the play of the sunshine that danced through sparkling clean portlights to highlight the dust-free, pollen-free oceanside air that filled our cabin.

This was the first time I'd actually seen sunshine inside my forepeak sleeping quarters. Ever since arriving in the shipyard, both of us had been working from dusk until long after dark, trying to be ready for what was definitely going to be a large and boisterous launching party. Larry had spent his time splicing wire to secure the mast that now towered in shining glory over the boat. I'd been running from one end of Newport Beach to the other, trying to cross items off the party shopping list and the boat gear list. Neither list seemed to grow shorter until our parents arrived to share a beachside home with a dozen other guests who'd come from far away to help launch us into this new phase of our lives.

I felt the first twinges of nostalgia as I worked contentedly under my mother's directions, glad for once to have her taking charge as we dragged planks and sawhorses out from under the boats and cradles laying idle around the weekend-quieted shipyard. Together we set them up to form carefully arranged ranks of tables. "Knowing your friends, there'll be tons of food arriving," Mom stated as she paused to let me get my breath. "Salads can go on that table, desserts on this one. Okay, now drag your new dinghy over there cause your brother's gone off to get a truckload of ice. Then grab your friend, the one who's over there talking to Larry, and get him to bring those boxes of champagne down off the deck of your boat. Put them in the dinghy ready to get chilled. Then you go grab Larry and get both of you cleaned up cause folks are starting to get here." I tried to give her a hug, to get her vibrant body to slow down and relax against mine just for a moment. But she was off yet again, orders floating behind her like confetti. I laughed to myself as I realized the conflict she must be feeling as she helped us launch the boat that would once again take us sailing far away from her watchful eyes, her close involvement in our lives. I sensed I'd miss the physical closeness, too.

Nostalgia seemed to build along with the crowd. "I'll miss your country parties," Mary said as she added a pile of shrimp to the growing mass of food. "I'll miss walking up the canyon roads with you," my sister commented as she arrived carrying my newest niece on one arm, a basket full of peanut butter cookies on the other. "I'll miss your turkey dinners," Jimmie said as he headed over to help Larry secure mooring lines on the boat. "I'll miss watching the boat grow," Grant stated as he turned to recall the lead-pouring day with another friend who'd been there, too.

At noon Larry and I stood closely alongside each other. I could sense he felt just like me, barely able to contain his excitement as we waited for the ceremonial champagne bottle to shatter against the bronze stem band of the creation we'd worked on for four long years. But even at that soul-filling moment I couldn't shake the feeling that I was leaving something very important behind.

Champagne dripping from her bow, the boat was slowly lowered into the water. *Taleisin* appeared smaller and smaller as the mass of her underbody was lost to view. A cheer went up as she lifted clear of her cradle to bob lightly and safely in her natural element. Larry swept me up into his arms, his eyes glowing, his face a study in absolute joy. It was just then, as I looked over his shoulder to soak in the sincere admiration of the people who'd come to share this day, that I realized that not one of our Bull Canyon neighbors had arrived.

Late that evening, as the last bottles of wine and champagne were being drained, the last bits of food nibbled by grazing late-stayers, my mother finally came to sit quietly by my side. Together we watched as Larry showed yet another friend how to carefully climb down the companionway and into our

new home. "I'm surprised no one from Bull Canyon drove down today, not even Ellie," I commented.

"Not surprised," Mom said curtly. "She was just a neighbor. These folks here are your friends."

"Guess you're right," I said. "But I'm going to miss the canyon."

Mom didn't hesitate, "No you won't," she said as she took one of my hands in hers then swept her other hand across the open vista of water and boats around us. "This right here is your world. Bull Canyon was just one more foreign land you visited."

Epilogue

I catch glimpses of the phallic-like peaks of Hiva Oa each time *Taleisin* rises to the crest of a tradewind-nurtured sea. White foam spreads from the boat's driving bow, rushes past her smooth white sides, then bubbles beneath her buoyant stern. Larry is asleep below decks. I lounge in the cockpit, utterly content, satisfied to do absolutely nothing but savor the first glimpses of the rising sun, the glistening sea around me. Over the hiss of foam I hear the cries of shorebirds that have flown offshore to fish along with the shearwaters and petrels that have followed in our wake over the past days. Their raucous squawking draws my mind back to the elegant echoing calls of the hawks that soared above *Taleisin*'s birthplace in Bull Canyon.

Mom had been right. Any nostalgia for the life we'd left behind in Bull Canyon slipped from my mind in the days following *Taleisin*'s launching. We moved from the shipyard to a berth in front of a friend's house where Larry was offered the use of a workshop. Within a few weeks, we were able to slip out onto the bay for the first taste of the sailing that lay ahead of us. Finishing details, sea-trials, planning and provisioning for the departure date we'd set, and just savoring life among our waterfront friends filled our days.

We had driven back to the canyon three times. On each visit the old stone cottage felt more like a ghost from our past. To insure we were clear of any potential financial problems following the foreclosures caused by the collapse of several large Savings and Loan companies, Jimmie and Barbara had taken over ownership of the cottage. In a very fair exchange, they'd given us clear title to a ten-acre parcel of land further up the canyon. Jimmie and Barbara retrieved Cindy from the farm where she had been a contented boarder and moved to Bull Canyon soon after we departed.

During the last foray to Bull Canyon, we cleaned out the boatshed, then headed down to the Lake Elsinore post office. I filled out the forms to close our post-office box and have our mail forwarded, then handed them to Joanne at the counter. "You're just one more of the folks deserting the town," she said. "This keeps up, might not be any need for me around here." The shuttered shops along Main Street, the foreclosure sale signs on partially completed and now deserted housing tracts seemed to support her concerns.

Over the next months, Jimmie had kept us informed about the neighbors we'd left behind. Each time he came to spend a few days away from the dust and heat of Bull Canyon, he'd stop by before heading onward to sail his boat. He was usually on his own. "Barb's off with her horses," he'd say, his indifference to this aspect of country life clearly discernable. "Shomler and Steele had a big falling out," Jimmie told us. "Seems Steele only let him use that access road across his land so he could share the power lines that ran up to Shomler's place, cheaper that way. Now that he's cut them off, Pete and Sandy can't do anything about it and they can't get down their own track when it rains. They have to scrape the money together to really improve their road. Got them in a bit of a bind cause their paintball hunting games have started to attract a lot of attention."

Just before we set sail for Mexico seven months later, Jimmie came by for a final catch up on Bull Canyon business, "Leave it to Steele. Somehow he convinced the local bank that all those roads, lakes and home sites made his land worth a fortune. They gave him a huge loan. Now he's done a runner with his lady and kids and all the money from the loan," Jimmie said. "Ellie hasn't changed at all, happy to chat if I drop in. Always has an extra dog biscuit for my shepherd. She's still waiting for the day when someone buys one of her pieces of land so she can build up top. Newhouse's place is like a trailer park; all five of his kids live there now. Lee's planted lots of bushes around the bottom to hide the wrecked cars everyone's piling there. Poor guy goes off to work each morning, everyone else just seems to laze around doing nothing..."

Each time Jimmie left, Larry and I talked long into the night reviewing not only the pleasures and successes we'd had but the lessons we'd learned as we built *Taleisin*. I'd learned that people who choose to live in a place like Bull Canyon are going to be oddballs, quirky, highly independent. We certainly fit the bill. Neighbors in an isolated place would almost always pitch in and be helpful just because of mutual needs. At the same time, the different outlooks and different financial situations of each of us meant anything we did could accidentally have unexpected affects on each others' lives. The prime example was the advent of electricity. Its arrival had helped us gain our dream more quickly and easily as it spurred on our boatbuilding project, but it cost Lee Newhouse his dream of retiring at 60 so he could ease back and enjoy the place he'd built.

My confidence as a writer had received an amazing boost during the canyon years. My respect for Larry had grown immensely. He'd often joked that I was earning the money so he could build the capital. Time has proven his words true. Now we had a brand-new handsome, perfectly outfitted boat plus some money in the bank to let us sail more comfortably toward new horizons. On top of this we had a piece of land we could sell to gain from the work that had gone into upgrading the cottage, the road and bringing utilities into the canyon.

Now both the canyon and the shores of California are thousands of miles behind us. I glance at the sails that tower above me, full-bellied and steadily grasping the winds to drive us toward our very first Polynesian landfall. My eyes are drawn upward along the length of the golden-hued mast and toward the clouds that are slowly changing from the blushing colors of sunrise to the clean white glow of a tropical day. And as I watch them scurry before the fresh tradewinds, I finally accept the difference between Old Man Payonessa and me. To him the tree-edged plateau and the stone cottage he'd created in the midst of a rocky desert canyon had represented the project of a lifetime. He'd come to Bull Canyon looking for somewhere to settle and spend the rest of his days, a place he could shape to be an unchanging reflection of his picture of perfection. I'd come to the canyon thinking I'd wanted just what he did — a home, a sense of belonging after years of being a foreigner. But I'd left knowing I am and always will be a foreigner wherever I live, for I am addicted to change. The challenge of new projects, the quest for new beginnings, new endings, is as necessary to me as food, as sleep.

I look through the companionway to where Larry is slowly wakening. "Come out! Take a look," I call to the man who shares this addiction with me. "Your navigation was spot-on. We're only a dozen miles away from a new land and a new adventure."

Acknowledgments

Bull Canyon has taken many starts and stops to reach its conclusion. Along the way I lost confidence in my ability to tell this story well, lost confidence that it was worth telling, or could find an audience. My deepest appreciation goes to my fellow adventurer, Larry, who never made me feel guilty when I decided to set the project aside and turn my mind to other books I knew would be easier to write. His editorial suggestions were often excellent, at other times I had to remind him that, unlike with the nautical books we usually write together, this story was from my perspective; the opinions expressed and vignettes chosen were mine alone. He accepted this with grace after he read the final draft of each chapter.

When I felt inclined to scuttle this project, Larry suggested I send the chapters I'd written to selected friends, hoping they might urge me onward. Patience Wales, editor of *Sail Magazine*, became an ongoing champion of this manuscript. Elizabeth Meyers, Tom Linskey, Gil Outerbridge, Beth Leonard, Maria Eugenia Bestani, Mariette Baldwin, Michael Marris, Sandra Farrell, plus the the Kawau Island Bookworms, including Jill Hetherington, Helen Jeffrey, Gael Archer, Lyn Hume, Ruth Henderson, Chic Vercoe, Jane Myers, Jenny Gibbons and Paddy Bartlett, all had faith in this project. Thanks to each of you. I hope you recognize changes you may have inspired. Catherine Miller has been a brave friend. As the first reader of each new chapter, she willingly challenged my ideas and tried to make sure I left few unanswered questions. To Oscar Lind and Lee Stanley, thanks for reminding me that readers of my sailing narratives might be disappointed to find that this book is definitely about voyages through the changing winds of relationships, not voyages across the sea. Kathleen Brandeis, editor extraordinaire, has been a keen supporter of this project since it was only a draft with ten chapters. I still laugh when I remember her writing, "enough rain, mud and flooding already." On her advice, I reduced three wet chapters to two.

Eric Kampmann of Midpoint Trade Book Distributors and Margot Atwell editor of Beaufort Books, which is an arm of Midpoint, encouraged me by offering to publish and distribute *Bull Canyon*. Though we chose another publisher, Margot's suggestion of certain name changes has been adopted. Thanks also to Spencer Smith, of Seapoint Publishing, Jim Mairs, long-time editor with W.W. Norton Publishing, and Dan Poynter of ParaPublishing. Ellen Reid used her book shepherding knowledge to help this project glide successfully out into the wide world. Ann Espuelas, edited this manuscript, JoAnne Neil, edited the final proofs, Moira Durham designed and set the book. I enjoyed working with each of you. Jim Morehouse of Paradise Cay Publication deserves a hug along with this thank you; he has always been available for encouragement and assistance.

Many people contributed to the life we led in Bull Canyon. They include all of my family, many of whom you have read about in this story. But I would like to add a note about Sam Zatkin, my father. He was a gentleman in every sense of the word — caring, gentle, so quiet he often appeared to fade into the background as he has in this book. But it was Dad who kept our big thickness planer working, who ensured everyone felt welcome at any gathering. He was there to hold my hand when a car careened out of control and almost hit the truck that was carrying *Taleisin* to the sea.

Jimmie and Barbara Moore shared far more than just the stone cottage with us. Jimmie has been a valiant supporter of this story in recent times, reminding me of incidents I'd almost forgotten. Shearlane and Robert Duke came through when I was feeling overwhelmed by canyon life, reminding me that someday I'd look back and see a story waiting to be told.

Among those friends who were not mentioned in this book, a special thanks to Linda Jensen, who gave us the big brass bed, her mother Gingerlee Field, who gave us two fine sets of sheets and blankets to warm it, Jerry Montgomery who loaned us his boat-moving trailer for three years to move timber. Others who offered help and tools include Bob Ramirez, Harry Vega, Jay Greer, Jerry Hampton, Dudley Rupert and Dean Wixom. They not only enabled us but enriched our lives.

Finally, a posthumous thank you to the late Bob Steele whose real name was Jim Crow. (We changed his name because there were far too many Jims to keep track of in this story and because the words Jim Crow have connotations that certain editors felt might distract readers.) He definitely had a big physical impact on my life in Bull Canyon. I didn't have to spend four years sweeping wood shavings out of the kitchen only because Jim Crow moved a hill for me.